100 CASES
in Clinical Ethics and Law

100 CASES
in Clinical Ethics and Law

Carolyn Johnston LLB LLM MA
Adviser in Medical Law and Ethics, King's College London School of Medicine,
London, UK; and Senior Lecturer in Law, Kingston University, Kingston, UK

Penelope Bradbury MBBS BSc (Clinical Healthcare Law and Ethics)
2006 graduate of King's College London School of Medicine at Guy's, King's and
St Thomas' Hospitals, London, UK

100 Cases Series Editor:
P John Rees MD FRCP
Dean of Medical Undergraduate Education, King's College London School of
Medicine, London, UK

HODDER
ARNOLD
PART OF HACHETTE LIVRE UK

First published in Great Britain in 2008 by
Hodder Arnold, an imprint of Hodder Education and a member of the
Hachette Livre UK Group, 338 Euston Road, London NW1 3BH

http://www.hoddereducation.com

Hachette Livre UK's policy is to use papers that are natural, renewable and recyclable products
and made from wood grown in sustainable forests. The logging and manufacturing processes are
expected to conform to the environmental regulations of the country of origin.

Whilst the advice and information in this book are believed to be true and accurate at the date
of going to press, neither the author[s] nor the publisher can accept any legal responsibility or
liability for any errors or omissions that may be made. In particular (but without limiting the
generality of the preceding disclaimer), every effort has been made to check drug dosages; however it is still possible that errors have been missed. Furthermore, dosage schedules are constantly
being revised and new side-effects recognized. For these reasons the reader is strongly urged to
consult the drug companies' printed instructions before administering any of the drugs recommended in this book.

British Library Cataloguing in Publication Data
A catalogue record for this book is available from the British Library

Library of Congress Cataloguing-in-Publication Data
A catalogue record for this book is available from the Library of Congress

ISBN-13 978 0 340 94575 9

2 3 4 5 6 7 8 9 10

Commissioning Editor:	Sara Purdy
Project Editor:	Jane Tod
Production Controller:	Andre Sim
Cover Design:	Laura DeGrasse
Indexer:	Laurence Errington

Typeset in 10/12 RotisSerif by Charon Tec Ltd (A MacMillan Company), Chennai, India
www.charontec.com
Printed in Spain

What do you think about this book? Or any other Hodder Arnold title?
Please visit our website: www.hoddereducation.com

CONTENTS

INTRODUCTION

The art of medicine is often dominated by the learning of facts. We are encouraged to collate symptoms, signs, results and imaging to produce diagnoses, prognoses, cures and palliations. Mrs Reeves becomes 'CCF in bed 7' and Mr Reynolds, 'acute-on-chronic renal failure in 10'. Learning ethics at medical school should be about remembering the humanity behind the diseases. Unfortunately, too many students are put off by believing that ethics is all about common sense or not relevant to them because it is often based around theories that are older than the patients they are treating. Lectures can be full of jargon and confusing terminology that seems to have no place by the bedside. We want this book to show you that this is not the case.

In its guidance *Tomorrow's Doctors* (2003) the General Medical Council states that medical 'graduates must know about and understand the main ethical and legal issues they will come across'. It identifies issues of confidentiality and consent, the withholding and withdrawing of life-prolonging treatment, and the treatment of vulnerable patients such as children and those with psychiatric illnesses. With these recommendations medical schools are looking to assess more than just a student's ability to memorize facts. They are looking to turn students into trustworthy and honest doctors with high levels of communication skills and professionalism. Studying ethics can help students with these skills as it makes them more aware of the patient as an individual rather than a disease process. It also gives them the skills to assess, evaluate and justify their views in the variety of emotionally draining and complex ethical, legal and social situations they will come across while practising as a doctor.

The aim of this book is to demonstrate some of these issues through clinical scenarios, which are based on realistic cases. As well as looking at the ethical and legal issues we also want to demonstrate what should happen from a clinical point of view and provide practical guidance that a medical student or junior doctor can use rather than focusing too much on different ethical theories and legal cases and statutes. The questions we have asked about each case scenario are by no means exhaustive. Every scenario will have different ethical and legal issues stemming from it and the answers are intended to be a springboard from which to develop your own analysis and understanding of the situation. With many of the cases there is no right or wrong answer and we implore you to think what your gut feeling is and go on to explore why you feel that way. We hope the cases will give you a taste of the myriad ethical dilemmas you could encounter on a hospital ward, and we have suggested further reading in each area at the end of the book to help you build on your knowledge.

Enjoy and good luck!

Carolyn and Penny
2008

ACKNOWLEDGEMENTS

The authors would like to thank those listed below for their comments and advice (although the authors remain responsible for any errors). Please note that the affiliations given were those at the date of first publication and may have been superceded by more recent appointments.

Dr Graham Behr, Consultant Psychiatrist, Central and North West London NHS Foundation Trust

Rachel Bingham, medical student, King's College London School of Medicine at Guy's, King's College and St Thomas' Hospitals

Dr Camilla Boyton, 2006 graduate of Barts and The London School of Medicine

Dr Caroline Bradbeer, Consultant in Genitourinary Medicine, Guy's and St Thomas' NHS Foundation Trust

Victoria Butler-Cole, Barrister

Dr Helen Daly, Consultant Anaesthetist, Guy's and St Thomas' NHS Foundation Trust

Ruth Gailer, medical student, Edinburgh University Medical School

Dr Natalie Hayes, former Specialist Registrar in Radiology, Addenbrooke's Hospital, Cambridge University Hospitals NHS Foundation Trust

Jehovah's Witness Hospital Information Services

Sabrieh Mazhary, medical student, King's College London School of Medicine at Guy's, King's College and St Thomas' Hospitals

Dr Ali Mears, Consultant in Genitourinary Medicine and HIV, Guy's and St Thomas' NHS Foundation Trust

Fiona Miles, medical student, King's College London School of Medicine at Guy's, King's College and St Thomas' Hospitals

Comfort Momoh, FGM Consultant/Public Health Specialist

Dr Franco Moscuzza, Consultant Anaesthetist, Guy's and St Thomas' NHS Foundation Trust

Dr Laura Nightingale, 2006 graduate of King's College London School of Medicine at Guy's, King's College and St Thomas' Hospitals

Dr Jo Nixon, GP and Tutor, Intercalated BSc Clinical Health Care Ethics and Law, King's College London School of Medicine, Department of General Practice and Primary Care

Brendan O'Brien, medical student, Cardiff University School of Medicine

Marilyn Peters, Research Co-ordinator, King's College London School of Medicine, Department of General Practice and Primary Care

Acknowledgements

Priyanka Saigal, medical student, King's College London, School of Medicine

Dr Annakshi Sen, 2006 graduate of Guy's, King's and St Thomas' School of Medicine, King's College London

Dr Tushar Vince, Consultant Paediatric Intensivist, King's College Hospital NHS Foundation Trust

John Withington, medical student, King's College London School of Medicine at Guy's, King's College and St Thomas' Hospitals

Dr Ann Wylie, Senior Tutor, King's College London School of Medicine at Guy's, King's College and St Thomas' Hospitals

Spiritual Health Care and Chaplaincy Team, Guy's and St Thomas' NHS Foundation Trust

FOREWORD

There are lots of reasons for reading this book. Perhaps you are facing an exam and need to revise. Maybe you did not really understand all the teaching you had and now want to make sense of things. But it might be that now on the ward or in practice you have come face to face with some things you do not know how to deal with, or you do not think are quite right.

You want to be a doctor, and presumably you want to be a good one. But demanding as it is to be on the mark in diagnosis and to know what treatment is needed, it will not always tell you actually what decisions should be made. Usually something more is needed. Deciding between treatments and their side-effects will be difficult without finding out about how the patient lives and the choices they would make. There may be a conflict, say between what doctors want to do and what the patient is prepared to accept. Perhaps what could be done is very expensive, or it does not seem worthwhile or fair to put someone through. The patient may be confused, a young child or in a new and foreign culture. Perhaps someone is putting pressure on you to do something you do not think is right, or even legal.

As soon as these sorts of questions appear, you are in the area where ethical (or moral – the words for our purpose mean much the same) and legal issues are important, which can only properly be resolved by the thinking in this book. A good doctor is prepared to ask 'Is this right?', 'Is this the best thing to do in these circumstances?' or 'What does the law say about this?'. Avoiding facing them will simply mean wasted effort, endless tension and anxiety, or worse. Sooner or later someone will make a complaint, or things will go wrong in a bigger way. Even if temperamentally you do not like to think about those possibilities, common sense will tell you that facing them is not going to be an easy experience, and if possible to be avoided. We hope you will see that finding good ways of thinking about the ideas raised here will be a much more happy and satisfying way to work.

Medical practice of necessity is often done at speed and in an atmosphere of uncertainty. Try as you will you cannot always expect to get it right all the time. But if you were doing your best at the time with the resources and help available that you had, you will feel that you should not be blamed if things went wrong. But even if they did not, you may still be uncertain what you should have done. How can you tell what's best?

One suggestion would be to take anything that has felt uncomfortable in your day's work, and think it through in more detail. You might most naturally do that with a close friend, but thinking and reading on your own may be as good. As you think, talk or read you may see what you missed, and see what you should do next time, but you may also be struck by a feeling: guilt about missing something, annoyance that someone did not help you out, or perhaps an awareness of some strong feeling that the patient had, which you could not deal with while getting the medicine right. My claim is that these feelings will nearly always point you to moral issues (often very practical ones) that need addressing.

Once those issues are clarified and if possible named, then the helpful thinking can start, and this book comes into its own. This claim may surprise you, but it is partly what the great Scottish philosopher David Hume (1739) was talking about when he said, 'Reason is and ought only to be the slave of the passions, and can never pretend to any other office than to serve and obey them'. So if you want to be a reasonable and good doctor, start by listening to what your emotions (Hume's 'passions') are saying to you, and then take your careful and rational thinking from there. (Without recognizing and addressing them, of course, those emotional feelings may continue to jangle on and spoil your work in unexpected ways.)

Giving an example might make things clearer. As a general practitioner (GP) I looked after a proud and private man who seldom asked for my help until in his late sixties he became seriously ill with lung cancer. (Rumour had it that he was one of the best diamond 'fences' in Europe, but that was not in the notes!) His wife called me after evening surgery to visit him. At his home I found he was jaundiced and very weak. I had just been part of a group that had opened a GP hospital that was designed to provide good terminal care. As it was late at night and not much could be done then, I suggested I admit him there. His wife was keen on this plan. His pain and other symptoms were well controlled with medication. When he got to the hospital and everything was sorted out, I came to say goodnight and told him I was in a bit of a hurry but would see him in the morning. He gave me a look that I did not understand. In the night he died, without distress. The nurses and the relatives, in spite of their own grief, were pleased with his care and his peaceful end: but there was that look, which had conveyed to me that in some way I had let him down. I shall not ever know what that was about, of course, or whether I had interpreted his glance correctly, but when I put myself in his situation I am sure he knew he was dying, was surprised I did not (or did not tell him), and wanted to talk about something important. He was alone, away from his family and the circumstances that he knew, with no chance to give important final messages. I was left with disquiet. Nobody could fault my clinical care. I had acted entirely within the law. No one was making a complaint. I had used the hospital exactly as it was intended. And yet some part of my care had not been right. Discounting my own sadness – I had liked him and we had worked hard together in his last illness – on a human level my care was deficient. It had not crossed my mind that this might be his last night. Even a company telephonist is trained to ask, 'Is there anything else I can help you with?' It's the moral equivalent of the old surgical joke: the operation was successful but the patient died. The medical care was excellent but there was still something wrong, something that could have been done better, and I had to learn it.

You may at this stage think I am setting the bar too high. How can we all possibly practise under pressure and still offer the best possible care? But that experience helped me to understand what 'a moral problem' really is: something that happens in the transactions between people that *could* and *should* have been done better. Ethicists often say 'ought implies can'. If something is impossible, there is no case to answer. In my situation, however, I *did* have the time and the opportunity to ask my patient that key question, and since I knew he was very ill I *should* have thought about what his needs were at that time. It is even possible, on a practical level, that by being so proud of my new hospital and moving an elderly ill man out of his home unnecessarily I had precipitated his death. The philosopher Geoffrey Warnock in his book *The Object of Morality* suggests 'it is the proper business of morality ... to expand our sympathies, or ... to reduce the liability to damage inherent in their natural tendency to be narrowly restricted'. Because we are all only human we sometimes give ourselves excuses for actions or thoughts that really ought, in the circumstances, all things considered, to have been better. Giving ourselves a let-out clause may help us get through the day, but may not help us get through the night.

This marks one difference between ethics and law. The law defines areas of right and wrong as they affect a whole society, and so is talking 'headlines' as it were: big issues or prohibitions that a whole society can sign up to and still be able to live together flexibly without everyone becoming lawbreakers. But these laws are usually derived from moral ideas. These ideas often only impinge on our private life and may be so obvious that we do not fully articulate them until something goes wrong. So, for instance, the law's thinking on contract derives partly from our ordinary thinking about promises, and the law of consent from our concern to have control of our own life and not to be harmed by other people. Though law (and medical ethics) may differ from era to era and country to country, and individuals (or cultures) may be free to make their own decisions about what is right or wrong in their interactions, the impulses to moral thinking behind these decisions are now realised to be universal. They are as much part of the make-up of *Homo sapiens* as the opposable thumb (Brown, 1991).

So the cases you will read here do not attempt to describe the limits of ethical or legal thinking. By defining the framework within which medical action is carried out (for instance, who can be thought of as doctors and how their powers and duties differ from people who are not), the law would have something to say about any case that we might like to raise; and ethics is just the same. We may want to raise questions about what is right or wrong *in the system of* medical care or about the *relationship* between people.

We have been brought up since childhood to act in certain ways that we think right – like telling the truth or being kind to other people when they are in distress – so we need ways to resolve the disagreement about what should be done when some of these ideas conflict, as they most certainly will do, in our work. This conflict is what at base makes each clinical situation described in this book a 'case' in terms of ethics and law. The law resolves a conflict (in the UK) by making a judgment in court set against both the common law, built up over hundreds of years, and more recent statutes or regulations, usually passed by Parliament.

The equivalent 'court' in medical ethics is more diverse. Official groups such as the General Medical Council produce guidelines. These are rules according to which doctors can be expected to work, but these may not deal adequately with the conflicts we perceive. In this then the 'court' has to be our own thought and conscience and the discussion we may have with colleagues and patients. Here we need the 'arguments' – the reasoning – of the different ways of thinking about morality that are described here. We can structure these in different ways – for instance by appealing to principles – or back up our decisions with reference to the *duties* we see people having, the *consequences* of different actions, or the best sort of characteristics we should like to have (*virtues*) when making that sort of decision; or by using some other cogent and consistent approach.

Just as in court, we need to acknowledge certain sorts of processes. We should listen to what other people have to say. We need to think if there are other points of view (other 'voices') that are not being expressed but which have a bearing on the decision (like the 'voice' of the unborn child). Even if a certain argument does not 'win' in deciding *what* we do, it should still be powerful in determining *how* we do what we do. Unlike philosophers (and sometimes lawyers) we have to do this in a tight time frame, so we have to set *limits* on the process. Others will have to know why in the circumstances we did what we did, so the decisions and their *reasons* have to be succinctly written down. And afterwards, we must go back with others to *check* if what we did was the best.

Luckily, in all this we learn more about our chosen profession, about good arguments and bad arguments, about how people tick, and about ourselves. Our decision making improves, and work moves from just being scary to being very exciting. That is why people admire doctors and envy us in our work, and why, if we find ourselves getting bored and this kind of book does not open things up again, we should probably go off and do something else.

Roger Higgs, MBE
Professor Emeritus and former deputy head of the Department of
General Practice and Primary Care, King's College London School of
Medicine at Guy's, King's College and St Thomas' Hospitals, London, UK

References

Brown DE. *Human Universals*. New York: McGraw-Hill, 1991.

Hume D. *A Treatise of Human Nature*. Book II, Part 3, section 3. [1739]

Warnock G. Quoted in: Ayer AJ, O'Grady JO (eds) *A Dictionary of Philosophical Quotations*. Oxford: Blackwell Reference, 1994.

GLOSSARY OF TERMS

Advance decision (directive)
Decision taken when a person is competent to refuse specified medical treatment if mental capacity is lost in the future.

Assisted suicide
The provision of means to enable a person to take the final act to end their life.

Autonomy
Self-rule, freedom from external constraint and the ability to exercise critical mental capacity.

Basic care
Procedures which provide comfort or alleviate symptoms or distress – includes oral nutrition and hydration.

Battery
Physical touching without consent or legal authority.

Beneficence
Provision of benefit and contribution to welfare.

Best interests
The criterion for determining whether treatment for patients lacking capacity is legally and morally justified. It includes consideration of the benefits and harms of the proposed treatment and the values and views of the patient, where known.

Capacity
The legal ability to make healthcare decisions.

Casuistry
The morally appropriate course of action determined by considering the particular features of a case and making a comparison with prior experiences from similar situations.

Competence
The ability to understand, retain and weigh up information in order to make a particular healthcare decision. This term tends to be used interchangeably with capacity.

Confidentiality
The obligation to keep safe and not to disclose health information provided in the course of a professional relationship.

Conscientious objection
The right to refuse to participate in certain medical procedures based on religious or ethical grounds.

Consent
The agreement to a treatment or procedure.

Consequentialism
A theory which states that the morality of an action depends on its (good) consequences, rather than the means by which those consequences are achieved.

Declaration
A statement from the court that proposed medical treatment is lawful because it is in the best interests of a patient who lacks capacity.

Deontology
A moral theory based on rights and obligations.

Doctrine of double effect
An action that has an unintended although foreseen harmful effect is permissible as long as the directly intended effect is beneficial. Often used in the context of pain relief for terminally ill patients where a side-effect may be that death is hastened.

Euthanasia
A 'good death'. An action to deliberately bring about the death of a person with the aim of relieving suffering.

Gillick competence
Children under 16 can consent to medical treatment if they have sufficient understanding and intelligence regarding the nature, purpose and likely consequences of the proposed treatment.

Informed consent
The choice of a patient to consent to medical treatment based on the provision of sufficient, understandable information.

Justice
Fair, equitable and appropriate decision-making. Distributive justice refers to considerations of fairness in the allocation of scarce resources.

Narrative ethics
Ethical issues explored through the values, experiences and perspectives of those involved.

National Institute for Health and Clinical Excellence (NICE)
NICE provides national guidance on the promotion of good health and the prevention and treatment of ill health and on new and existing medicines and treatments.

Negligence
Conduct that falls below the standard reasonably expected in the circumstances. Damages can be awarded in compensation for harm caused. The purpose of damages is to compensate the claimant for harm caused/loss suffered as a result of negligence.

Non-maleficence
'Do no harm' – the obligation to avoid or minimize harm.

Parental responsibility
The duties and rights which parents have in respect of their children.

Paternalism
Overriding a person's known preferences based on the justification that this will benefit them or avoid harm to them.

Passive euthanasia
Withholding or withdrawing life-prolonging medical treatment resulting in that person's death, for example turning off an artificial ventilator.

Psychiatric advance directive
A document which sets out a person's instructions or preferences regarding future mental health treatment in the event of loss of capacity due to psychiatric illness.

Quality-adjusted life year (QALY)
A measure of calculating the cost effectiveness of treatment, combining the quality and quantity of life achieved through a medical intervention.

Quality of life
The value of life assessed by reference to certain attributes including mental and physical ablities, rather than its length.

Sanctity of life
All life has intrinsic value irrespective of the features or quality of a particular life.

Saviour sibling
A child created by *in vitro* fertilization in order to treat brothers and sisters with genetic disorders.

Suicide
An act performed by an individual with the knowledge and intention that the action taken will result in their death.

Surrogacy
An arrangement under which a woman carries a baby on behalf of another.

Therapeutic privilege
Deliberate withholding of information about risks of treatment in order to prevent harm to the patient.

Utilitarianism
A consequentialist moral theory which provides that the right course of action is that which promotes the greatest happiness for the greatest number.

Virtue ethics
A moral theory which provides that an action is morally right if it is what a virtuous agent would do in those circumstances.

Section 1
ETHICAL PRINCIPLES

CASE 1: PRINCIPLISM

Ophelia is a 27-year-old woman who has struggled with anorexia nervosa since she was 11 years old. She is extremely intelligent and having gained a first in history at Oxford University she is now halfway through her PhD. It is at times when her life is most stressful that she struggles with her anorexia. The first time she was admitted to hospital was when she was 13. She was being badly bullied at school and had stopped eating in order to become thin to prevent being teased about being overweight. Being able to lose so much weight gave her the sense that she had some control over at least one aspect of her life.

Ophelia has spent the past 14 years in and out of hospital. On two occasions she had to be admitted to intensive care as she had lost consciousness. During these admissions she was fed by a nasogastric tube. She also has a history of obsessive-compulsive disorder and has been receiving cognitive behavioural therapy. A year ago she had managed to stabilize her weight at 50 kg – she is 1.7 m tall. With the stress of her PhD and the breakdown of her relationship with her boyfriend, when you initially see Ophelia she weighs less than 35 kg. Although you want to feed her by nasogastric tube to prevent her needing a third admission to intensive care, she adamantly refuses to have this. She tells you that she does not want to die, but nor does she want to be force fed. She is extremely frail and needs constant supervision by a healthcare assistant. Due to a shortage of beds on the psychiatric ward Ophelia is currently being nursed on a general ward. The older women in her bay are complaining about the amount of personal attention she is receiving, as when they need assistance to change position or to go to the bathroom there is often a long wait due to staff shortages.

Questions
- What is principlism?
- How can the four principles be applied to this case scenario to offer guidance to the doctor about whether Ophelia should be force fed?

ANSWER 1

Beauchamp and Childress are American bioethicists who coined the four principles approach (principlism) for analysing ethical dilemmas in medicine.

! Principlism

The four principles are the *'prima facie'* moral obligations of:

- Respect for autonomy
- Beneficence (promote overall benefit)
- Non-maleficence (avoid causing harm)
- Justice

The four principles approach is the most well-known ethical theory. Medical students are often taught this theory to demonstrate how to approach (and solve) medical dilemmas.

The first step is to analyse how each principle may be relevant to the situation, i.e. what is the scope of the principle. The principles are non-hierarchical although respect for autonomy has gained in importance in the era of patient-centred care. Respect for autonomy requires that the decision-making capacities of the individual are acknowledged. A person may not be fully autonomous in all situations but increasingly the views of those with limited autonomy are being recognized and respected. Just because a patient lacks capacity to make a particular decision does not mean that a doctor should override their wishes. When a patient voices an opinion, every effort should be made to respect that decision, unless it is contrary to their best interests.

The moral obligation of beneficence is not owed to everyone in general. However, there is a moral obligation for healthcare professionals to benefit their patients. This is underscored by the legal duty of care and a doctor must act in a patient's best interests when they lack the autonomy to make decisions about their healthcare. In contrast, the *prima facie* obligation of non-maleficence is a general requirement to avoid causing harm. Most medical treatment incurs an element of potential harm. However, the risk of harm may be justified by balancing it against the anticipated benefits. The principle of justice often takes a back seat to the other principles. It is used in ethical arguments to ensure that there is fair allocation of services and treatment within society. At an individual level, it is used to promote equality among patients from all walks of life, irrespective of nationality, culture or religion.

When there is conflict between the principles then a choice must be made to prioritize one over another. If Ophelia is not sectioned under the Mental Health Act (MHA), the doctor can only impose treatment if there is evidence that she lacks capacity. Anorexia nervosa is a complex illness. Affected individuals feel that they do not have control over their life and so use refusal of food to demonstrate that there is some aspect of their life that they can control. But does this mean that Ophelia lacks autonomy? It may be in her best interests to force feed her if she is at a critically low weight to avoid irreparable harm and restore her autonomy for future decision making. However, restraint and force feeding may destroy any trust she has built with her doctors. The principles of beneficence and non-maleficence should be balanced to produce the outcome with overall net benefit. It could be claimed that the special nursing that Ophelia is receiving is an unfair allocation of limited health resources.

CASE 2: CONSEQUENTIALISM

Pippa has a 3-year-old son and a 13-month-old daughter. Her son had the triple measles, mumps, rubella (MMR) vaccination just over a year ago after Pippa had been reassured that it was extremely safe and would protect her son against dangerous childhood illnesses. Unfortunately he had a bad reaction to the injection, with a high temperature, a rash around the injection site and a seizure. Although he seems fine now Pippa is worried that having a seizure is an indication that he will become autistic or develop bowel problems. She has read the contradictory evidence about the risks of the triple MMR vaccine in newspapers and recognizes that the evidence suggesting a link between MMR and autism has now been disproved. However, she is still concerned about having her daughter immunized against MMR, in case the same thing happens to her.

Questions
- What is consequentialism?
- How can this ethical theory be applied to the case scenario to determine whether or not Pippa should have her daughter immunized?

ANSWER 2

Consequentialist theory states that the morally correct course of action is that which results in the best overall outcome, irrespective of the means used to achieve those consequences. The inherent wrongness or rightness of an act is not considered. One example of consequentialist theory is utilitarianism, which was first proposed by Jeremy Bentham in the late eighteenth century and further established by John Stuart Mill in the nineteenth century. Utilitarianism is the most influential consequentialist theory. The principle of utility provides that the morally correct course of action is that which promotes the greatest happiness of the greatest number. So the right thing to do is determined by the action that will result in the greatest overall happiness. The term 'benefit' is now used in the context of healthcare. Intuitively this seems an attractive and simple theory, but it does require impartiality since the theory does not allow room for the promotion of individual interests nor those of family and friends. The consequences of an action must be considered across time. There is no preference for happiness now, and the consequences for both the present and future generations should be taken into account.

The net happiness must be calculated taking into account any unhappiness that a course of action will cause. The theory not only considers the consequences of actions but also the consequences of failures to act. It is a hugely demanding theory because it requires us to constantly analyse the potential outcomes of everything that we do or do not do and thus allows insufficient moral breathing space.

Consequentialism can be considered to conflict with the demands of justice. Plucking a healthy person off the street and using his body parts to save the lives of six people who need organ transplants may produce the greatest happiness. But does this mean that we can do disagreeable things if the consequences are good enough? The theory is so obsessed with ends that it overlooks the importance of means, in contrast with deontological theory.

The main problem with consequentialism is that it is difficult to apply to real-life scenarios because accurately predicting the possible consequences of an action is impossible. In this case scenario there are several possible outcomes of Pippa having her daughter immunized against MMR. In theory, she may suffer immediate short-term harm (fever) but gain long-term benefits (disease resistance). Although it is not possible to predict whether this child will benefit from vaccination there is scientific evidence to suggest that childhood vaccination schemes offer overall benefit to society. If sufficient numbers of children are immunized, 'herd immunity' is achieved and eventually diseases may be eradicated altogether. This will protect future generations from the side-effects of disease and subsequently increase happiness. The future benefit of immunization outweighs the unhappiness caused by any potential side-effects to this child and other children receiving the vaccination.

CASE 3: DEONTOLOGY

Patrick is a 45-year-old mature student nurse in his last year of training. His friend Carlos has had human immunodeficiency virus (HIV) infection for many years. He is now in the terminal stages of the disease and is in constant pain and suffering. Carlos and Patrick have been friends for a long time and Patrick has always said that he would be there to support Carlos. Carlos now asks him to travel with him to Dignitas in Switzerland so that he can be assisted to end his life. Patrick wants to be there for his friend. Personally he does not have any ethical quandaries about whether he should prevent Carlos from making a decision to seek assistance to end his own life. However, he is worried that he now has professional responsibilities and duties, which would be compromised by travelling to Switzerland with Carlos.

Questions
- What does deontological theory say about duties and obligations?
- To what extent must duties be followed irrespective of the consequences?
- According to deontological theory is it morally acceptable for Patrick to take his friend to Dignitas?

ANSWER 3

Deontological (Greek '*deon*' = duty/obligation) theory focuses on duties and rules rather than consequences. Some acts are intrinsically wrong irrespective of the good consequences that may follow, for example torture, lying, murder. Immanuel Kant, who propounded the deontological theory 'Kantianism', considered that duties arise from application of reason by rational human beings and that moral rules must apply universally, i.e. to all people in similar situations. This may seem particularly harsh as it does not take into account either the consequences of an action or the emotions and needs of an individual. The rule 'never kill' may echo intuitive moral understanding but should this constraint apply in all situations? Would it be ethically justifiable for the police to shoot one terrorist to prevent him blowing up a train full of people?

In his work on the categorical imperative, Kant stated that an individual should 'act only according to that maxim by which you can at the same time will that it should become a universal law' (*Groundwork of the Metaphysics of Morals*, 1785) This implies that moral rules should be used only if they can be applied to every situation equally. Deontological theory can be criticized because it does not provide a definitive list of duties, nor does it state what should be done where two duties conflict. On the other hand it provides 'moral space'. People can act freely so long as they do not violate moral constraints. In comparison consequentialist theory could be said to be far more demanding as it constantly requires an assessment of consequences.

Deontological constraints are usually negatively formulated, e.g. do not kill, do not lie. What is outside these boundaries is not forbidden; it could be argued that withholding the truth is morally acceptable because it does not amount to lying. It is also important to consider the nature of the constraint on action and how narrowly it is framed. For example, Kant considered that it is always wrong to deliberately end the life of an innocent human being. Therefore it does not preclude killing of animals or murderers. It is more concerned with action rather than inaction. It may be wrong to take life but what about not saving it?

Does the application of deontological theory help in deciding whether it is morally permissible for Patrick to go with his friend to Dignitas? According to the theory it is wrong to deliberately end the life of an innocent human being. If Carlos is injected with a lethal dose of barbiturates then the person doing this would breach the moral imperative, but what if Carlos is supplied with the drug to self-inject? Patrick is not acting to kill his friend, he is merely enabling such an act to take place. But Kant's categorical imperative requires us to act in a way that we would wish to be treated, which could be applied as a universal law. A universalizable law may forbid assisting a suicide.

CASE 4: VIRTUE ETHICS

Scenario 1

Sara, a 15-year-old girl, has suffered from leukaemia since the age of 6 years. She has had multiple courses of chemotherapy and a bone marrow transplant which have all failed. She is constantly in hospital and as such has had a disrupted education and little opportunity to make lasting friendships. She and her parents have accepted that further treatment is unlikely to be beneficial, and she wishes to return home to die in peace. Her doctors are unwilling to accept her decision as she is only 15.

Scenario 2

Tasha, a 15-year-old girl, was born with a congenital heart defect that was repaired at birth. She now needs a heart transplant to enable her to live an active life. She is, however, adamant that she does not want to live 'with someone else's heart beating inside me'. The prognosis of recovery after the heart transplant is good. Her parents are prepared to accept whatever decision she makes as they believe she will have to live with the consequences.

Questions

- What is virtue ethics?
- Which virtues do you think would make a good doctor?
- Can virtue ethics be applied to these two case scenarios to offer guidance to the doctor about whether Gillick competent children should have the right to refuse life-saving treatment?

ANSWER 4

Virtue ethics was first introduced as a concept by Aristotle in his *Nicomachean Ethics* and as such was one of the first true moral theories to shape the history of civilization. According to virtue theory every action taken by a virtuous individual achieves 'eudaimonia'. Philosophers have attempted to translate this and describe it as 'human flourishing'. Aristotle believed that to be virtuous is to be able to rationally analyse a specific characteristic (virtue) and then act on the decision, which would ultimately result in human flourishing. Virtue theory does not comment on which particular virtues are important.

! **Some virtues of a good doctor**

- Honesty
- Compassion
- Respect
- Non-judgemental
- Courage
- Benevolence
- Conscientiousness
- Confidence
- Humility

- Empathy
- Trustworthiness
- Self-awareness
- Enthusiasm
- Professionalism
- Personable
- Altruism
- Discernment
- Integrity

Typically in a doctor–patient relationship the main virtues seem to be honesty, compassion, integrity and justice, although the list is not exhaustive. The application of which virtues to consider in specific situations is highly subjective. This is both a strength and a weakness of the virtue ethics theory. Can virtue theory be used to assess whether Sara and Tasha should be allowed to refuse potentially life-saving treatment?

The virtuous doctor should have a good knowledge of both the *facts* of the cases and the *emotions* of the patients. She should also consider her own emotional response and then reflect on which virtues should be applied in order to attempt to reach a moral conclusion. Benevolence, compassion and discernment are three virtues which could be applied to the two scenarios.

When applied to medicine, *benevolence* means to act in a way which best serves the interests of the patient. Sara is suffering and has little prospect of recovery. It is in her best interests to value the time she has left. Tasha, however, has a good chance of leading a normal life. It would not be in her best interests to die. *Compassion* means being able to identify with the patient's situation and show empathy. A discerning doctor would weigh complex emotional issues and understand the reasoning behind the patient's decision. She would perhaps understand that Tasha does not want to die but that she has fears surrounding the operation and the consequences of having a transplant. These issues should be discussed with the patient to enable her to cope with her fear.

Thus it would seem that virtue theory would suggest that Sara's wishes should be respected but Tasha's should not. Virtue theory does not give definitive answers to moral dilemmas, but it can help guide decision making after careful analysis. It enables individuals to reflect on the dilemma in question and come up with workable solutions.

CASE 5: CASUISTRY

You are the F1 doctor on call when you are called to the ward to see an elderly confused man. He is wandering around and crying out. The nurses have tried persuading him to stay by his bed or at least in his bay, but he is refusing to listen to them. One female patient has become upset because he keeps going to stand at the end of her bed and stares at her. The nurses are worried that as well as upsetting other patients, he is very unsteady on his feet and they fear he may fall over and injure himself. You read his notes to try to find a cause for his confusion. You learn that Micky, 76 years old, was an elective admission yesterday for a laparoscopic cholecystectomy. Two weeks earlier he had been admitted to accident and emergency with shortness of breath and pleuritic chest pain. He was kept in for 3 days and treated with intravenous antibiotics. There are at least two possible causes for his confusion: a recurrence of his pneumonia (or other sepsis) or a reaction to the general anaesthetic. You decide to speak to Micky and try to take some blood. Micky refuses to co-operate and actively pushes you away from him, shouting and swearing. He then tries to leave the ward, claiming he is well enough to go home and it is illegal for you to keep him a prisoner. The nurses suggest he should be physically restrained so that you can take blood and assess him, and that it may be a good idea to give him a sedative so that he does not continue to upset the other patients.

Questions
- What is the ethical principle of casuistry?
- Should you use restraint in this case?

ANSWER 5

Casuistry is a method of applying theories rather than a theory in itself. It is much more practical than other theories and consequently is considered easier to use in clinical practice. Casuistry is broadly defined as a 'case-based' approach to solving an ethical dilemma. A case with a clear-cut course of action is used as a 'paradigm' case. New cases are analysed in detail, paying particular attention to the minutiae, and then compared with the paradigm case. If a new case is similar to the paradigm case then the same course of action can be taken. If it is significantly different, then a different course of action should be taken. Therefore, choices are made depending on what decisions were previously made in similar cases. It is also a reflection of what happens in common law, where individual cases are examined and judgments are made based on precedent.

In deciding whether to restrain Micky, any of the other ethical theories could be used. Deontology may argue that a patient should never be restrained against their will, but consequentialists may argue that it would be ethical to restrain the patient because it would prevent the other patients from being upset and prevent possible harm occurring to the patient himself. Casuistry would examine similar cases and assess the outcome based on previous decisions. The most striking difficulty with this method of decision making is that in reality junior doctors often do not have the experience to make difficult ethical decisions based on what they have done previously. In the above scenario the F1 doctor rang her senior to ask for his advice on whether it would be appropriate to restrain the patient to assess and treat him.

In this specific case, the patient was given a little longer to calm down and when this failed he was safely sedated and assessed. He turned out to have a relapse of his pneumonia, which responded to intravenous antibiotics, and 24 hours later his confusion had resolved and he did not remember anything that had happened. This indicates that biochemical restraint to treat a patient can be argued as ethically justifiable. However, compare it with a slightly different case. A patient with dementia and acute-on-chronic renal failure does not understand what is wrong with him. The doctor knows that his chances of survival without dialysis are poor. However, the patient is unable to comprehend that he needs to stay seated for several hours a day, several days a week. He finds the dialysis sessions extremely traumatic. It is suggested that he is sedated while he is having dialysis. This was considered inappropriate because it was not thought to be in his best interests, and the decision was made to discontinue dialysis.

Casuistry forces the decision maker to examine all the facts of a case carefully before employing appropriate ethical theory to make a decision. A very slight change in case detail can shift the emphasis and can lead to a different decision and, hence, a different outcome.

CASE 6: NARRATIVE ETHICS

You are the F1 doctor attached to a general medical firm. During a typical on-call you admit a 78-year-old man with shortness of breath. He is acutely unwell. Investigations reveal that he has right lobar pneumonia. He also has dementia and ischaemic heart disease. Despite intravenous antibiotics and fluids he does not make much improvement over the next few days. He is lethargic, yet occasionally agitated and needs full nursing care. You decide to discuss his medical issues with his wife and son to see how they had been coping at home before the pneumonia. You discover that there had been a gradual decline in his general wellbeing over the past 6 months. In particular, his son comments how his father seemed to have had increasing difficulty swallowing. He used to hold food in his mouth for long periods of time before swallowing and had choked on several occasions. You decide to get a swallowing assessment. The speech and language therapist grades him as unsafe to swallow and he is made nil by mouth. A nasogastric tube is inserted so that he can continue to be fed but he pulls it out on three occasions. He continues to deteriorate and his albumin drops due to sustained lack of intake. The only way to improve this would be to insert a percutaneous endoscopic gastrostomy (PEG) tube but you feel that in a patient with so many comorbidities this may not be in his best interests. You once again discuss the pros and cons of PEG feeding with the patient's relatives. You explain to them that without a PEG you can let him return home and continue to eat as much as is possible but that this would likely result in a fatal aspiration pneumonia at some point. The alternative is a PEG tube and keeping the patient nil by mouth permanently. A PEG tube is associated with a mortality of 3 per cent and serious complications. You inform the relatives that the medical opinion of the team is to allow the patient to return home but that you would be willing to consider a PEG if the family felt that the patient would continue to have a good quality of life with one.

Questions
- What is narrative ethics?
- Which 'voices' should be listened to in this scenario?

ANSWER 6

Medical ethics is not just about hugely controversial issues, such as euthanasia and abortion, but is central to every decision made about the welfare and treatment of a patient. It is impractical to assume that every doctor will know the details of ethical theories. However, there is one theory that it has been suggested can help improve the doctor–patient relationship by enabling the doctor to take account of the views of those involved.

Good doctors have been using narrative theory instinctively for centuries. But the theory and its role in medicine have only been fully explored in the past few decades. The theory has two essential elements, which in practice are often intertwined: (i) use of cases as stories for their content, and (ii) analysis of these stories to create an analytical and reflective approach to learning. It has a more substantial role than other ethical theories in the education of healthcare professionals and in the solving of everyday medical dilemmas.

Looking at a case as a story gives a holistic approach to medicine. Every individual's role in the story is examined and analysed. Every character's narrative is listened to in order to determine their beliefs and wishes and to act in their best interests. However, the patient's voice should always be listened to first. This is reflected in the way doctors start by taking the patient history. The patient's story is the first clue in discovering how the illness is affecting them – physically, psychologically and socially. A joint narrative is constructed by the doctor listening to the patient without interrupting them and then filling in any gaps with more direct questioning. Non-verbal cues displayed by the patient should also be picked up.

The scenario above is an interesting one in which to examine the application of narrative theory since the primary voice you should listen to is silent. The patient has severe dementia and cannot voice his wishes. However, body language and actions are often a subtle but significant indication of what a patient wants. In this case, the patient keeps removing his nasogastric tube. We do not know if this is an expression of his wishes not to be fed or because he finds the tube uncomfortable. The doctor should also listen to the patient's relatives and take into account their wishes and what they think the patient would have wanted. Nursing staff and other healthcare professionals involved in his care should also be listened to. Do they think the patient should have a percutaneous endoscopic gastrostomy tube? Do they think the patient would be happier at home in his own environment, irrespective of the risk of aspiration?

Application of narrative ethics is essential when practising medicine. It enables the doctor to focus on the individual rather than the disease. However, it does not give clear-cut guidance about how to solve an ethical dilemma. In this respect it may be argued that the theory is best used in conjunction with other ethical guidance, where, for example, the four principles framework could be used to decide on a course of action with narrative ethics providing a more detailed understanding of the different voices involved.

CASE 7: RIGHTS AND DUTIES

Xavier is a 72-year-old man who is admitted to the intensive care unit where you are an F1. He was clearing out a gutter when he fell off the ladder and hit his head on the pavement. Passers-by immediately called an ambulance and he was taken straight to theatre where a large subdural haematoma was drained. Subsequent tests indicate that he fell from his ladder because he suffered a massive myocardial infarction. He has yet to recover consciousness and it is thought that he has had irreparable brain damage due to anoxia. He is married and has three sons. His eldest son works as a radiographer in the hospital. His second son is an evangelist with the Pentecostal church, is married and has three young children. His youngest son is travelling around Australia. The intensive care unit has a family room which has been taken over by Xavier's family. It is also constantly filled with well-wishers from the church who hold prayer and song meetings around the clock. Relatives of other patients are complaining about the lack of access to the family room and the noise levels. However, when the senior staff nurse asks them to keep the noise down, Xavier's son threatens the hospital with legal action for religious discrimination. He also says that the hospital is impeding the chances of his father's recovery because if they cannot hold a prayer meeting the hospital is preventing the possibility of a miracle from God. Despite full active medical treatment and round-the-clock prayers, Xavier makes no improvement over the next 6 weeks. The medical team decide to discuss the possibility of allowing him to die in peace by withdrawing supportive medical intervention. He has multi-organ failure and has not regained consciousness. Xavier's wife and one son refuse point blank to allow this to happen and insist that everything be done for him, including resuscitation. The staff on the unit are becoming upset that Xavier is not being allowed to die with peace and dignity.

Xavier's eldest son supports the advice of the medical team and attempts to discuss it with his brother and mother. However, they threaten him with becoming a family outcast and divine retribution. They also continue to threaten the hospital with lawsuits as they do not believe that Xavier is being cared for properly. No joint decision is ever made, and after 11 weeks Xavier dies during a 60-minute cycle of resuscitation.

Questions
- What are 'rights' and 'duties'?
- What is the difference between positive and negative rights?
- Who has 'rights' in the above scenario?

ANSWER 7

There are different types of rights: political, religious and personal rights, such as a right to bodily integrity and a right to life. Rights are also attached to groups within society, for example students' rights, patients' rights and parental rights. One important distinction is between rights which are legally recognized and moral rights. Some might argue that only rights which are substantiated in law are true rights and sanctions cannot be imposed on anyone who interferes with a moral right. If someone has a moral right to something it could be said that they ought to be given it. But not all moral claims involve a claim of rights that should be legally upheld. There may be a moral obligation of fidelity within marriage, but to involve the law to uphold such a right seems inappropriate.

There is a difference between positive and negative rights. A negative right implies a right to non-interference, for example a right not to be killed. In contrast, positive rights impose positive duties of support or assistance on others. A positive right to life imposes the duty to provide proper healthcare and ensure that life is saved. It is only the person with the right who can demand that the duty is performed or who can waive that right.

There are very few absolute rights. An absolute right is one that may not be justifiably overridden in any circumstances. What counts as an absolute right – a right to life? In some countries the death penalty is still used as a form of punishment. Healthcare professionals may decide to withdraw life-supporting treatment from a patient whose quality of life is considered extremely poor. It could be argued that there is no right to a life of intolerable suffering. There are also situations where rights conflict, for example, the right to life and the right to self-defence. How and who should determine which right should predominate in such situations?

Consider the rights of all the characters in the above scenario:

- Who has rights?
- Why do they have them?
- What duties does the existence of these rights impose on other people?

Xavier has a *prima facie* 'right to life'. However, a tragic accident led to deterioration in the quality of his life. The duty of the medical team to provide intensive medical care and support for him has been fulfilled but is proving futile. With the patient incompetent to make a decision about whether the duty to provide medical care should be continued, who should make the decision? The law states that treatment should be provided in a patient's best interests and that no one has a right to insist on the continuation of futile treatment. Xavier's family do not have a legal right to insist on treatment.

Xavier's son also complains about the interference by hospital staff with his right to religious expression. In the UK, there is both a legal and moral right to allow people to express their religious, cultural and political beliefs. However, this is not an absolute right and can be outweighed where the exercise of the right infringes on the rights of others. In this case the constant singing and praying is causing distress to other patients and families on the intensive care unit, which may be an infringement of their rights.

HOW TO DEAL WITH AN ETHICAL DILEMMA IN CLINICAL PRACTICE

Identify the ethical issue
- Determine why you feel that there is an ethical dilemma.
- How would you frame the ethical dilemma?
- Is this a clinical issue that you need more information about?

Clinical information
- Is the diagnosis clear?
- What other information do you need and how will you get it?
- How are you going to clinically manage this case: what options are possible, what prognoses are possible?

Do you know what the patient wants?
If the patient is *competent*

- Have they expressed a preference (informed/after dialogue)?
- Can the patient's expectations/choices be met – legally/clinically?
- Is the patient making an 'unusual' choice indicating that further dialogue is necessary and/or capacity is formally assessed?

If the patient is *not competent*

- Is there an advance decision – is it valid and applicable?
- Has the patient appointed a proxy to make decisions?
- What treatment option is in the patient's best interests?
- Can the patient's relatives/carers provide insight into what the patient would have wanted?

If the patient is *a child*

- Have the parents been informed and consulted about the treatment options and likely outcomes?

Resolving the ethical dilemma
Identify the main ethical principles that are relevant, including:

- Patient autonomy
- Confidentiality
- Provision of information
- Duties – to the patient, to colleagues, to oneself, to others
- Best interests
- Avoid/limit harms
- Competence

Is there a tension between any of these ethical principles – which ones?

Which ethical principle do you think carries most weight? Justify why.

Seek advice or a sounding board
- Always speak to your consultant, your educational supervisor or another consultant.
- Does professional guidance clarify the issue?
- Can you refer the matter to a clinical ethics committee?

Make a decision

- Who should be involved in the decision-making process?
- When does the decision need to be made?
- What are the foreseeable consequences of your decision?
- What would be the implications of your decision if it applied in all similar cases?
- Can you justify this decision to: the patient or the patient's family; to your consultant; and to your peers?

Review your decision with the benefit of experience and learn from it!

Section 2
ETHICS AND LAW IN CLINICAL MEDICINE

BEGINNING OF LIFE

CASE 8: *IN VITRO* FERTILIZATION

You are a newly qualified general practitioner and you run a weekly sexual health and fertility clinic. During your first clinic three couples come to see you to request *in vitro* fertilization (IVF) treatment on the National Health Service (NHS). The first couple have been married for 3 years; both are well-paid professionals and have failed to conceive since they got married. Tests have not identified any medical reason why they cannot have children. The second couple is not married and receive state benefits. The woman cannot conceive as she has polycystic ovarian syndrome. The third couple is a lesbian couple wishing to have a child who is genetically related to one of them but is carried by the other.

Questions
- What does the National Institute for Health and Clinical Excellence (NICE) guidance say about IVF?
- How does the law regulate assisted conception?
- Is there a 'right' to assisted conception?

ANSWER 8

Childlessness and infertility are different issues. Should limited NHS resources be used to fund IVF for single women or lesbian couples where childlessness is not necessarily due to an absence of fertility? In 2004, NICE issued guidance on the assessment and treatment of people with infertility problems. These guidelines recommend that women aged between 23 and 39 who have diagnosed fertility problems, or unexplained infertility of 3 years' duration, should receive three free cycles of fertility treatment on the NHS. However, a survey by the British Fertility Society in 2006 revealed that only one cycle is offered in most cases. This survey also shows that primary care trusts apply a wide variation of social criteria to determine who should qualify for NHS-funded fertility treatment, including the existence of previous children, high body mass index (BMI) and smoking. In practice the absence of infertility in lesbian women may be used as a reason to deny them publically funded assisted reproduction. The British Fertility Society recommends that single women and same-sex couples should be treated in the same way as heterosexual couples.

The Human Fertilisation and Embryology Act 1990 (updated in 2008) regulates medically assisted reproduction. The Human Fertilisation and Embryology Authority (HFEA) is responsible for licensing clinics carrying out assisted reproduction. A licence is required for the use, storage and disposal of gametes and embryos and the creation of embryos outside the body. There are currently over 80 IVF centres in the UK licensed by the HFEA.

Welfare of the child

The Act states that a woman shall not be provided with treatment services unless account has been taken of the welfare of the child to be born as a result of the treatment and of any other child who may be affected by the birth. Originally the 'need of that child for a father' was to be considered in the assessment of welfare. However that requirement was considered to be too open to interpretation, unjustifiably offensive to many, impossible to implement and of questionable practical value in protecting interests of children born as a result of assisted reproduction (House of Commons Science and Technology Committee, Fifth Report, session 2004/5). The Human Fertilisation and Embryology Bill (2007) proposes to remove the term 'need for a father'.

In 2005 the HFEA published *Tomorrow's Children*, setting out a more focused interpretation of the welfare requirement under the Act. It states that there is a presumption in favour of providing treatment for those who seek it unless there is any evidence that any child born to an individual or couple, or any existing child of the family, would face a serious risk of medical, physical or psychological harm. This may be because of previous convictions relating to harming children, child protection measures or serious violence. Other risk factors to be taken into account include any aspect of the patient's past or current circumstances which is likely to lead to an inability to care for the child to be born – this includes mental or physical conditions and drug or alcohol misuse. It is also relevant to consider whether the child to be born may be at risk of suffering from a serious genetically inherited disorder. Where the child will have no legal father, the treatment centre is expected to assess the prospective mother's ability to meet the child's needs and the ability of other persons within the family or social circle willing to share responsibility for those needs.

Although clinicians have some responsibility in creating new life, the assessment of welfare must be practicable and appropriate to their knowledge and skills. Treatment centres now only contact GPs if they have a cause for concern about the welfare of the child to be born.

The Human Fertilisation and Embryology Act 2008 still requires that the welfare of the child is taken into account in providing fertility treatment, but the 'need for a father', has been replaced by the 'need for supportive parenting'.

A 'right' to have a child
Article 12 of the European Convention on Human Rights provides a 'right to found a family'. However this is not an absolute right. A refusal to fund infertility treatment for women over an age where it is clinically less effective may be justifiable in the light of limited resources.

Donor anonymity
Children born as a result of gamete donations made after 1 April 2005 can, when they reach 18, find out identifying information about the donor, including the donor's name, date and place of birth, appearance and last known address.

Ethical issues
In the UK there is no limit to the number of children that a person can have. Social services only become involved in the welfare of a child after birth and then only if a child is at serious risk of harm or neglect. People with a history of child abuse are not prevented from becoming pregnant again. It could, therefore, be considered ethically unjust for the state to become so involved in the suitability of people with fertility problems to become parents. It could also be argued that to be born is better than to never have an existence. Conversely, it could be argued that because assistance is being provided by a third party, an ethical duty is owed to ensure that the child being created is going to be adequately cared for. This is comparable with the checks that are carried out on individuals who wish to foster or adopt children.

 KEY POINTS

- There is no right to access fertility treatment. The 'welfare of the child' requirement and funding issues regulate access.
- The first and second couples can access treatment on the NHS (regardless of their ability to pay) if they meet the NICE criteria.
- Lesbian couples are not barred from having IVF; indeed it would be discriminatory to do so on that ground alone. However, NICE guidelines limit access to free treatment on the basis of infertility. Lesbian couples may obtain sperm privately and self-inseminate, which is clearly not subject to supervision or currently subject to regulation.

CASE 9: CONSENT TO USE OF GAMETES

A 35-year-old woman, Samantha, had been in a relationship for 3 years. She and her partner wanted to start a family but were unable to conceive naturally. They attended a private fertility clinic for *in vitro* fertilization (IVF) and both gave consent for fertilization of their gametes and for the resulting embryos to be stored. In the meantime Samantha was unfortunately diagnosed as having ovarian cancer. She received chemotherapy and had her ovaries removed, so she will never be able to conceive naturally. Through this difficult time her partner reassured her that he did want to have children with her.

Then the relationship broke down. Samantha's ex-partner contacted the clinic to withdraw his consent to the continued storage of the embryos. Samantha is devastated. She considers that as he gave consent to storage of the embryos he cannot now withdraw it to prevent her becoming a mother.

Questions

- Can consent to the use and storage of embryos be withdrawn by either party prior to implantation?
- Is it *lawful* to destroy healthy gametes/embryos?
- Is it *ethical* to destroy healthy gametes/embryos?

ANSWER 9

Legal issues

The Human Fertilisation and Embryology Act 1990 (updated in 2008) states that consent in writing must be given by both parties for the use and storage of embryos. The terms of the consent should be specified – the maximum period of storage and what should be done in the event of death or incapacity. The parties should be offered counselling. The Act states that consent must be 'effective', i.e. it has not been withdrawn.

Samantha may argue that her ex-partner gave consent because he had agreed to the creation and storage of the embryos and now it is too late to withdraw consent. This issue was considered in *Evans* v. *UK* (2006). It was decided that 'effective' consent means consent that is ongoing from commencement of treatment up to the point at which the embryos are implanted. One partner's withdrawal of consent means that the embryos must be destroyed. This decision may seem 'unfair' as it denies Samantha the chance to have a genetically related child, and some may consider that it infringes an embryo's 'right' to life. The Human Fertilisation and Embryology Act 2008 now provides for a 'cooling off' period of up to a year following the withdrawal of consent to embryo storage by one of the parties whose gametes were used.

Article 8 of the European Convention on Human Rights (ECHR) provides a 'right to respect for private and family life', and this right incorporates the right to respect for a decision to choose whether to become a parent. Samantha's ex-partner's Article 8 rights are not necessarily considered less worthy of protection than Samantha's, and interference with Samantha's rights can be considered proportionate and necessary to ensure that her ex-partner does not become a parent against his will.

Ethical issues

Does an embryo have a 'right' to life? If so, it would be unlawful to destroy it. The European Court has decided that, in the absence of any European consensus on the scientific and legal definition of the beginning of life, the issue of when a right to life begins can be decided by each State. The provisions of the Human Fertilisation and Embryology Act requiring destruction of the embryos following a withdrawal of consent is not a violation of the embryos' 'right to life'. However, although the legal position may be clear, there is scope for disagreement about the moral status of gametes and embryos.

 KEY POINTS

- The Human Fertilisation and Embryology Act 1990 (updated 2008) sets out requirements for consent for the use and storage of gametes and embryos.
- The Act places a legal obligation on a clinic carrying out IVF treatment to explain that a gamete provider can terminate the process at any time up to implantation.
- Destruction of embryos and gametes may be lawful but this may be considered unethical by those who believe life begins at fertilization.

For further information on reproductive autonomy, *see* Case 14: The moral status of the fetus, page 39.

CASE 10: PRE-IMPLANTATION GENETIC DIAGNOSIS

Mike and Lauren, both in their late twenties, have been happily married for 4 years. They are both profoundly deaf and there is a history of congenital deafness in both families. They use sign language to communicate with friends and relatives, and their home and places of work are fully adapted to meet their needs. They have never considered them-selves to be disadvantaged by their condition and met while studying at Gallaudet University, Washington DC, USA, one of the leading academic institutions for people who are deaf or hard of hearing.

Now settled in the UK, Mike and Lauren are keen to start a family and believe passion-ately that their child should have first-hand experience of deaf culture, language and his-tory. They have heard of a technique called pre-implantation genetic diagnosis (PGD) and would like to use this to ensure that they have a child who is deaf like themselves. As an F2 doctor completing your general practice rotation, you have been asked to give them more information.

Questions
- What is pre-implantation genetic diagnosis?
- Under what circumstances is it licensed for use?
- What ethical issues are raised by this case?

ANSWER 10

Legal issues

Pre-implantation genetic diagnosis (PGD) is a technique which involves the genetic testing of embryos created *in vitro*, followed by the selection of specific embryos for implantation. Its main application is in screening for serious, genetic conditions that are known to be present in the family seeking treatment. The regulation of PGD varies widely from country to country. In the UK, the Human Fertilisation and Embryology Authority (HFEA) has licensed testing for over 50 heritable conditions, including sickle cell anaemia, Huntington's disease, cystic fibrosis and certain familial cancers.

At present, PGD may not be used to determine the sex of a child unless there are strong medical grounds for doing so (e.g. where there is a risk of an X-linked condition) nor can it be used to decide physical characteristics such as hair and eye colour, intelligence or particular aptitudes. The HFEA Code of Practice states that clinics offering PGD are obliged to consider the welfare of any resulting children and may refuse treatment if they believe that this will be compromised.

The idea that a couple might wish to use reproductive technologies to have a child with an impairment came to light in 2002, when a deaf lesbian couple in the USA sought a deaf donor from a sperm bank. Their application was refused but they went on to have two deaf children using the donor sperm of a friend with five generations of deafness in his family. The Human Fertilisation and Embryology Act (2008) provides that deliberately screening in a disease or disorder is prohibited.

Ethical issues

The status of the embryo

An inevitable consequence of the technique is the destruction of embryos deemed unsuitable for implantation. For those who believe that morally significant life begins at fertilization, this is clearly unacceptable. On the other hand, many believe that discarding very early embryos is preferable to a termination later in the pregnancy, when a serious genetic condition may become apparent.

Parental autonomy

From the moment of conception, all parents make decisions that will shape their child's future. Should they be allowed to decide the genetic make-up of their child, particularly when this involves denying it a natural faculty such as hearing?

Disability

Since PGD seeks to eliminate undesirable genes, some argue that it is tantamount to discrimination against disabled people. It has even been suggested that it will pave the way for full-scale eugenics. However, the ethicist Julian Savulescu argues that parents have an obligation to select the embryos 'most likely to have the best life, based on available genetic information'. The interpretation of 'best life', of course, is open to discussion.

The scenario also invites questions about the term 'disability'. The World Health Organization defines this as 'a restriction or lack of ability to perform an activity in the manner or within the range considered normal for a human being.' This tends to emphasize the intrinsic failings of the individual and some – like Mike and Lauren – prefer to view 'disability' as a social problem created by the prejudices and intolerance of society.

The following remark (Davis A, From where I Sit. London: Triangle, 1989, p. 19) illustrates the point neatly:

'If I lived in a society where being in a wheelchair was no more remarkable than wearing glasses and if the community was completely accepting and accessible, my disability would be an inconvenience, and not much more than that. It is society which handicaps me, far more seriously and completely than the fact I have spina bifida.'

KEY POINTS

- Pre-implantation genetic diagnosis is used to select out embryos with genetic diseases before implantation to prevent children being born with genetic diseases.
- It cannot be used to test for desirable physical characteristics or to select in genetic conditions, such as deafness.
- Destruction of embryos is morally contentious if it is considered that life begins at fertilization.

CASE 11: SAVIOUR SIBLINGS

Yousef and Maria, a couple in their mid-thirties, have a son aged 4 years and a daughter aged 2 years. Shortly after birth, their son was diagnosed with β-thalassaemia major, an inherited disorder of haemoglobin in which there is reduced or absent production of the β globin chain. It is characterized by profound anaemia and failure to thrive.

Their son requires regular medication and blood transfusions every 3–4 weeks. In the long term, however, stem cell treatment represents his only hope of a cure. This treatment usually involves a bone marrow transplant from a tissue-matched donor but could also take the form of a stem cell transplant from the umbilical cord blood of a tissue-matched baby. At present, there is no suitable donor for their son. His sister is only a 50 per cent tissue match and although Yousef and Maria are keen to have more children, there is only a 25 per cent chance that the new child would be an exact match.

Yousef and Maria have recently read an article on the internet about 'saviour siblings' and understand that it might be possible to create a tissue-matched sibling for their son using pre-implantation tissue typing. They are very excited about this and would like to find out more. As an F2 doctor completing your general practice rotation at their local surgery, you have been asked to discuss the main issues with them.

Questions
- What is pre-implantation tissue typing?
- Is the creation of 'saviour siblings' legal?
- What ethical problems are raised by the use of this technique?

ANSWER 11

In pre-implantation tissue typing, embryos that have been created *in vitro* are tested for the appropriate histocompatibility antigens before implantation. Only those that are a suitable match for the existing sibling are transferred into the woman's uterus.

Legal issues

Applications for pre-implantation tissue typing are considered by the Human Fertilisation and Embryology Authority (HFEA) on an individual basis. Three cases merit particular attention. The first was about a child with β-thalassaemia and the other two involved children suffering from Diamond Blackfan anaemia.

- *Hashmi 2001*: Zain Hashmi had β-thalassaemia and by the time he was 2 years old he was extremely ill. The HFEA granted a licence for pre-implantation tissue typing to be carried out at the same time as genetic screening (pre-implantation genetic diagnosis [PGD]) for β-thalassaemia, but this was challenged by the campaign group Comment on Reproductive Ethics. The House of Lords said that tissue typing was a practice which 'assisted' women to carry children as it was designed to determine whether embryos are 'suitable' to be placed in a woman. Mrs Hashmi could regard an embryo as unsuitable unless it would be free from abnormality *and* a perfect blood match for Zain.
- *Whitaker 2002*: In this instance, the HFEA refused a licence on the grounds that the unborn child should not be exposed to pre-implantation testing without direct benefit to itself. Although similar to the Hashmi case, there was one crucial difference: Diamond Blackfan anaemia is a sporadic condition for which there is no genetic test. Pre-implantation testing of the embryo would therefore confer no direct benefit to the newly created child.
- *Fletcher 2004*: Following a review of its policy on pre-implantation tissue typing, the HFEA granted a licence to the Fletchers. The embryo being selected need not be at risk of suffering from the condition affecting the existing child.

Ethical issues

In the absence of PGD to exclude serious genetic disease, tissue typing confers no immediate benefit to the newly created embryo. Concerns have been raised about the long-term psychological and physical impact of being a 'saviour sibling', and the child could be considered at risk of exploitation. Others argue that in creating a child for a specific purpose, it would be seen as a commodity rather than a person, an argument that has its philosophical roots in Kant's dictum: never use people simply as a means but always treat them as an end in themselves.

In contrast, others suggest that the child would derive psychological benefit from helping the older sibling and from being born into a family that has not already suffered the loss of a child. Supporters of the technique argue that the new child would enjoy the same legal rights and protections as anyone else. Others point out that children are conceived for a whole range of reasons (e.g. to balance a family, save a relationship or provide an heir), none of which meets the Kantian ideal.

> **KEY POINTS**
> - Several cases have been discussed in court and it has been declared lawful for tissue typing to be performed even when the embryo being tested is not at risk of an inheritable disorder.
> - The creation of a 'saviour sibling' could be considered unethical since it is creating a child as a means to another's end.

CASE 12: SURROGACY

Tilly and her husband come to see you, their GP, to ask for advice on fertility treatment. She is 30 years old and has had five miscarriages. She does not have any problems conceiving but is unable to carry a pregnancy to term. Recent tests have diagnosed her with antiphospholipid syndrome – a condition which causes her blood to clot and disrupt the supply of blood to the placenta. Tilly and her husband are still desperate to have their own children. They have discussed their situation with their friends and family and Tilly's best friend has offered to act as a surrogate mother. She is 34 years old, married and has three children of her own and her husband has recently had a vasectomy as they felt their family was complete. Tilly wants to know what the law in England says about surrogacy and whether she could have *in vitro* fertilization (IVF) so that the child would be genetically hers and her husband's but carried by her friend. She also wants to know who will be considered the 'mother' of the child.

Questions
- What does surrogacy involve?
- Who are the legal parents of a surrogate child?
- Is surrogacy lawful?
- Is surrogacy ethical?

ANSWER 12

Legal issues

Surrogacy is the practice by which a woman becomes pregnant with the intention of handing the baby to the commissioning couple after birth. Surrogacy can involve either implanting an embryo into another woman so that the child will be completely genetically related to the commissioning parents or artificially inseminating a woman so that the child is genetically related to the father but not to the commissioning mother.

The Surrogacy Arrangements Act 1985 was introduced in response to 'Baby Cotton', a highly publicized case of a baby born to a surrogate mother. The Act is unusual in that although it is not unlawful to enter into a surrogacy arrangement, it does not make it easy for surrogacy to occur. It is illegal to advertise for a surrogate mother and the birth mother cannot be paid for her role, although usually some provision is made to cover the expenses of the birth mother. Any surrogate contracts drawn up between the commissioning couple and the surrogate are legally unenforceable. Therefore the surrogate cannot be sued if she fails to hand over the baby.

By law the birth mother is the legal mother of the child and her name will go on the birth certificate. If the birth mother is married, her husband will be named as the father unless he declares that he did not agree to the arrangement. If this happens, or if the birth mother is single, the genetic father can be named as the father on the birth certificate. Between the ages of 6 weeks and 6 months the commissioning couple must apply for a parental order, which allows parental responsibility to be vested in them.

Ethical issues

The Warnock Report (1984) and later the Brazier Report (1998) looked at the ethical aspects of surrogacy. Surrogacy can be seen as an extension of an individual's right to reproductive autonomy. Carrying a child for another person can be seen as an act of virtue and love. There is no evidence that any potential child would be harmed by being separated from its birth mother straight after birth. Parallels here can be drawn with children whose mother died during childbirth.

The arguments against surrogacy are principally about the indignity of having a market in selling babies. It is said to be an affront to the dignity of the surrogate and her marital relationship. The virtue of carrying a baby for another woman is outweighed by any potential health risks of pregnancy and childbirth. It also has the potential to take advantage of vulnerable woman who may enter into an agreement to gain financial reward. Relatives may also feel coerced into surrogacy by being unable to say no to a request from someone they love. Some people feel that surrogacy can never be truly altruistic.

 KEY POINTS

- Surrogacy is lawful under specific conditions, but contracts are unenforceable.
- Surrogacy can be considered an altruistic act, but opponents believe it uses women and may have adverse psychological effects on the child.

CASE 13: TERMINATION OF PREGNANCY

A 30-year-old lawyer, Charlotte, is happily married and has a good income. She has just discovered she is pregnant. She does want children at some point but has also just been nominated for promotion at work. She knows she would not get the promotion if she told her boss she was pregnant. She decides that, at this time in her life, the promotion is more important to her than having this baby. She goes to see her general practitioner (GP) a few weeks later, having finally decided that she would like to have an abortion. She asks the GP about whether she has a right to an abortion.

Questions
- What are the grounds for a lawful termination of pregnancy?
- Does the potential father have any legal rights?

ANSWER 13

Legal issues

The Offences Against the Person Act 1861 (OAP) made it a criminal offence for a woman to procure her own miscarriage. To prevent the high levels of mortality and morbidity associated with illegal abortions the Abortion Act 1967 was introduced to provide limited defences to the criminal offences under the OAP. The Abortion Act was amended in 1990 and currently sets out four grounds for termination. Abortion is lawful only if it fulfils the criteria of the Abortion Act.

The grounds for abortion

The most commonly used ground is that the pregnancy has not exceeded 24 weeks and two doctors are of the opinion, formed in good faith, that the continuation of the pregnancy would involve risk, greater than if the pregnancy is terminated, of injury to the physical or mental health of the pregnant woman or any existing children of her family. This is sometimes called the 'social' ground and is the only ground which sets a time limit. There is no restriction based on the viability of the fetus and although most abortions take place within the first 12 weeks of pregnancy, theoretically the results of a late scan may give rise to a choice to terminate *after* the point at which the fetus is viable. There have been calls to lower the time limit for abortion but the Human Fertilisation and Embryology Act 2008 did not effect such a change.

The second ground is that the termination is necessary to prevent grave permanent injury to the physical or mental health of the pregnant woman. This could include the situation where the pregnant woman is suffering from severe hypertension and continuation of the pregnancy might result in permanent kidney damage.

The third ground allows termination where the continuation of the pregnancy would involve risk to the life of the pregnant woman, greater than if the pregnancy were terminated.

The fourth and most contentious ground is the 'fetal abnormality' ground. Terminations may be performed until birth provided that two doctors agree that there is a substantial risk that if the child were born it would suffer from physical or mental abnormalities as to be seriously handicapped. Approximately 1 per cent of all abortions in England and Wales are carried out under this ground. There are two issues here – the *likelihood* of risk and the *nature* of the risk. There will be some situations where antenatal tests show that the baby *will* be born with disabilities. In some cases, however, a positive diagnosis cannot be made. The Royal College of Obstetricians and Gynaecologists (RCOG) has stated that a strict definition of serious abnormality is impracticable. There are insufficient advanced diagnostic techniques to detect malformations accurately and it is not always possible to predict the 'seriousness' of the outcome (in terms of the long-term physical, intellectual or social disability on the child and the effects on the family). The RCOG believes that the interpretation of 'serious abnormality' should be based upon individual discussion agreed between the parents and the mother's doctor (*Abortions for fetal abnormality and syndromatic conditions indicated by cleft lip and/or palate*, RCOG, July 2008).

In 2003 Reverend Jepson, who herself had been born with a congenital jaw defect (corrected by surgery), discovered that in Birmingham an abortion had been carried out at 28 weeks on a fetus with a cleft palate. She argued that terminations after 24 weeks should only be carried out for extremely serious conditions and therefore the doctors who authorized the termination for fetal abnormality under the fourth ground were not justified in doing so. Following an investigation by the Crown Prosecution Service, the doctors were not prosecuted as they had decided in good faith that there was a substantial risk of serious disability.

Rights of the father

The father-to-be has no right to insist that a woman continue with the pregnancy. This was clarified in the case of *Paton* v. *Trustees of British Pregnancy Advisory Service* (1979). Mr Paton tried to prevent his wife from having an abortion using both his right as a potential father and the right to life of the unborn child as justification. He failed on both accounts. The only way in which a potential father could prevent a woman from undergoing an abortion would be to argue that the abortion would be illegal and would not comply with the Abortion Act.

Practicalities

Usually the two doctors signing the form would be the GP and a consultant gynaecologist. It is not a legal requirement for the doctor performing the abortion to sign the form. All abortions must be notified and recorded. The information required includes the gestation of the pregnancy, how this gestation was calculated and which section of the Act was used to justify the abortion. If a fetus is being aborted on the grounds that it is at risk of physical or mental abnormalities, these must be stated as well as the methods used for testing for such afflictions.

 KEY POINTS

- There is no 'right' to abortion. Doctors can be seen as gatekeepers to a woman's access to termination services and they have discretion in interpreting the applicability of the grounds of termination.
- The decision to have an abortion is entirely the woman's and the father of the potential child cannot prevent an abortion from being carried out. This recognizes a woman's bodily integrity.

CASE 14: THE MORAL STATUS OF THE FETUS

A 30-year-old lawyer, Charlotte, is happily married and has a good income. When she discovered she was pregnant she discussed the possibility of a termination with her general practitioner (GP). However, she was undecided at first and the conversation she had with the GP made her realize that she did, after all, want to proceed with the pregnancy. Her husband, family and friends were all delighted. Charlotte has received antenatal care at her GP practice and local maternity hospital and until now the pregnancy has proceeded well. However, the 18-week scan shows that the fetus has increased nuchal thickness and has a high risk of being born with Down's syndrome. Charlotte and her husband are distraught; they had not considered the possibility that the baby would not be 'perfect' and they do not feel they can cope with the continuation of the pregnancy. Despite counselling, Charlotte is now sure that she wants to terminate the pregnancy.

Questions
- What is the extent of a woman's reproductive autonomy?
- At what stage of gestation, if at all, does the moral status of the fetus limit a woman's right to choose?

ANSWER 14

When a woman wants to terminate a pregnancy her reproductive autonomy is in direct conflict with the interests of the fetus. Although a fetus has no legal rights it could be argued that it has a moral claim to a right to life, which trumps the woman's right to procreative autonomy. However, there are various ways in which abortion can be defended morally.

The personhood argument states that only 'persons' can claim rights and rights are exercised by autonomous beings. The definition of 'person' is therefore crucial. If 'person' is defined as someone who can make choices, is self-aware, has a conception of their future, and can evaluate from past experience, then a fetus is clearly not a person and has no claim to a right to life. However, according to this definition, patients in a persistent vegetative state and neonates will not count as persons and therefore will lack a right to life, but surely it is precisely those who lack autonomy who need protection.

A contrasting view is that an embryo is a human being with full moral status, and therefore has a right to life, from the moment of conception, or less conservatively, at some point during its development. Rights are acquired by virtue of being human, and therefore any 'human' (born or not, conscious or not) would have a right to life. This accords moral status to a clump of cells by virtue of being a member of the human species – it is therefore 'speciesist'.

The potentiality argument states that although an embryo is not yet a person it should nevertheless be treated as such because it has the *potential* to become one. John Harris in *The Value of Life* (1985) says that if the fertilized egg is potentially a human being (provided it implants and does not spontaneously abort) then the unfertilized egg and sperm also have the potential to become a human being (provided they meet and then do not encounter a contraceptive!).

So at what point of development would a fetus gain a right to life – conception, the appearance of a nervous system, viability? If such a right is acquired from conception onwards then all abortion would be wrong, but if such rights are acquired from viability, early abortions would be permitted but not late ones (and there would be no differentiation between damaged and healthy fetuses).

Even if fetuses are accorded full moral rights from conception then does this justify harm to the woman whose life or health is at risk? Should not a woman's right to determine what happens to her body override any rights of the fetus even where there is no harm to her?

 KEY POINTS

- Abortion highlights the conflict between the moral status of an embryo and a woman's right to procreative autonomy.
- There are many different ethical perspectives about when a moral claim to a right to life is acquired.

CASE 15: CONSCIENTIOUS OBJECTION

A 30-year-old lawyer, Charlotte, is 18 weeks pregnant. A routine scan carried out 2 days ago showed that the fetus has increased nuchal thickness and is at an increased risk of being born with Down's syndrome. Charlotte and her husband are distraught; they had not considered the possibility that the baby would not be 'perfect', and they do not feel they can cope with the continuation of the pregnancy. Despite counselling, Charlotte is now sure that she wants to terminate the pregnancy. She goes to see her GP to request a termination. However, the GP is a practising Roman Catholic with a strong faith, and she does not wish to participate in abortion services.

Questions
- In what circumstances can a healthcare professional refuse to carry out a termination of pregnancy because of religious, cultural or ethical beliefs?
- Are there any other medical situations when conscientious objection can be relied on by a healthcare professional?

ANSWER 15

Doctors, nurses and midwives are permitted to refuse to 'participate in treatment' by virtue of a conscientious objection clause in the Abortion Act 1967. Section 4 provides that 'no person shall be under any duty ... to participate in any treatment authorised by this Act to which he has a conscientious objection, except where treatment is necessary to save the life of or prevent grave permanent injury to the pregnant woman'. The onus is on the person claiming to rely on conscientious objection to prove it, on religious or ethical grounds. As there is no statutory definition of conscientious objection there may be practical difficulties in interpreting these grounds.

Conscientious objection applies only to *participation* in treatment. The British Medical Association (BMA) takes the view that 'general practitioners cannot claim exemption from giving advice or performing the preparatory steps to arrange an abortion if the request for abortion meets the legal requirements' (*The Law and Ethics of Abortion*, BMA, 2007). Doctors relying on the conscientious objection clause must facilitate a referral to another doctor without delay.

> The Royal College of Midwives considers that 'the interpretation of the conscientious objection clause should only include direct involvement in the procedure of terminating pregnancy'. 'Thus all midwives should be prepared to care for women before, during and after a termination in a maternity unit under obstetric care'
> Royal College of Midwives, *Conscientious Objection*,
> Position Paper No 17. London: RCM, April 1997

Medical students can use the conscientious objection provisions to opt out of witnessing abortions. The BMA advises that those who have a conscientious objection should disclose that to the appropriate supervisor/manager 'at as early a stage as possible so that this fact can be taken into account when planning provisions for patient care' (*The Law and Ethics of Abortion*, Conscientious objection clause; BMA, 2007).

In any event conscientious objection does not apply to necessary treatment in an emergency when the woman's life may be jeopardized. Healthcare practitioners are obliged to provide care, thus the duty of care takes precedent over conscientious objection. In this case scenario, the pregnancy is now quite advanced so delay will increase emotional trauma and risk. Other health professionals in the area may also object because the pregnancy is second trimester and not first.

Other situations

The Human Fertilisation and Embryology Act 1990 provides conscientious objection to those participating in assisted conception. Objecting to the treatment of lesbians or single women would not come within the exception. Those who conscientiously object to participating in withdrawing life-sustaining medical treatment should, where possible, be allowed to hand over the care of the patient to a colleague (*Treatment and care towards the end of life: good practice in decision making.* London: General Medical Council (GMC), 2010). The Assisted Dying for the Terminally Ill Bill proposed by Lord Joffe in 2004 included a conscientious objection clause. In March 2008 the GMC published *Personal Beliefs and Medical Practice* which sets out grounds for conscientous objection (www.gmc-uk.org).

KEY POINTS

- Healthcare professionals may refuse to participate in certain procedures because of their religious or cultural beliefs.
- That refusal is limited by the overriding health interests of the patient, and treatment must always be given when life is at risk.

CASE 16: WRONGFUL BIRTH

Scenario 1

Josephine was 8 weeks pregnant when her 3-year-old daughter was covered with red spots and diagnosed as having German measles. Josephine told her general practitioner (GP) that she would want a termination rather than risk giving birth to a disabled child. She had two blood tests but the results were contradictory. The GP did not check with the laboratory nor did he run new tests. Instead he reassured her that all was well. In fact, Josephine gave birth to a boy who was blind, deaf and severely brain damaged.

Scenario 2

James and Anna are planning to have children. They inform their GP that a nephew of James has a severe chromosomal abnormality and is profoundly disabled. They ask whether tests should be carried out to ensure that a genetic abnormality is not passed on to children that they may conceive. However, the GP does not take a family history nor does he refer the couple to a clinical geneticist for testing. James and Anna's first child, a girl, is born with multiple mental and physical disabilities, as a result of chromosomal abnormality. She is now 2 years old and cannot walk, talk or recognize her parents.

Questions

- Can the parents of a child who is born disabled make a legal claim for costs incurred in their upbringing?
- Can a child who is born with severe disabilities make a legal claim for 'being born'?
- Are there any situations in which it could be argued that a child would be better off not having been born?

ANSWER 16

There are many ethical arguments that support the moral right of a fetus to be born. But it could be argued that a damaged fetus has a right *not to be born*. If so, what is the threshold at which it could be said that it is better for a child never to have existed, because of the extent of their disabilities?

Wrongful birth

This is a claim made by the parents of the child. It is alleged that a negligent act or omission, e.g. failure to correctly interpret scan results, has resulted in the birth of a disabled child. Had the mother received adequate and accurate medical information she would have had the choice to avoid the harm by requesting a termination (although the woman is not obliged to have a termination even if she were properly informed). Such actions are recognized in many jurisdictions around the world, including the UK. An award would be made for the costs attributed to raising a disabled child. The healthcare professional acted negligently in failing to avert the harm, e.g. by negligently failing to advise of/test for a risk of genetic disability.

Wrongful life

The child claims it has been wronged by being born and should be compensated. This claim is not recognized in the UK because it is impossible to compare a life of poor quality with no existence whatsoever (although a very poor quality of life is used as a justification for withdrawing treatment). The case of *McKay* v. *Essex Area Health Authority* (1982) recognized that such a claim would mean 'regarding the life of a handicapped child as not only less valuable than the life of a normal child, but so much less valuable that it was not worth preserving'.

In the above two scenarios, failure to carry out genetic tests that were reasonably indicated (scenario 2) and unreasonable failure to chase/interpret test results accurately (scenario 1) enables a wrongful birth action to be brought by the parents. However, the disabled child cannot bring a claim for wrongful life.

To what extent is an unborn child entitled to protection? A woman cannot be sued for harm she causes the fetus, e.g. by taking drugs and alcohol throughout pregnancy. The only claim that can be made against a mother, by her child, is where damage arises through driving accidents.

 KEY POINTS

- Parents may make a claim for wrongful birth if a negligent act or omission resulted in the birth of a disabled child, and had they been properly informed, the woman could have exercised her right to have a termination.
- A claim that a child has a *right not to be born* implies that there are some conditions where the child is better off not having been born, i.e. a comparison of existence with disabilities and non-existence.

CASE 17: NEONATAL CARE: LEGAL ISSUES

Rebecca was born at 26 weeks' gestation weighing 1.3 kg. She had severe respiratory failure requiring ventilation for the first 3 months of her life, and now she has pulmonary hypertension resulting from the damage to her lungs. She also has recurrent urinary tract infections and her renal function is worsening. She has not left hospital since her birth and 2 months ago she was transferred to the paediatric intensive care unit with a severe infection. Since that time her respiratory and neurological functioning have profoundly and persistently deteriorated. Rebecca is now 8 months old and although her weight is increasing it is not matched by growth in head circumference which is indicative of brain damage and limited potential brain growth. She does not respond to stimulation although she does experience pain and distress and it is considered that she will be able to experience pain of future treatment. She will have minimal cognitive function and she is very likely to develop epilepsy. After considerable debate, the clinical team decides that it would not be in Rebecca's best interests to perform cardiopulmonary resuscitation if she has a respiratory arrest. Her parents disagree.

Questions
- Does Rebecca have a right to life?
- How should the doctors proceed if the parents' views conflict with those of the medical team?

ANSWER 17

Right to life

Article 2 of the European Convention on Human Rights (ECHR) provides that everyone's right to life shall be protected by law. This applies to all persons, irrespective of age and competence. However, this does not mean that life must be prolonged in all circumstances. Withholding and withdrawing medical treatment will not breach Article 2 when it is in the best interests of the patient.

Article 3 of the ECHR states that no one shall be subject to inhuman or degrading treatment. Invasive treatment where the only benefit is a brief extension of life, and death cannot be averted, could breach Article 3. In the case of *A National Health Service Trust* v. *D* (2000) a decision not to resuscitate a baby with irreversible lung disease and multiorgan failure taken in the best interests of the baby did not amount to a breach of Article 2. Article 3 required the hospital not to impose futile and burdensome measures to prolong the baby's life and to allow the baby to die with dignity.

Views of the parents

The courts have stated that there is no legal distinction between withholding or withdrawing life-prolonging treatments and that the best interests test applies equally to both situations. The Royal College of Paediatrics and Child Health acknowledges that there are circumstances in which treatments that merely sustain 'life' and that do not restore health nor confer any other benefit are not in the child's best interests (*Witholding or Withdrawing Life-sustaining Treatment in Children: A Framework for Practice*, 2nd ed. London: Royal College of Paediatrics and Child Health, 2004). In this case scenario the clinical team considers that resuscitation is not in Rebecca's best interests. To what extent should the clinical view be balanced against the views of the parents about Rebecca's best interests?

Parents of young children have legal authority to make healthcare decisions on their behalf, acting in the child's best interests. Because of their knowledge and understanding of the child, parents' views about their child's best interests may have particular value. Would this also be true of a very ill premature baby who has spent all her life in intensive care? The assessment of best interest is an objective one. A useful approach, adopted by the courts, is to make a list of the benefits/advantages and the burdens/disadvantages of continuing or discontinuing the treatment in question. Although parents' wishes regarding the treatment of their child should be accorded respect, they cannot request treatment that is contrary to the professional judgement of doctors.

Except in emergency situations doctors should not withhold or withdraw treatment from a child without parental consent unless they have sought authority from the court. The court would be involved in determining which course of treatment is in the best interests of the child. However, a court will not order doctors to provide a course of treatment which they are unwilling to give.

 KEY POINTS

- If there is abject disagreement between the clinical team and the child's parents, timely legal advice should be sought.
- Doctors cannot be compelled to give treatment that in their properly held view is not in a child's best interests.

CASE 18: NEONATAL CARE: ETHICAL ISSUES

George was born after a 24-week pregnancy. He weighed 2.8 kg and did not breathe spontaneously. He was resuscitated but he remained ventilator dependent after 96 hours. Serious brain injury was indicated by cerebral magnetic resonance imaging. Clinical evidence indicated that George, if he survived, would have severe quadriplegia, severe learning difficulties and would be entirely dependent on his carers. His parents were informed of his prognosis and were involved in the discussion about withdrawal of mechanical ventilation. However, they felt that if they agreed to withdrawal of ventilation they would be 'abandoning' their son. The clinical team is considering what options they have and how to proceed.

Questions
- When, if ever, is it morally justified to withdraw or withhold medical treatment from a neonate?
- Is the deliberate ending of the life of a severely handicapped baby morally acceptable?
- Should costs of treatment be taken into account in critical care decision making?

ANSWER 18

In 2006 the Nuffield Council on Bioethics published a report that considered the issues of *who* should make decisions on behalf of a baby and *how* their interests can be identified and protected.

Sanctity of life

The ethical principle of sanctity of life states that there is an intrinsic value in human life, irrespective of whether it is valuable to the person concerned or to anyone else. This is why it is considered wrong to cause the death of a human being, even one who is terminally ill or severely disabled. However, sanctity of life is one of a cluster of relevant ethical principles:

- Respect for the dignity of the individual
- Beneficence (acting in the best interests of a person)
- Non-maleficence (do no harm)
- Justice (including consideration of resources).

Although there is a very strong presumption in favour of a course of action which will prolong life, quality of life is a consideration in deciding what course of action is ethically, clinically and legally acceptable. The Nuffield Council on Bioethics report stated that there is no ethical obligation to act to preserve life where imposing or continuing treatment to sustain life results in a level of irremediable suffering. It considered that distressing and futile interventions that do no more than delay death would impose an intolerable burden on the baby and would not be in its best interests.

In this case scenario it is necessary to consider whether it is in George's best interests to continue to receive mechanical ventilation. This requires consideration of the pain and suffering he is experiencing and the quality of life he has now and can expect to experience. Clearly without mechanical intervention he will die. The decision should be made by the treating team, based on clinical evidence and after discussion with his parents.

Active means to end the life of a severely impaired neonate

In the Netherlands the Groningen Protocol sets out circumstances in which active means can be authorized to end the life of babies who are so ill and their suffering so severe that they have no prospect of a future. There has been widespread condemnation of this Protocol. The Nuffield Council rejected the argument that withholding/withdrawing treatment and deliberately ending life are equally morally acceptable. Doctors have a professional obligation to preserve life and taking active measures to end life, even where suffering is intolerable, is regarded as a violation of that duty.

Economic considerations

To what extent should the high costs of treatment and perhaps ongoing care of premature babies be relevant factors in decision making? Although treatment decisions taken for any newborn baby should made on the basis of the best interests of the patient, resource restraints at national and local levels may limit the availability of best treatment options.

 KEY POINTS

- Assessment of the best interests of a neonate requires objective consideration of the clinical evidence.
- Parents' views should be taken into account as they will bear responsibility for the care of the child.

For a discussion of acts and omissions, *see* Case 63: The distinction between acts and omissions at the end of life, page 157.

CHILDREN AND ADOLESCENTS

CASE 19: PARENTS REFUSING TREATMENT FOR THEIR CHILD

Mandy and her partner, Kev, are delighted to be the parents of their first child, Zac. Mandy is human immunodeficiency virus (HIV) positive. She has not taken any antiretroviral medication but instead has maintained a healthy diet and lifestyle and she considers that she is fit and well. Kev is HIV negative. Mandy and Kev did not seek antenatal care as they did not want conventional Western medicine imposed on them. Mandy had a planned home birth with a midwife. Zac is now 6 weeks old and seems happy and healthy. He is being breastfed. However, the health visitor says that Zac should be tested for HIV because he is at risk and if he is found to be HIV positive he can be given prophylactic treatment.

Mandy and Kev prefer alternative medicine and they are very concerned about the effects of prophylactic medication. They explain to the health visitor that two of their friends have had very bad reactions to such medication and they do not wish to expose Zac to that risk. They are obviously caring parents and they are prepared to monitor the situation themselves. Despite the health visitor's explanations of the comparative risks, and the intervention of their general practitioner, they refuse to agree that Zac should be tested to see if he is HIV positive because, even if he is, they do not want him to then be subjected to aggressive medical intervention in which they have little faith.

Questions
- Is it in Zac's best interests to be tested to see if he is HIV positive?
- To what extent is the assessment of a child's best interests left to the discretion of the parents?
- What can be done if both parents are adamantly against medical intervention that is objectively considered to be in the child's best interests?

ANSWER 19

The test to be applied here is the 'best interests' of the child – is it in Zac's best interests to be tested to see if he is HIV positive? In assessing best interests, medical evidence holds great weight. However, 'best interests' does not just mean best *medical* interests but rather best *overall* interests and parents will be able to give input into the wider interests of their child. Parental views about best interests of their child will carry greater weight where there is scope for a difference of opinion, and, in the case of refusal to consent by the parents, where the risks to the child are minimal. Where evidence of medical benefit is compelling, less weight will be attached to their views because they are not consistent with promoting the welfare of the child.

The advantages of an HIV test for Zac are overwhelming: it involves minor intrusion, there are benefits of a certain diagnosis and, if treatment is necessary, it is relatively effective and carries minimal risks. (The parents' perception of harms of treatment experienced by their friends should be explored.) It is clearly in Zac's best interests to ascertain his medical status so that appropriate informed decisions can be taken in the event of future illness. In contrast there are significant risks if he is HIV positive and does not receive medication.

Although the advantages of the test are very substantial it is worth considering the effect on the parents of interfering in their personal realm of decision making. In a similar case (*Re C* [A Child] [HIV Testing] 2000) the judge noted the disadvantages of imposing decisions on parents: the affront to them, the stress of medical intrusion into their lives and the prospect of further conflict with orthodox medicine, and even perhaps with the law, in the wake of the test result.

Although autonomous decisions of the family should be respected, children themselves have rights which may justify a limitation on the exercise of parental rights. If the matter cannot be resolved by discussion, the involvement of the court may be necessary.

 KEY POINTS

- Although parents have the right to be involved in healthcare decisions for their children, this is always subject to the overriding principle that such decisions are in the best interests of the child. Children have separate rights of their own.
- Best interests means that the procedure or treatment is therapeutic. This is given a wide interpretation and may incorporate non-medical benefits.
- Refusal of treatment solely on religious grounds does not promote the best interests of the child.
- There is scope for a difference of perspective – the autonomous decision of the parents will be respected where the procedure is one which is elective and a refusal will have no major adverse outcome on the child's health, for example, immunization.

CASE 20: CONSENT AND YOUNG CHILDREN

A 4-year-old boy, Bobby, has nephrotic syndrome. For the past 3 years he has been under the care of a consultant renal physician at a city teaching hospital. The consultant considers it necessary to carry out a renal biopsy to check the extent of renal damage. It is likely that in the future he will need treatment including possibly a kidney transplant. Bobby lives with his mother in a commune over 240 km from the hospital. She is a caring mother and there is no issue that she is failing in her duties towards her son, but she says that she cannot cope with the long journey away from where she feels safe. Bobby has always attended hospital appointments with his grandmother, who has been supportive of his care.

Questions
- Who can consent to medical treatment on behalf of young children?
- What happens in an emergency?

ANSWER 20

A person with 'parental responsibility' has decision-making authority regarding the child, including the right to make healthcare decisions in the child's best interests. Mothers automatically have parental responsibility. Both parents have parental responsibility if they are married. For children born after 1 December 2003 (in England and Wales) both of the child's legal parents have parental responsibility, whether or not they are married, if they are registered on the child's birth certificate. Generally it is not necessary, nor reasonable, for a healthcare professional to make enquiries of the adult bringing a child for medical treatment, about whether or not she has the right to give consent. However, if a carer brings a child for treatment the views of the parents should be sought.

Legally consent is needed from only one person with parental responsibility. However, it is clearly good practice to involve both parents where possible, particularly if treatment is invasive or the benefits of treatment do not overwhelmingly outweigh the burdens. Where there is disagreement between the parents, and discussion fails to reach agreement, the lead clinician may take the decision whether or not to proceed if there is good evidence that it is in the child's best interests. In some situations best interests are not quite as clear cut. When conflict arises in these situations, either between parents and the doctors or between parents, a court order should be obtained before any treatment is given where there is tine to do so. There is not a specific list of when this should be done but some examples include non-therapeutic neonatal male circumcision and refusal to have the measles, mumps and rubella (MMR) vaccine.

It is possible for another person to acquire parental responsibility through a court order, but there is nothing to suggest that Bobby's grandmother has done so. Nevertheless the Children Act 1989 authorizes a person with care of a child to do 'what is reasonable in all the circumstances of the case for the purpose of safeguarding or promoting the child's welfare'. This would apply to childminders who can consent to necessary routine treatment. Grandparents can be authorized to take medical decisions. One way to resolve the practical difficulty of obtaining consent for Bobby's biopsy is for his mother to provide documentary evidence that his grandmother can give consent. However, it is essential that the mother and grandmother are both adequately informed about the biopsy and the implications for further investigations and treatment and that this is clearly recorded.

In an emergency where no parent is present or contactable, urgent treatment which is in the child's best interests may be given.

 KEY POINTS

- Those with parental responsibility can make healthcare decisions in the best interests of the child.
- A temporary carer, such as a teacher or childminder, can consent to essential medical assistance following an accident.

CASE 21: CONSENT FOR NON-THERAPEUTIC TREATMENT

Michael, a 6-month-old baby, is referred by a general practitioner to one of the surgeons at the hospital where he has been a patient previously. Both his parents are in full agreement that they wish to have him circumcised for religious reasons. Their two older sons have also had circumcisions for religious reasons. The eldest had his performed by the (non-medical) person used by their local religious community. The second son was treated in the local hospital as the parents found it too distressing for them and the child for the procedure to be done without an anaesthetic.

The surgeon to whom Michael is referred has performed religious circumcisions previously, but only in cases where the children were all fit and well. The team has taken the view that although the operation is not clinically necessary, the risks to the child are extremely low and therefore it is in the child's best interests to have it done under general anaesthesia with good pain relief and with expertise readily available should there be a rare complication such as bleeding. However, when the surgeon reviews Michael's history he realizes that Michael has serious cardiac disease which has a significant risk of deteriorating under general anaesthesia. Michael will also require antibiotic prophylaxis. The surgeon discusses the situation with Michael's cardiologist and the anaesthetist. They all agree that there is a significant risk to him and that in their collective view this risk is too high to perform a procedure that is not clinically essential. They discuss this with Michael's parents and tell them that in their opinion it is not in his best interests for them to proceed with the circumcision. The parents then say that they have no other option but to go to the lay person and ask him to do it which would mean that their baby will be subjected to an even higher risk.

Questions
- Is it in Michael's best interests to have the circumcision performed in hospital?
- Can parents request a procedure or treatment that is not in the child's best medical interests?
- Does the 'threat' that the parents will seek an alternative, less safe, procedure affect the assessment of best interests?

ANSWER 21

'Parents should be entitled to make choices about how best to promote their children's interests, and it is for society to decide what limits should be imposed on parental choices'
British Medical Association, *The Law and Ethics of Male Circumcision – Guidance for Doctors*. London: BMA, 2006

In the case of female genital mutilation (FGM) the law has limited parental choice; it is illegal in all circumstances in the UK. The harms of neonatal non-therapeutic circumcision are not as extreme as FGM and in some cases the benefits of the infant's identification with a religious or cultural group could swing best interests in favour of the procedure. The potential risks *for this baby*, arising from his serious cardiac disease, overwhelmingly outweigh any benefit of following the religious traditions of his family.

The parents' view of their baby's best interests is seriously at odds with the medical view to the extent that they are willing that Michael undergoes a non-therapeutic procedure with significant inherent risks. If the procedure is not performed at a National Health Service (NHS) hospital they say that they are willing to ask a lay person in their religious community to perform the procedure. Doctors should not be coerced into performing non-therapeutic treatment that is not in the best interests of a child, simply to prevent the procedure from being performed by a lay person in a situation which may pose an even greater threat to the child's health. This would ignore the duties of the healthcare professional – to act in the best interests of the child and to 'do no harm'.

Medical treatment often inadvertently harms the patient while providing an overall benefit. The benefits of circumcision should be balanced against the burdens. As there is no medical need to perform the circumcision, and in this case to do so would actually cause harm, the principle of non-maleficence should be the overriding factor in determining whether to proceed. Alternatively, it could be argued that the clinician's duty is to *minimize* harm. Performing the circumcision in hospital may be safer than allowing it to be performed by a lay person. However, it is a supposition that the parents would, if properly informed of the risks, proceed with circumcision by a lay person. Even if the only two options were NHS or lay circumcision, the surgeon can anticipate a real likelihood of harm, which means that surgery cannot be justified.

 KEY POINTS

- Parents can give or refuse consent for medical treatment or procedures, but this must be in the best interests of the child, without regard to their own interests.
- If there is abject disagreement between the parents and the clinical team about what is in the child's best interests then the matter should be referred to court.
- Doctors cannot be compelled to perform a procedure that they do not consider to be in the best interests of a child.
- There will be a point at which society's interest in protecting its vulnerable members will limit the choices parents can make for their children.

The legal and ethical issues of circumcision are discussed in Case 90: Female genital mutilation, page 223, and Case 91: Neonatal male circumcision, page 227.

CASE 22: ASSESSING COMPETENCE IN MINORS

Ruby, a 14-year-old girl, has had asthma since she was a young child and regularly uses beclomethasone and salbutamol inhalers. She occasionally gets teased at school, where she is a boarder, because she cannot join in all the sports that are played due to cold weather and extreme exercise exacerbating her asthma. Despite this she is compliant with her medication and has only had to be admitted to hospital once, when her inhaler ran out. Ruby goes to see her GP and tells him that everyone at school is suffering with flu and she has caught it off the other boarders. She feels terrible but her main worry is that her asthma has become much worse. By the end of the history taking she is struggling to catch her breath and has to take a couple of puffs of salbutamol. The GP listens to her chest and diagnoses a chest infection. The GP suspects that she may benefit from intravenous antibiotics but is told by Ruby that she has an important examination coming up and does not want to go to hospital. The GP gives her a choice of taking oral antibiotics and steroids but tells her she has to stay in sick bay for a few days to get some rest.

Questions
- When is a young person considered competent to make healthcare decisions?
- Are there any limitations on what treatments a young person can consent to?
- What is the role of parents of a competent minor in healthcare decision making?

ANSWER 22

16–17-year-olds

At 18 years a person is an adult and has legal capacity to consent to medical treatment. Young people under 18 have legal capacity to consent to treatment in the same way *if* they can understand the treatment and its effects, i.e. if they have sufficient competence. Young people aged 16–17 years are presumed to be competent to give effective consent to surgical, medical and dental treatment, and associated procedures such as investigations and anaesthesia. There is no presumption of competence to consent to organ donation, non-therapeutic procedures or research although this could be shown using the Gillick test. Consent is not also necessary from the parents.

Under-16s

Young people under 16 years of age can consent to medical treatment if they demonstrate that they are competent to do so. This is sometimes called 'Gillick competence' because the legal principle was clarified in the case of *Gillick* v. *West Norfolk and Wisbech AHA* (1985). If a young person has sufficient intelligence and understanding to appreciate the treatment issues then they can consent to the procedure or treatment without either the knowledge of or the consent of their parents. Sometimes the term 'Fraser competence' is used. In the Gillick case, Lord Fraser set out guidelines for when doctors could provide contraceptive advice/treatment to teenage girls without the consent of parents. Fraser competence refers to competence in the context of contraception and is narrower in its scope.

The Age of Legal Capacity (Scotland) Act 1991 provides that minors younger than 16 may consent to medical treatment if, in the opinion of the health professional, they are capable of understanding the nature and possible health consequences of the procedure or treatment.

The ability to consent depends on competence not age, although clearly experience of life, and perhaps particularly of illness itself, will point towards the ability to weigh issues in the decision-making process and to predict outcomes. Competence is functional, i.e. it depends on the nature of the decision to be taken, and a high level of understanding would be expected for an invasive procedure. However, in such cases, the parents of a young person will normally be involved in the decision-making process. The assessment of competence is a matter for the healthcare professional conducting the examination/providing the treatment. If there are doubts about the young person's capacity then a second opinion should be sought.

Where a minor is not competent to give or withhold informed consent, a person with parental responsibility may give permission for investigations or treatment which are in the minor's best interests. This is the case whether the minor is 17, 16 or younger than 16 years.

 KEY POINTS

- Children under 16 have the legal capacity to consent to medical examination and treatment if they can show sufficient maturity and intelligence to understand the nature and implications of the proposed treatment, the alternatives and the risks involved.
- The nature and amount of information provided can influence capacity.

CASE 23: UNDER-AGE CONTRACEPTION

Sarah has come to accident and emergency late one evening with a girlfriend. She says that she has had unprotected sex with her boyfriend and wants to be given emergency contraception. After some discussion, she reluctantly tells you that she is 13 and that her boyfriend is a 'bit older' than her. You talk to her about the risks of sexually transmitted infections through unprotected sex. She says, 'Yeah I know all about that, now give me the tablets so I can go home before my Mum notices that I have gone.'

Questions
- Is it lawful to provide Sarah with emergency contraception?
- If so, do you have to let her Mum know?
- As Sarah is under the legal age for sexual intercourse should this be reported?

ANSWER 23

Legal issues

In 2004, the Department of Health issued *Revised Guidance for Health Professionals on the Provision of Contraceptive Services for the Under-16s*. This recommends that when a person under 16 requests contraception, doctors and other health professionals should discuss the risks of pregnancy, sexually transmitted diseases and the pros and cons of the various contraception options. A doctor or health professional can provide contraception (and sexual and reproductive health advice and treatment) without parental knowledge or consent, to a person under 16, provided that:

- she understands the advice provided and its implications
- her physical or mental health would otherwise be likely to suffer and so provision of advice or treatment is in her best interest.

In addition it is good practice for healthcare professionals to follow the Fraser guidelines.

The courts have recognized the importance of maintaining confidentiality of young people who access contraception and abortion services – without this reassurance they may not engage with such services, which would put them at risk of becoming pregnant and contracting a sexually transmitted disease. In this case scenario, it seems likely that Sarah would be considered competent to consent to emergency contraception. She should be counselled to speak to her mother, although she must not be contacted if Sarah refuses.

Although it is an offence for a man to have sex with a girl under 16 it would not normally be in the girl's best interests to involve the authorities. However, Sarah would be considered vulnerable because of her age. If there was a power imbalance in the relationship, because of age difference or the nature of the relationship, a referral should be made to the appropriate authority. Young people over 16 and under 18 are not deemed able to give consent if the sexual activity is with an adult in a position of trust or a family member as defined by the Sexual Offences Act 2003. Children under 13 are not deemed competent to consent to sex (Sexual Offences Act 2003) and consideration would have to be given as to whether it would be in the young person's best interests to report to a statutory agency. This would usually be the case, and although there is no requirement for mandatory reporting, the case should always be discussed with the child protection lead.

Ethical issues

An individual's choice about her sexual activities and preferences is an aspect of private life which deserves respect. Respecting the autonomy of a competent young person provides a benefit in itself – an increased sense of worth and dignity. However, this must be balanced against the potential for harm. As Sarah is having sex with her boyfriend in any event there would be a harm in refusing to provide her with emergency contraception, but the long-term harm of having unprotected sex should also be considered.

 KEY POINTS

- Doctors and health professionals have a duty of care and a duty of confidentiality to all patients, including those younger than 16.
- If a doctor is concerned about a young person having sexual intercourse, and fears that their vulnerability is being abused, the doctor should seek advice from a senior colleague or social services.

CASE 24: ADOLESCENT REFUSAL OF LIFE-SUSTAINING TREATMENT

Kylie, a 16-year-old girl who lives with her parents and young brother, was diagnosed with cancer 2 years ago. She has received two courses of chemotherapy. She has shown maturity and understanding with respect to treatment decisions and she has a good relationship with the clinical team. Now she has got to the stage where she is 'fed up' of being in hospital and receiving unpleasant treatments. She is due to have another round of chemotherapy and she refuses to consent. Kylie is told that without this next round of chemotherapy, it is likely that she will die within 3 months, but with treatment she has a 30 per cent chance of survival for 3 years. Her parents are supportive of her decision – they wish her to have a peaceful and dignified end to her life.

Questions
- Can Kylie legally refuse treatment?
- Should she be 'forced' to have treatment?
- Can her parents give consent?

ANSWER 24

Legal issues

Minors aged 16 and 17 are presumed to be competent to consent to treatment. However, in this case Kylie is *refusing* to consent. It could be assumed that if a person is competent to consent, then she would be competent to refuse. Competence is essentially assessed on a sliding scale in proportion to the importance or seriousness of the outcome and the ratio of risks to benefits of the treatment. Court decisions have shown that an exacting standard is required for a minor to be considered competent to refuse medically indicated treatment. If a minor is not considered competent to understand the implications of treatment refusal then the minor's parents can give consent to the procedure. Kylie's parents support her wish not to receive further treatment.

Kylie has shown understanding and maturity in the decisions she has made about her treatment. She seems well informed and rational in her refusal of further treatment. Her experience of illness is likely to promote her comprehension. The courts have indicated that even competent refusals may be overridden where it is in the young person's best interests to do so. However, this would be only in extreme cases where the young person is seeking to refuse treatment in circumstances which will in all probability lead to her death or to severe permanent injury. Reasonable force may be used to carry out the treatment/procedure. Imposing invasive treatment which offers only a small hope of preserving life against the wishes of a competent adolescent would not be considered to be in her best interests.

Could it be considered to be in Kylie's best interests to start a new round of chemotherapy which carries a fairly low chance of success? The assessment of her best interests should include the importance of respecting her autonomy and dignity and the harm done to her, and her family, of enforcing treatment which they have not agreed to. If this course of chemotherapy had a higher rate of remission, the objective medical considerations would have greater weight in determining Kylie's best interests.

Ethical issues

Kylie's experience of illness and previous treatments indicate that she has a concept of where her best interests lie. On the other hand, she has limited life experience and is in a vulnerable position. There is a conflict between respecting her autonomous wishes now and protecting her long-term interests. Enforced treatment may have a grave negative effect, not only on Kylie and her family but also on the healthcare professionals who treat her – they may be very reluctant to impose regular ongoing treatment against her wishes.

 KEY POINTS

- Establishing dialogue and respect between the patient, the family and the healthcare professional is essential to promote considerate decision making.
- Carrying out medical treatment against the wishes of a competent adolescent has been allowed by the courts in extreme circumstances but could be subject to challenge under the Human Rights Act 1998.

CASE 25: ADOLESCENT REFUSAL OF PREVENTIVE SURGERY

A 16-year-old boy, John, needs orthopaedic surgery on his knee, under general anaesthesia (GA), to avoid serious mobility problems in the future. He understands clearly why the procedure is needed and he wishes to have it done. His parents are also in full agreement, and they want it done as soon as possible to ensure no problems develop. However, he expresses particular concern regarding the GA and also the surgery. He is extremely frightened of being put to sleep and the possibility that during the operation complications may arise and he will die. He is fit and well, and his surgeon and anaesthetist speak to him at length and explain exactly what is going to happen. He appears to be reassured. A date is planned for the operation and his parents have arranged leave from work so that they can be with him on the day of the operation and to look after him when he is discharged from hospital. On the day of admission he is fine and says he does not want to take any premedication as he does not need it.

However, on arrival in the anaesthetic room John suddenly becomes panic stricken and says that he cannot allow himself to be put to sleep as he is afraid he will die. The anaesthetic team and his parents try to reassure him but to no avail. His reasons for refusal are expressed in considered terms. He agrees he needs the operation and he wants to have it done. He is ashamed of himself that he is so afraid. However, he is very clear he does not want the GA. He says he needs more time and he will take a premed. The anaesthetist agrees with this and the decision is made to send him back to the ward, have a premed and then return to theatre later. This is done and he is sleepy when he arrives in the anaesthetic room, but as soon as he is in there he has the same objections. The staff try to convince him to have a cannula inserted into his vein but he will not let anyone hold his arm, nor will he accept the anaesthetic gas. He again declares that he is afraid of dying. The team decides that they cannot proceed now as the surgery is not urgent and can be done in a few months' time. The anaesthetist informs John's parents, but they want him to be held down and given the GA. The anaesthetist says she cannot do this, as it is not appropriate in the circumstances and also because John is expressing concerns and making a choice that many adults would be allowed to make. The parents are now very distressed and angry with their son and the clinical team.

Questions
- Does John have capacity to refuse the operation?
- Can his parents insist that he has the treatment now?

ANSWER 25

Legal issues

Consent must be obtained prior to administering GA and surgery. If the patient is competent, he can give consent to the surgery. At 16, John is considered to have sufficient maturity and intelligence to understand the implications of the treatment and the risks. He agrees 'he needs the operation and in fact he wants to have it done'. However, he is refusing to consent to having the GA. When he arrived in the anaesthetic room he suddenly becomes panic stricken and says that he cannot allow himself to be put to sleep as he is afraid he will die. The fact that he is panic stricken may affect his capacity.

In *Re MB* (1997), a 23-year-old woman was 40 weeks pregnant with her second child. The baby was in a breech position and a caesarean section was considered necessary. The woman originally consented, but she had an irrational fear of needles and refused the insertion of a Venflon as she was not prepared to undergo anaesthesia by way of injection. She was not capable of making a decision at all because at the moment of panic her 'fear dominated all'. In some circumstances fear may be so overwhelming that it paralyses the will and destroys capacity to make a decision. But fear of an operation may be a rational reason to refuse it. In the present case scenario, the anaesthetist considers that John is refusing for considered reasons.

John's parents want him to have the operation. They can provide valid consent for the GA and for the operation if John lacks capacity. Parents can also give consent even if the child is competent and refuses, although legal advice should be sought. In the case of *Re W* (1993) the judge referred to a legal 'flak jacket' which protects a doctor from a charge of battery. Consent could be obtained from the child *or* the parents (and in some situations the court). This is contentious from an ethical perspective as it fails to respect the young person's autonomy and is now questionable in the light of the Human Rights Act 1998.

Ethical issues

The clinical team has a duty to act in John's best interests. The harm caused by violating John's choice to refuse treatment now must be balanced against the harm of failing to treat him. The consequences of holding him down to give him the GA, the impact on his dignity and of failing to respect his decision, and the possible consequence that he will lose trust in the clinical team outweigh the beneficial consequences of performing the operation *at this stage*.

 KEY POINTS

- Consent for treatment can be obtained from a Gillick competent child, a 16–17-year-old or someone with parental responsibility.
- The clinical team is not obliged to perform a procedure that it does not consider to be in a patient's best interests, despite the insistence of the parents.
- Fear can be so overwhelming that it temporarily removes capacity to consent to treatment.

CASE 26: WITHHOLDING INFORMATION FROM A MINOR

When Sandra was 2 years old her mother noticed that her daughter was very listless and had a yellow tinge to her skin. She was admitted to hospital and underwent tests to try to discover the cause. She was eventually diagnosed with hereditary spherocytosis, a hereditary haemolytic anaemia. The severity of the disease can vary enormously between patients and some people may go throughout life without any symptoms. The doctors tell Sandra's parents that she will most likely need a splenectomy at some point, but, if possible, they would prefer to do this when she is an adolescent because there is an increased risk of infection by encapsulated organisms in childhood, which may result in death if the spleen has already been removed. Sandra has regular tests for red blood cells and liver function throughout her childhood. She also has periods when she has to take folate tablets due to periods of rapid cell turnover. However, she has been fortunate and has never had to be admitted to hospital with an aplastic or megaloblastic anaemic crisis.

Sandra is now 14 years old. Her parents have spoken to the consultant haematologist and asked him not to tell Sandra that she has hereditary spherocytosis. She is a studious girl and they are concerned that such information will cause her unnecessary worry and may affect her examination results. The consultant doesn't want to go along with their wishes, especially as Sandra is a bright girl and is asking questions about the drugs she sometimes has to take and why she needs so many blood tests. But her parents are adamant about the harm that such knowledge will do to her.

Questions
- Do doctors have a duty not to deceive their patients?
- Is there a moral difference between lying and deception?
- If Sandra does not ask what is wrong with her then should the doctor inform her of her condition?

ANSWER 26

Legal issues

The duty of the consultant is to act in *the patient's* best interests. Respecting the treatment choices of a competent informed young person will usually be in her best interests. Sandra has enquired about her treatment and at her age she has the potential to make competent treatment decisions. Without knowledge of her diagnosis she is deprived of the information she needs to exercise her autonomous choice. It is both a legal and ethical requirement to seek consent before treatment of a competent person. She should be informed of her diagnosis so that she can give consent to future treatment.

Ethical issues

From a consequentialist perspective the morally correct course of action is that which produces the best overall consequences, both in the long term and in the short term. Thus there is no intrinsic moral difference between lying and deception as both give rise to the same consequences. What are the consequences of not telling Sandra of her diagnosis now? On the one hand, when she later finds out or is told about her diagnosis, she may feel that she cannot fully trust her doctor, which may affect compliance with treatment. It may also adversely affect the relationship she has with her family, who wish to continue to conceal her diagnosis. On the other hand, it is likely that she will be upset if she is told that she has hereditary spherocytosis, but this will happen at some time in the future in any event.

There seems something intrinsically wrong with the idea of a healthcare professional deliberately lying to a patient regardless of the 'good' consequences (e.g. not upsetting the patient). It breaches the duty of trust which is essential to the doctor–patient relationship. In contrast with a consequentialist approach, a rule-based theory of ethics assumes that there is a moral obligation to tell the truth. Lying and deception are wrong in themselves, irrespective of the consequences.

The exercise of autonomous healthcare choices relies on provision of sufficient information. The patient here is a bright girl with long-term experience of her (yet to be explained) illness. She is approaching the age when she can make informed treatment and lifestyle choices. Yet lack of knowledge of her diagnosis undermines her ability to do so. To give effect to patient-centred care the autonomy and choices of the patient should be enhanced and valued. Should her autonomy be preferred over what is considered 'best' for her? Her parents have her interests at heart, and parents could be considered to be in the best position to make this assessment. That is true of a very young child; however, Sandra at 14 years has the potential to determine her own choices and with sufficient information and support can be in a position to do so.

 KEY POINTS

- Most patients value candidness and wish to be given the information necessary to make an informed choice.
- Autonomous choices should be promoted where possible.

For a discussion of a child's right to know/not to know of a genetic diagnosis, *see* Case 39: Genetic testing of children for adult-onset conditions, page 97.

CONSENT, CAPACITY AND CONFIDENTIALITY

You are the surgical house officer on call. A patient comes in acutely unwell. He is reviewed by your seniors who tell him he needs an operation to investigate the cause of his symptoms. They ask you to obtain consent for laparoscopy and a laparotomy and proceed. When you see the patient he is still uncomfortable and he tells you that although he understood everything that he was told, he is not sure whether he wants an operation. He says he does not want to know what risks there might be, 'You do whatever is best doctor.'

Questions
- Why is consent legally necessary?
- What are the essentials of valid consent?
- Is consent valid if the patient is not informed of risks because he does not want to know?

ANSWER 27

Legal issues

> 'Every human being of adult years and sound mind has a right to determine what shall be done with his own body; and a surgeon who performs an operation without his patient's consent commits an assault for which he is liable in damages.'
>
> *Schloendorff* v. *Society of New York Hospital* (1914)

Consent is the agreement of a patient to being examined or having a procedure performed. Touching a patient without consent is a battery (although prosecutions are uncommon). Consent does not have to be given in writing; it can be given orally or even implied from the circumstances, e.g. holding an arm out for an injection, nodding the head, although care must be taken to ensure the patient has understood what is going to be done and why.

In some situations, such as organ donation and fertility treatment, written consent is compulsory. Written consent should also be obtained from the patient if the investigation or treatment is complex or involves significant risks; there may be significant consequences for the patient's employment, or social or personal life; providing clinical care is not the primary purpose of the investigation or treatment; where the treatment is part of a research programme or is an innovative treatment designed specifically for the patient's benefit (*Consent: Patients and Doctors Making Decisions Together*, GMC, 2008). This guidance also states that "If, after discussion, a patient still does not want to know in detail about their condition or the treatment, you should respect their wishes, as far as possible. But you must still give them the information they need in order to give their consent to a proposed investigation or treatment" (including information about level of pain and discomfort and serious risks). In the present scenario it might be tempting to 'just get the form signed' and it is important to document when consent has been given. However, although a signed consent form is *prima facie* evidence of consent, the form itself does not mean valid consent has been given, for example the patient may later claim that his consent was not voluntary.

There is also the question of who should obtain consent. Most agree that it is good practice for the healthcare professional performing the procedure to obtain consent as it is their responsibility, but in practice this does not always happen. The process of taking consent can be delegated but the person seeking consent must be suitably trained and qualified, have sufficient knowledge of the proposed investigation or treatment, and understand, and be able to explain, the risks involved.

! Essential elements of consent

- The patient must be competent to give consent.
- It must be voluntary, and not coerced.
- The patient must be provided with information about the procedure.

Competence is presumed in patients aged 16 and over unless there is evidence to the contrary. Arguably a certain amount of coercion occurs in almost all cases as the doctor has relevant knowledge and can be seen as holding the key to treatment, but consent is only considered not voluntary in cases where there is undue, excessive or unwarranted exercise of power or trust. One example of this occurring is when a young woman originally agreed to a blood transfusion but after a private discussion with her mother, a devout Jehovah's Witness, she then refused to consent (*Re T: Adult refusal of medical treatment* [1992]).

To make a valid choice a person must be given information of the broad nature and purpose of the proposed treatment at the very least – what the procedure involves and why it is needed as well as the likely outcomes. Failure to provide this basic information could give rise to a claim of battery. But this may not be enough to prevent an action for negligent failure to provide sufficient information about risks and alternative treatments. How much information the patient needs is difficult to judge because particular risks may have significance to certain patients. Doctors have a powerful role as dispensers of information as well as medicines and treatment.

Consent is limited to the procedures which the patient has been informed of and agreed to. Except in an emergency it cannot be exceeded to include other procedures. In the American case, *Mohr* v. *Williams* (1905), the plaintiff consented to an operation on her right ear. When she was anaesthetized, her surgeon made the decision to operate on her left ear instead, because this was found to be more seriously diseased. Despite no harm having occurred to the patient, a claim in battery was successful as the patient had only consented to surgery on her right ear.

Ethical issues

A patient can be competent to make a decision even if the decision is not one that most patients in that position would make, thus giving effect to patient autonomy. Can patients be truly autonomous? There is an imbalance of power between the informed and experienced doctor and the vulnerable patient, whose autonomy may be compromised by illness. Although full autonomy may be difficult to achieve, a patient can be sufficiently autonomous. The nature of information given to a patient and the way in which it is presented can affect the patient's choice, and ultimately whether or not they consent to the procedure proposed. In this scenario the patient is exercising his autonomy in saying that he 'doesn't want to know'. From a legal perspective this is problematic because consent must be based on an informed decision.

Requiring consent for all procedures also protects a patient's dignity, bodily integrity and respects the patient's values. When examining a patient it is important to establish your role in the relationship. Medical students have an ethical obligation to inform the patient that they are learning by being permitted to examine the patient, rather than the patient receiving the only benefit from the examination.

 KEY POINTS

- Continuing dialogue is important in obtaining consent. Consent that is merely ritualistic does not serve to respect the autonomy of the patient.
- Consent is limited to the procedures which the patient has been informed of and agreed to. Except in an emergency it cannot be exceeded to include other procedures.
- Consent can be withdrawn prior to the procedure.

CASE 28: ADULT CAPACITY TO CONSENT TO TREATMENT

Celeste, a 29-year-old woman, presents to accident and emergency in extreme pain. She fell over on Astroturf in the afternoon the day before while playing hockey and grazed her knees. Her left knee is now extremely painful, swollen and erythematous and she cannot bend her leg or weight bear. You suspect that she has a septic arthritis secondary to her knee injury. This is a medical emergency, and without immediate drainage and antibiotic treatment there is a risk of destructive joint damage and permanent disability. You explain to Celeste that she needs to have the joint aspirated and the risks associated with aspiration. You are not sure that she is taking in what you are telling her because she is in pain and scared.

Questions
- Is the patient competent to make such a decision?
- How is this assessment made?
- Who makes this assessment?

ANSWER 28

Legal issues

Adults have the legal capacity to make healthcare decisions and can do so if they are competent to make the relevant decision (the terms capacity and competence tend to be used interchangeably, and 'capacity' will be used here). There is a presumption of capacity for adults, although this can be rebutted on medical evidence. Mental capacity is a legal concept informed by clinical advice which has been developed by the courts over time. In England and Wales, the Mental Capacity Act 2005 (MCA) now sets out a statutory test for capacity for those aged 16 and over.

Capacity is assessed at the time the relevant decision is taken. Persons lack capacity if they cannot make the decision because of an impairment of or a disturbance in the functioning of the mind or brain, due to, for example, mental illness, dementia or learning disability. The MCA states that a person lacks capacity if they cannot do one or more of the following:

- understand the information relevant to the decision
- retain that information
- use or weigh that information as part of the process of making the decision
- communicate the decision (whether by talking, using sign language or any other means).

Capacity is decision relevant so that a high standard of capacity will be required for procedures which carry a high risk, which are complex and where there are significant implications for the patient. There is a cognitive bias in the assessment of capacity; values and emotions are not mentioned in the legal test. The MCA provides that persons should not be treated as unable to make a decision merely because they make an unwise decision. Reference to age, appearance or an aspect of the person's behaviour is not sufficient to establish lack of capacity. The courts have said that they will be guided by the view of the medical profession regarding capacity. Where there is doubt about a patient's capacity, a medical assessment should be carried out, usually by a consultant psychiatrist.

Ethical issues

Capacity and autonomy are linked. The characteristics of an autonomous person are those of a competent person; someone who can understand the information, weigh it up and make judgements in accordance with their values. So an autonomous person will be one who is competent to make that decision. The exercise of autonomy depends on the provision of sufficient, understandable information on which to base that decision. Thus provision of information on treatment options can directly impact on the patient having capacity to make the decision and being able to exercise an autonomous choice.

 KEY POINTS

- Capacity can evolve and fluctuate over time, and treatment should be postponed if capacity can be restored.
- It is task specific – a person may have capacity to make a particular decision but lack capacity for other more complex decisions.
- Before it is concluded that someone lacks capacity to make a decision all possible steps should be given to help them to reach the decision.

CASE 29: REFUSAL OF TREATMENT

You are an F2 on an obstetric rotation. Mary has been referred to the hospital by her general practitioner as she is now 40 weeks pregnant with her third child. Her previous two children, now aged 5 and 2, were delivered by normal vaginal delivery. Unfortunately her husband has abandoned her in this pregnancy and she is finding it difficult to cope. She has received good antenatal care and is well apart from having iron deficiency and anaemia. The baby is breech, and the consultant obstetrician suggests that the baby is turned by external cephaloversion. However, Mary refuses to consent to this and she seems very frightened at the suggestion. The consultant considers that the only alternative is a caesarean section. Mary is unwilling to undergo a caesarean section as she is a Christian Scientist, and her faith forbids medical intervention. You explain to her that both she and her baby will be at serious risk if a caesarean section is not carried out immediately.

Questions:
- Can a competent adult refuse any treatment including life-sustaining treatment?
- In what circumstances can medical intervention be performed on a non-consenting competent woman to preserve the life of a viable fetus?

ANSWER 29

Legal issues

If a patient has been provided with relevant information about the proposed treatment and available options, and mental capacity is not questioned, then a refusal by the patient must be respected by healthcare professionals. This is so even if they believe such a decision is not in the patient's best interests and even if the patient is refusing life-sustaining treatment or treatment which may risk death or serious harm to a viable fetus. Mary is making a decision which may seem to others to be irrational, but this does not mean that she necessarily lacks capacity. The courts have highlighted the importance of separating the outcome of a decision with an assumption of incapacity.

> 'It is most important that those considering the issue should not confuse the question of mental capacity with the nature of the decision made by the patient, however grave the consequences. The view of the patient may reflect a difference in values rather than an absence of competence and the assessment of capacity should be approached with this firmly in mind.'
>
> *Ms B* v. *NHS Hospital Trust* (2002)

Legal obligations of a pregnant woman

A pregnant woman may be considered to owe a moral obligation to the fetus. However, a fetus has no legal rights until it is born and has a separate existence from its mother. Mary appears overwhelmed by her circumstances but this does not mean that she lacks capacity to make the decision about treatment. If there is no doubt about her capacity this refusal must be respected and documented. But if her capacity is seriously in doubt an assessment should be made and if necessary legal advice should be sought.

Ethical issues

If due respect is given to patient autonomy, then the patient's choices regarding healthcare treatment must be given effect, even if they conflict with what is objectively considered to be in the patient's best interests. An autonomous person is considered to be the best judge of their own interests. The principle of sanctity of life yields to the principle of self-determination. Maternal autonomy is not compromised by any interests of the fetus and the woman's bodily integrity must be respected.

 KEY POINTS

- A woman has a right to refuse treatment even if this may result in the death of a viable fetus. Her rights are not diminished by any 'duties' owed to the fetus.
- An assumption of incapacity should not be made merely because a patient is refusing treatment which the doctor considers appropriate.

CASE 30: ASSESSMENT OF BEST INTERESTS

Scott is 63 years old and has been severely cognitively impaired since birth. A few years ago he was brought to hospital with an enlarged bladder, which was assumed to be secondary to prostatitic hypertrophy. However, he is terrified of being outside of his home environment and finds it hard to trust anyone. He refused all investigations and the doctors treating him at the time did not feel his condition was serious enough to warrant investigation under restraint. He has now come to hospital again with acute urinary retention. He needs a catheter to relieve the short-term problem and is likely to need a transurethral resection of the prostate (TURP), which requires general anaesthetic. Without treatment recurrent retention and renal failure seem inevitable. However, Scott is clearly uncomfortable and frightened in hospital and he is terrified of needles. It will be difficult to carry out treatment without his co-operation. He lives in a home and has a good relationship with his carers. His sister visits him frequently.

Questions:
- What factors should be considered in assessing the 'best interests' of an incompetent adult patient?
- Who makes the decision about Scott's best interests?
- What if the clinical team and Scott's relatives disagree about what treatment is in his best interests?

ANSWER 30

Legal issues

Scott has severe cognitive impairment, therefore he would not be competent to make a treatment decision of this magnitude. Any decision made on behalf of a person who lacks capacity must be made in that person's best interests. Assessment of best interests is wider than a purely objective assessment of the clinical best interests. Case law has indicated that best interests encompasses medical, emotional and all other welfare issues, and given the range of issues to be considered it will be a difficult assessment to make.

The Mental Capacity Act 2005 (MCA) sets out a legal framework for the care and treatment of persons lacking capacity. Although it does not define the term 'best interests', it sets out a checklist of factors that must be considered when determining best interests. The person making the decision must consider, as far as is reasonably ascertainable, the patient's past and present wishes, and the beliefs and values and other factors that could have influenced their decision if they had capacity. This assessment of best interests looks to what the person lacking capacity would have wanted, and should also take non-medical issues into account. In addition to the checklist, 'all relevant circumstances' should be considered. For example, a doctor would need to consider the 'clinical needs of the patient, the potential benefits and burdens of the treatment on the person's health and life expectancy and any other factors relevant to making a professional judgement' (MCA Code of Practice, paragraph 5.19) when making a decision about major medical treatment.

The assessment of best interests is carried out by the doctor or other healthcare staff responsible for carrying out the particular medical treatment or procedure. The MCA requires that where practical and appropriate, others who are close to the patient should be consulted about what might be in the patient's best interests and, wherever possible, the patient should still be involved in the decision-making process. Thus Scott's views and those of his carers and sister should be considered. It seems unlikely in this case that the views of those who care for him will differ from the clinical team with regard to which procedure is in Scott's best interests. When there is a conflict of opinion about whether a particular treatment is in the patient's best interests, which cannot be otherwise resolved, the Court of Protection may be asked to adjudicate.

Lasting power of attorney

A lasting power of attorney (LPA) is a legal document which allows a person (donor) to appoint someone to take decisions (attorney) for him in the event of loss of capacity (Scott has never had sufficient capacity to make an LPA). The attorney can then make decisions that are as valid as if made by the donor, but only if the donor lacks capacity. Personal welfare LPAs allow the attorney to make decisions about medical treatment, although there may be restrictions about the types of decision that can be taken. An attorney can only consent to or refuse life-sustaining treatment on behalf of the donor if he has been given authority to do so in the LPA document. Healthcare staff must discuss their proposed care plan with the attorney and obtain the attorney's agreement to it. They must also consult with the attorney about what action is in the patient's best interests. The attorney must always act in the patient's best interests. Where the healthcare team disagrees with the attorney's assessment of the best interests of the patient the case should be discussed with other medical experts. Ultimately, the issue may have to be resolved by the Court of Protection.

Independent mental capacity advocate

Independent mental capacity advocates (IMCAs) are independent advocates who represent the views of vulnerable people lacking capacity to make important decisions about serious medical treatment when there are no family members or friends who can be consulted. They act as a check to ensure that proposed treatment is in the person's best interests and therefore have the right to see relevant healthcare records. They can challenge decisions that they do not think are in the patient's best interests, and they must be instructed and consulted in certain circumstances, e.g. providing, withholding or stopping serious medical treatment and where the person will stay in hospital longer than 28 days.

Ethical issues

Scott is clearly unhappy in the hospital setting and is reluctant to have treatment. Respect for patient autonomy entails that a person's views are considered and factored into the decision-making process. To what extent does Scott have autonomy that should be respected? Autonomy can be defined as freedom from external constraint and the ability to exercise critical mental capacities. Capacity is the prerequisite for legal recognition of autonomy, but although Scott's views may not be decisive they are nevertheless relevant.

The assessment of a person's best interests uses consequentialist criteria. A 'balance sheet' could be drawn of the benefits and harms of treatment. A procedure that is invasive and has harmful side-effects may be in a patient's best interests only if it has a commensurate benefit, but would not be so if the harms outweigh the benefits to be gained. Scott will benefit from insertion of a renal stent – indeed he will suffer serious irreparable harm if he does not receive such treatment. The assessment of best interests could therefore take into account overall *future* benefit despite the immediate harm of carrying out treatment which Scott does not want.

> 'Unfortunately, the best interests standard has sometimes been interpreted as highly malleable, permitting values that are irrelevant to the patient's benefits or burdens and incorporating intangible factors of questionable value to the incompetent person.'
> Beauchamp TL, Childress JF. *Principles of Biomedical Ethics*, 4th edn.
> Oxford: Oxford University Press, 1994

 KEY POINTS

- Scott lacks capacity and therefore treatment decisions must be taken in his best interests.
- His views and those of his carers/relatives should be taken into account.
- Where an incompetent patient has no one to represent his best interests an IMCA must be consulted in connection with decisions about major medical treatment.
- A 'best interests' assessment is not relevant where a person has made a valid and applicable advance decision.
- Consider whether a person has been appointed under an LPA with authority to make the relevant decision.

See case 67 for more information on advance decision, page 167.

CASE 31: TREATMENT OF INCOMPETENT ADULT PATIENTS

Susie is 24 years old and has Down's syndrome and a mental age of 10. She is very loving and has a happy-go-lucky personality. She is also extremely pretty. She lives with her parents and younger sister. For the past 10 years she has gone to a daycare centre four times a week to socialize with other people and to give her parents some respite from looking after her. Recently, she has been bad tempered and tearful. Susie's mother is worried by this change in temperament and brings her to see you, her GP. You ask Susie what is making her upset. Reluctantly she tells you that she is cross because people at the daycare centre will not let her play with her new friend, a 30-year-old man called Steve. You contact the daycare centre and find out that Susie and Steve have been separated because they keep being discovered kissing each other and, on one occasion, Steve had undressed Susie. The daycare centre explained that it was not a punishment, but that neither Susie nor Steve had any understanding of what they were doing and were acting on instinct. They did not understand the implications of a sexual relationship or the risks of pregnancy. They had not wanted to tell Susie's mother as they felt they would be in trouble for letting things get out of hand in the first instance. You suggest that everything should be discussed openly and honestly.

A month later Susie's mother comes to see you with her husband. Susie's temperament has not improved and the atmosphere at home is very tense. Susie often talks about Steve and how much she misses him. Her mother feels that it is unfair to keep them separated, but she is worried that they may end up having a sexual relationship and that Susie may get pregnant. Her mother does not want to deprive Susie of a life that can be enjoyed to the utmost but she feels that Susie will not understand the changes in her body if she became pregnant and feels that Susie would find it a terrifying experience. She asks you whether you can arrange for Susie to be sterilized.

Questions
- What legal authority does a healthcare professional have to treat a person lacking capacity?
- It is lawful for Susie to be sterilized?
- Is sterilization in her best interests?
- Is it necessary to seek court approval?

ANSWER 31

A person who has severe intellectual disability is not competent to give valid consent for medical treatment. Under common law, no one could give consent on behalf of an incompetent person; however, the doctrine of necessity provided a justification for the provision of treatment, including a wide range of routine acts. The Mental Capacity Act 2005 now gives statutory protection to carers (whether paid or family members) and social and healthcare professionals for acts performed in connection with the personal care, healthcare and treatment of those who lack capacity, where they are acting in the patient's best interests. 'Section 5' acts are stated widely to cover acts carried out *in connection with the care or treatment* of a person who is believed to lack capacity. There is no requirement to obtain formal authority to act. It includes major healthcare and treatment decisions although a careful determination of best interests is required and the choice of treatment must be the least restrictive option. Section 5 authority applies only where no one can give valid consent. A person appointed under a lasting power of attorney has authority to consent and refuse procedures and treatments within the scope of their authority, and therefore consent must be obtained from that person.

Is sterilization lawful?

Sterilization of an intellectually disabled person can be lawfully performed where it is in that person's best interests. The courts have authorized a hysterectomy for therapeutic reasons for an incompetent woman who had excessively heavy periods which had a serious effect on her and caused her great distress. A distinction can be made between a procedure which addresses an existing harmful situation (distressing menstruation) and one which is speculative about future risks (distress arising from an unintended pregnancy). By comparison, sterilization for contraceptive purposes was held by the court not to be in the best interests of a woman with severe learning disabilities where the woman was adequately supervised in the day centre she attended and the risk of pregnancy was unlikely. In another case it was not considered to be in the best interests of a man with Down's syndrome to perform a vasectomy. The court weighed up the benefits (foolproof contraception, greater freedoms) and burdens (apprehension, risk and discomfort inherent in the operation). In Susie's case whether the harms of the proposed procedure are outweighed by countervailing benefits depends from whose perspective best interests are assessed. Her mother clearly considers that sterilization will benefit Susie and enhance her freedoms, but it will also benefit her by enabling her better to meet the obligations of caring for Susie.

It is not necessary to seek approval from the court where the sterilization is for therapeutic reasons. However the Court of Protection must be asked to make decisions relating to proposed non-therapeutic sterilization, for example, for contraceptive purposes.

 KEY POINTS

- The Mental Capacity Act gives authority to healthcare professionals to provide medical treatment to those who lack capacity.
- Consider treatment options which are least restrictive of the person's rights or future choices and which promote the greatest freedom.

CASE 32: INTIMATE EXAMINATION OF A PATIENT UNDER ANAESTHESIA

Pamela, a 34-year-old woman with fibroids, was clerked in yesterday by a fourth year medical student on an obstetrics and gynaecology rotation. Pamela is scheduled to have surgery today for removal of the fibroids and the consultant asks the student if she would like to scrub in to assist during the operation. The student has assisted the anaesthetist before the operation and has reassured Pamela about the planned operation. Once Pamela is anaesthetized, the consultant asks the student how she would perform an internal examination on a female patient. The student realizes that Pamela was not asked for permission to do this and feels that it would be wrong to carry out the examination. However, she also thinks that it would be a good learning opportunity and she is slightly in awe of the consultant, who she is sure would shout at her if she refused. The student decides to point out that she does not have Pamela's consent, but the consultant reassures her that as Pamela is anaesthetized she will not know anything about it.

Questions
- Should the student perform an internal examination on Pamela?
- What should she say to her consultant if she refuses?

ANSWER 32

Professional guidance underscores the requirement of consent for intimate examinations performed under anaesthetic.

> 'You must obtain consent prior to anaesthetisation, usually in writing, for the intimate examination of anaesthetised patients'
>
> General Medical Council, *Maintaining Boundaries*. London: GMC, 2006

There is no justification that the procedure is performed in a teaching hospital, and that the patient must, therefore, be aware that students will perform examinations as part of their training.

Ethical issues

There is a conflict between respecting the patient's dignity and autonomy, the desire of the student to gain experience and the need to train competent doctors. Should the interests of individual members of society be outweighed by the need to promote the training of competent doctors? A consequentialist justification for examination without express consent is that the overall benefit to society in having well-trained doctors outweighs the harm to individual patients. Intimate examinations carry no real risk, may add to patient anxiety and may meet with a refusal, thus reducing the opportunity for training. The experience will increase the student's practical skills and knowledge, which she may use to diagnose a similar condition in the future, possibly preventing harm to other patients.

However, the patient may suffer discomfort, loss of privacy and dignity, perhaps some psychological harm, and loss of trust in the medical profession. Do the consequences of informing the patient and requesting consent impede medical education and training? There is no evidence that a significant number of patients would withhold consent to impact on training. In comparison, Kantian ethics state that people should always be treated as ends in themselves, and never only as a means to another's ends. Medical procedures performed for training purposes only without any benefit to a particular patient use the patient as a training aid and merely as a means to enhance the doctor's training and *her* goals of becoming a better doctor.

Clinical issues

It can be hard to stand up to consultants and students may often fear the repercussions on their clinical involvement and assessment if they do not do as a consultant asks them to do. Many medical schools now have a pro forma which must be completed by the student and the patient in order for the student to perform any internal examination on an anaesthetized patient. It is the responsibility of the student to ensure that written consent has been given by the patient. In the present case the student should remind the consultant of this and state that she is not prepared to perform the examination as she does not have the patient's consent. However, she would very much like the opportunity to come to theatre with the consultant at some point in the future so that she can examine a patient who has been consented prior to being anaesthetized.

 KEY POINTS

- The requirement to practise ethically and lawfully supersedes the need to practise techniques without consent of the patient.
- Students and trainee doctors must take responsibility for their conduct.
- A patient who gives voluntary and informed consent to a training procedure should not be used merely as a 'means' to an end.

CASE 33: NEEDLESTICK INJURIES

Scenario 1

You are taking blood from a patient with dementia when she jerks her hand and the blood-filled needle punctures your glove and your hand. The patient does not understand much of what is happening to her. She is disorientated in time and place and usually becomes distressed around people she does not recognize. She is being treated for a chest infection, but is due to be sent back to her nursing home if the blood results from the vials you have just taken show an improving white cell count and C-reactive protein.

Scenario 2

In accident and emergency (A&E), a medical student is taking blood from a comatose patient who was admitted after being found collapsed in the street. It is thought he is comatose due to high alcohol levels. When filling the blood bottles the student slips and stabs herself in the finger. She immediately squeezes her finger and holds it under running cold water for 10 minutes.

Scenario 3

A mother and her young child are visiting a family friend on a hospital ward. The friend has been given some bad news about his prognosis and is extremely upset. While the mother is comforting him, her child wanders off and accidentally puts her hand in the yellow sharps bin. She is in a lot of pain and her hand is covered in cuts.

Questions

- What is hospital policy regarding needlestick injuries?
- Is consent needed to test a patient's blood for bloodborne viruses?

ANSWER 33

Clinical issues

All hospitals should have a needlestick injury policy to advise doctors and members of the public on what to do in the event that they are injured by a contaminated needle. Generally, the first thing to do is to assess the risk. The doctor should discuss what has happened with the patient, explaining what the risks are and sensitively asking the patient if she knows about any transmissible diseases she may have and whether she has ever injected drugs or had a blood transfusion, tattoos or piercing, or unprotected sex within the past 3 months. The incident should be documented and occupational health should be informed (or A&E if the event occurs out of hours).

A blood sample should be taken from the recipient of the injury and from the source but consent must be obtained both to take and to test blood for viruses such as hepatitis B and C and human immunodeficiency virus. The risk of bloodborne virus transmission determines what action should be taken.

Legal issues

In scenario 1, it will be unlawful to take blood from the woman with dementia because she will not be able to give consent. It would be difficult to show that performing an unnecessary test would be in her best interests because it is unlikely that she would be a high-risk patient. Although the comatose man in scenario 2 is potentially high risk, his blood cannot be tested until he has come out of his coma and his consent has been given. The little girl in scenario 3 is at high risk of being infected but it is impossible to identify a specific source, so she should be given post-exposure prophylaxis (PEP) and her parents should be offered support. The hospital would also have to address how it could have been possible for a child to have access to a yellow sharps container. If the little girl did become infected, the hospital would be potentially liable.

Ethical issues

An incompetent patient lacks the autonomy to make healthcare decisions, and it is the duty of a doctor to ensure that the patient is treated in their best interests until autonomy can be restored. However, healthcare workers have rights too, and it is the responsibility of an employer to ensure that the rights of an employee are also respected. This can lead to conflict between the rights of patients and employees. It is questionable, therefore, whether there should be a limit to the rights of a patient, where there is a risk of harm to another individual. Consequentialists would argue that it is justifiable to test an incompetent patient's blood as a blood test is of minimal harm to the patient but can provide information that will prevent harm to a healthcare worker. For example, the test may be negative for bloodborne viruses so PEP, which may have unpleasant side-effects, would not have to be continued.

 KEY POINTS

- Needlestick injuries are common in medical practice and can pose a threat to the health of a healthcare worker.
- Consent is needed to test a patient for communicable diseases. Comatose patients and patients with dementia cannot be tested unless it is in their best interests.

CASE 34: PERSONAL DATA

Scenario 1

While getting a trolley in a supermarket, a person finds a discarded shopping list. On the back of the list are the names, hospital numbers and dates of birth and current medical problems of all the patients on a local hospital ward.

Scenario 2

A staff nurse was worried about a neighbour who had recently been to a hospital clinic appointment and had returned home very upset. The neighbour had not been forthcoming about the matter and had said they would rather be left alone. Thinking she was only trying to help, the nurse logs on to the hospital's patient records system and looks up her neighbour's latest blood and radiology results. She discovers that her neighbour has metastatic liver cancer.

Scenario 3

A consultant in a hurry one morning decides to do a quick 'board round' before leaving his juniors to do a proper ward round. While discussing the results of one patient, he is unaware that the patient's wife is standing within earshot and has heard about the poor prognosis before the bad news can be broken to her husband in a more sensitive manner.

Questions

- Why is confidentiality important?
- What is the Data Protection Act?
- What are the Caldicott Principles?

ANSWER 34

Medical problems can often be embarrassing and frightening and can be associated with stigma. Keeping patient information confidential helps to ensure that the patient will trust their doctor sufficiently to divulge personal information to enable optimum healthcare. Although few healthcare professionals purposefully break confidentiality it is important to be aware how easily information can be shared between people who do not have a right to that information.

Legal issues

The Data Protection Act 1998 deals with the use and handling of confidential information. The Caldicott Report (1997) gives guidance on how the Data Protection Act should be employed within the framework of the National Health Service (NHS). The aim of both these publications is to set standards on the use of personal and identifiable data. Data protection principles state that personal data shall be processed fairly and lawfully, obtained only for one or more specified lawful purposes, be adequate, relevant and not excessive, be accurate and up to date, and not be kept for longer than necessary.

The Data Protection Act entitles patients to view their own medical records. Individuals can request to see their medical records, but a doctor has the right to remove any information in the records that pertains to a third person. To help support and implement the Data Protection Act 1998 within the framework of the NHS, Dame Fiona Caldicott recommended that each NHS trust appoint a 'Caldicott guardian'. A Caldicott guardian acts as an adviser in situations in which confidentiality is at risk of being breached. This is a varied job and includes ensuring that waste paper containing patient information is disposed of in a secure way, dealing with drug companies that may want anonymous prescribing data and general practitioners who want to make email referrals without having in place encryption protection on their personal computers. The Caldicott Principles recommend that a healthcare professional must always: justify the need for information; use the minimum amount of information possible; ensure that patient information is shared on a strict need-to-know basis only; and ensure that the people with access to information are aware of the importance of keeping the information confidential.

All of the above scenarios are possible in real life and demonstrate how easily confidentiality can be unintentionally broken. Simple measures such as destroying patient lists after they are out of date, not sharing passwords with colleagues or remaining logged on to computer programs, and only ever discussing patient cases in private areas can prevent accidentally sharing private information with other people.

The National Programme for IT, which will provide online electronic patient records, will present real challenges for maintaining confidentiality.

KEY POINTS

- Maintaining patient confidentiality is necessary to ensure that patients trust doctors with personal and sensitive information.
- Personal data should be kept safe, used for the proper purpose and only be shared with relevant healthcare professionals.

CASE 35: REFUSAL OF HUMAN IMMUNODEFICIENCY VIRUS TESTING

Celia, a 50-year-old Caribbean woman, has a 5-year history of intermittent sinusitis, unexplained rashes, anaemia and tiredness, oral thrush, shingles, and slightly positive autoimmune tests. Her health has been gradually deteriorating. Although human immunodeficiency virus (HIV) infection has been part of the differential diagnosis, she has always refused to have an HIV test. Two months ago, she presented again with parotid and lymphoid enlargement. Although HIV was again suspected she refused an HIV test and a diagnosis of sarcoidosis was made. Despite the suspicion that HIV was possibly the cause of all her symptoms, she was treated with steroids for the presumptive diagnosis. Three weeks later she was admitted to the intensive care unit (ICU) unconscious and was found to have cryptococcal meningitis. As this is an acquired immune deficiency syndrome (AIDS)-defining illness there was technically no further need to do an HIV test. A man arrives at the ICU claiming to be Celia's partner and asking for information about her.

Questions
- When Celia initially presented should you have carried out an HIV test despite her refusal?
- Could you do this without her knowledge?
- Should you divulge the diagnosis to her partner while she is still unconscious?
- If Celia dies because of meningitis, without regaining consciousness, what should you say to her partner about the cause of death?

ANSWER 35

Legal issues

Any procedure carried out without the consent of a competent adult amounts to battery. Celia cannot be tested for HIV without her consent. She should be informed about the potential risk to her health if she remains untested but if she refuses she cannot be tested. The doctor looking after her can say he thinks she has HIV (despite her refusal of testing) and that, in her best interests, he would advise that she is seen by the HIV team. He should ask a second doctor to review the patient and liaise with the HIV team.

Acting in the patient's best interests here is tricky and conflict can easily occur. For example, steroids for sarcoid can be detrimental to Celia's health if she is immunosuppressed because of HIV infection, so it may be the wrong thing to do. The doctor should explain to Celia that her presumed sarcoid would not be treated in this setting if the risks outweighed the benefits (i.e. until the patient had an HIV test). She should be warned that she is putting her health at grave risk by refusing to be tested and that the doctor thinks that she is at very high risk of having HIV. The doctor should provide advice about safe sex.

Case law and professional guidance underscore the importance of maintaining confidentiality. However, in some situations there may be a conflict between the doctor's duty to maintain confidence and their legal and/or moral duty to reveal information to others, such as family members, public health authorities, and the police, to avoid risk of harm.

Guidance from the General Medical Council states that confidential information can only be disclosed where failure to do so may expose others to risk of death or serious harm. Disclosure to Celia's partner may enable him to get an HIV test and receive treatment if the test is positive. The duty to maintain confidentiality is owed to unconscious patients and continues after death. If Celia dies, the cause of her death could be disclosed to her partner where disclosure can be justified to prevent harm to him.

Ethical issues

Respect for patient autonomy entails that a person determines what is done with their body and their health information. Generally, it could be considered that maintaining confidentiality will produce good consequences; patients must be able to trust that their medical details will be kept secret; without such assurance they may not divulge all information necessary for their optimal treatment. Failure to provide a secure confidential environment for discussion of sensitive issues will have a negative impact on encouraging those at risk to seek help and this has widespread public health implications. The virtues of trust and integrity are important in caring for patients who have, or may have, HIV.

 KEY POINTS

- It is important to document everything carefully, including whether Celia is competent and, in particular, that it has been explained to her that she could die if she has advanced HIV and does not receive treatment.
- It is difficult to treat Celia in her best interests without a clear diagnosis of HIV.

CASE 36: CONFIDENTIALITY WITH REGARD TO HUMAN IMMUNODEFICIENCY VIRUS INFECTION AND DISCLOSURE OF RISK TO KNOWN PARTNERS

James, a 25-year-old white man with no symptoms, attends the genitourinary medicine clinic. He reports that Tom, his boyfriend of 2 years, has advised him to attend. He says Tom was diagnosed and treated for syphilis the week before at the same clinic. James has had no other partners since his last negative tests 2 years ago and says Tom had a negative human immunodeficiency virus (HIV) test last year. James consents to all tests including an HIV test.

While the patient is waiting for his tests the doctor pulls out Tom's file. She confirms that Tom was diagnosed with syphilis last week but also notices that Tom is HIV positive and has attended this centre for the past 4 years for HIV care. Tom's next appointment is in 2 days.

Questions
- How should the doctor proceed with this consultation? What should she say to James?
- Does the fact that both patients are under the care of the same clinic affect the doctor's decision?
- What should be said to Tom at his next appointment?
- Would the doctor be liable if she breached Tom's confidentiality *or* if she did not inform James of his ongoing risk?

ANSWER 36

Following James' consultation, the doctor is now aware that Tom has concealed his HIV-positive status, which may have put James at risk of HIV transmission. She should proceed with the consultation ensuring appropriate sexual health advice is provided and address any of James' concerns. At this stage, the doctor would not be justified to disclose to James any of the information she has found out about Tom as it would result in a breach of confidentiality. The doctor has not yet had the opportunity to discuss issues of disclosure with Tom, and unless Tom himself consents to the disclosure of his HIV status, or disclosure is necessary in the public interest she has both a moral and legal duty to maintain confidentiality.

Taking a full sexual history from James is important to assess his risk (and it is important not to make assumptions). Other information which may be useful in consultation includes their sexual practices, e.g. whether they have anal sex and if they use condoms regularly. An uninfected individual is thought to be most at risk of acquiring HIV by unprotected receptive anal sex. The results from James' tests will also crucially determine how he will be managed. If he is found to be HIV positive he will need to be counselled sensitively. James will also need to be seen by an HIV specialist within two weeks (the standard for HIV clinical care). Even if James is now HIV negative, failure of disclosure from Tom may result in HIV transmission to James in the future. As both James and Tom are patients under the care of the same clinical team, they are both owed a duty of care. The important but difficult issue is identifying in which circumstances the duty of confidentiality is outweighed by the interests of others.

During Tom's next consultation it would be important to ascertain his feelings regarding disclosure of his status to his partner. It is the doctor's duty to properly advise him of the nature of the disease and ways of protecting others from infection. Tom should be encouraged to disclose his HIV-positive status to James, regardless of condom usage. It would be important to inform Tom that lack of disclosure and choosing not to use condoms could amount to 'reckless' transmission of HIV, which has recently been seen in UK courts as a criminal offence resulting in prosecution. (This was recently clarified by the Court of Appeal in *R* v. *Dica* [2004].) Acting 'recklessly' means that the individual must have been aware that he was placing others at an unreasonable risk. Tom should be advised that sharing information about his HIV diagnosis with his partner allows for informed decision making about their sexual behaviour. Also, disclosure would enable James to seek post-exposure prophylaxis following accidental unprotected sex and therefore reduce the risk of transmission. The case would be discussed by a multi-disciplinary team and a deadline agreed with Tom by which he needs to have disclosed. It would be made clear to Tom that if this deadline was breached the clinic would step in and inform James that he has been at risk and needs HIV testing (but not telling him outright that Tom has HIV). It is rare for a person to refuse to disclose when supported. Any disclosure to Tom – about James attending the clinic – needs to be authorized by James first.

If James was to become HIV positive as a result of Tom failing to disclose, it is questionable whether the doctor could be held accountable for failing to prevent onward transmission of HIV. Some court decisions have suggested that the doctor could be held civilly liable (that is liable in damages) if the third party was also a patient of the doctor and independently owed a 'duty of care'. Therefore, in the event that the doctor has sufficient reason to believe Tom is not following the advice given and cannot be persuaded to do so, and is putting James at ongoing risk, it may become necessary to disclose information. In these circumstances the doctor should inform Tom before the disclosure is made, and must be prepared to justify the decision to disclose.

In the UK, it is unlikely that doctors would be held civilly or criminally liable for failure to prevent onward transmission of HIV (see Chalmers 2004). The General Medical Council's guidance on confidentiality and disclosure should be followed. The guidance does not suggest that there is a 'duty' to disclose ongoing risk to a third party, but indicates the ability to disclose if the doctor, in discussion with the patient and with other colleagues, feels that ongoing risk to a known individual outweighs the risk to the existing patient relationship and trust in confidentiality (see British Association for Sexual Health and HIV post-consultation HIV/STI guidelines, 2006).

Ethical issues

Individuals have a moral obligation to avoid harming others where possible. But they also have a responsibility to protect themselves from known harm. A person consents to assume and accept a risk which they were aware of (where there is a choice to avoid that risk). But can James be said to have assumed the risk of acquiring HIV when he has been deceived by Tom about the reality of the risks? Society places strong emphasis on an individual's autonomy. James's decision to have sex with Tom can only be said to be truly autonomous if he is made aware of all the facts (as condoms do not protect against HIV 100 per cent). This does not negate the public health message that everyone should take responsibility for their own health (and not put themselves at risk), which is particularly prudent given that a third of all cases of HIV in the UK remain undiagnosed.

 KEY POINTS

- The duty of confidentiality is an important cornerstone of the provision of medical care but it is not absolute.
- Disclosure can be justified to prevent a person from risk of death or serious harm, e.g. sexual contact of patient with HIV who has not been informed.
- Inform the patient before disclosure.
- Do not disclose to others who are not at risk of infection.

CASE 37: INTERPRETERS

Vladimir, a Russian man, is admitted to hospital with pain in the abdomen. He moved to the UK only 6 months ago and his understanding of English is limited. He is able to tell you that it hurts and where but not how long the pain has been present or the nature of the pain. He is also unable to communicate to you his medical history or other useful information needed as part of the history. On the basis of the limited history and examination you suspect that he has acute appendicitis, and you feel that he should be consented for emergency surgery, However, you want to clarify a few details in the history and explain the risks involved in the procedure so that your patient can give valid consent. You attempt to phone an online interpreter but are told that due to lack of funding the interpreter service is only available from 9 am to 5 pm, Monday to Friday. You decide to ask the cleaning staff if any of them speak Russian. One of them happens to know a little, and you use him as an interpreter. Unfortunately the cleaner's understanding of English does not extend to medical terminology. You feel, however, that the basics have been covered, and the patient is consented and taken to theatre.

Questions
- What services should a hospital provide in order to communicate with people who are unable to speak English or communicate with the hospital staff?
- Is it ethical to use cleaning staff in this situation? Does this impinge on patient confidentiality?
- What other scenarios can you think of where communication may be problematic?

ANSWER 37

Clinical issues

Effective communication with patients can be extremely difficult, and language barriers are just one example of this. It is very common to encounter patients with expressive or receptive dysphasia. Being able to understand the patient is important as it enables the doctor to take an accurate and detailed history and also enables him to explain what he is planning to do to treat the problem. When consent is needed it is also essential to be able to explain (in a way in which the patient can understand) the procedure, any alternatives and the associated risks.

All hospitals should have in place an interpreter service. Interpretation is often done over the phone by professionals who have had some medical training and can interpret accurately. Medical professionals from other countries or with linguistic skills are often used by their colleagues to assist in these situations. Sometimes other people within the hospital are used too. Although this may seem to be more convenient than using a telephone interpreting service, it is associated with risks. The translations may not be accurate or the questions may not be answered honestly due to embarrassment associated with discussing medical problems with non-medical staff.

Ethical issues

Using interpreters raises several ethical issues. The most common issue is how to ensure that patient confidentiality is maintained. Professional interpreter services are run by trained professionals who have a professional code of ethics and are subject to the same standards of confidentiality as other healthcare professionals. However, when other people within a hospital are used, such as cleaning staff, there is a risk of breach of confidentiality as there are no professional sanctions. It is also difficult to expect members of the family to remain entirely confidential. Patients may also be reluctant to discuss embarrassing problems through an interpreter. Having a third party in the room can inhibit the development of a good rapport. Unless someone is trained to interpret medical or disease-related information, there is a possibility of inaccurate translation so that the doctor is given the wrong information.

Increasingly, children are being used to act as interpreters for their parents. Although this can be useful in straightforward clinical consultations, it is not a practice that a doctor should encourage. Children will not understand the implications of what they are interpreting. If a child's parent has a disease it may also cause the child unnecessary distress and anxiety to interpret their parent's symptoms and pain. However, it may help children feel valued by the rest of their family.

 KEY POINTS

- Hospital and general practices have a legal obligation to provide interpreter services for patients with disabilities, deaf patients or patients who speak a different language.
- Using interpreters can inhibit the doctor–patient relationship and raises issues of translation mistakes and confidentiality.
- Family members should only be used as interpreters when there is no other option.

CASE 38: SHARING GENETIC INFORMATION WITH FAMILY MEMBERS

Hannah is 52, and there is a history of breast cancer in her immediate family. Her mother died from breast cancer and her two sisters have had successful treatment for breast cancer – they now appear to be doing well and are in remission. Hannah has been very affected by this. She has undergone tests for *BRCA1* and *BRCA2* mutations to gain peace of mind and avoid the stress of uncertainty of whether she may be at increased risk of breast cancer. The test results show that she does carry a *BRCA1* mutation and she is considering whether to undergo elective mastectomy.

Hannah has a 19-year-old daughter, Sophie, who is in her second year at university. Hannah does not want to burden Sophie with the 'bad news' that she is a carrier of the gene mutation which puts her, and therefore Sophie, at an increased risk of developing breast cancer. Hannah considers that Sophie should be enjoying a trouble-free time at university, and this information would only trouble her and 'what could she do anyway'? Also, Sophie was very young when her grandmother died and her aunts had breast cancer and she is not aware of the implications for her future health.

Questions
- Should genetic information belong to individuals or families?
- Does Hannah have an ethical obligation to tell her daughter that she may be at risk of breast cancer?

ANSWER 38

Genetic tests can give individuals information that allows them to make choices and plan for the future. If Sophie is informed about her potential increased risk of breast cancer she can exercise her choice to be tested, and if she is found to be a *BRCA* mutation carrier she could make health and lifestyle choices, e.g. whether to opt for prophylactic surgery or be closely monitored through screening. Provision of information would allow her to make informed autonomous choices regarding her future health.

Legal issues

Although some genetic information may be considered highly sensitive, because of its ability to predict future health, not all genetic information will be sensitive, highly predictive, nor indeed private (because it is observable). Information generated by genetic testing is confidential in nature but the obligation of confidence is not absolute and there may be good reasons for disclosing it. Although the law permits disclosure in the interests of others this is usually where there is an identifiable risk to others, which is serious in nature, and where disclosure can go some way to avoid the anticipated harm. In this scenario relevant factors will be the severity of the disorder, the level of predictability of risk, the actions Sophie could take if told of the risk and the weight given to Hannah's reasons for not wishing to disclose. There is also the possibility that Sophie will be 'harmed' by receiving unsolicited information of this nature.

Ethical issues

Genetic information allows inferences to be drawn about the genetic status of relatives, and therefore it could be considered 'family' information rather than information belonging to an individual. The Human Genetics Commission has discussed whether genetic knowledge may bring people into a special moral relationship with one another. It uses the term 'genetic solidarity', which may take priority over a person's self-determination concerning their genetic information.

> 'Arguably, the familial nature of genetic information compromises the possibility of making an autonomous decision about genetic testing on two counts. First, an individual's DNA test results have direct implications for biologically related kin and second, the persons who undergo testing have social obligations towards these kin.'
>
> Hallowell N *et al.* Balancing autonomy and responsibility: the ethics of generating and disclosing genetic information. *J Med Ethics* 2003;29:74–9

 KEY POINTS

- Genetic information may not be considered to be private where it is observable.
- The harms of breaching confidentiality by informing a relative 'at risk' without consent must be weighed against the benefits of disclosure: is there a cure or lifestyle measures that can be taken to prevent or ameliorate harms?
- Those who have inherited genetic susceptibility could be said to owe a moral duty to assist others within that group to avoid harm.

CASE 39: GENETIC TESTING OF CHILDREN FOR ADULT-ONSET CONDITIONS

Janice and Dean have been married for 12 years and have a 6-year-old son. Dean's father and grandfather died from cancer when they were in their early forties. Because of the strong family history of cancer Dean wanted to have a genetic test to find out his level of risk. Although no clear diagnosis was possible, tests indicated that he was at risk of hereditary non-polyposis colorectal cancer. Now Dean is feeling tired and unwell, and has a colonoscopy. The test reveals that he has inoperable bowel cancer. Janice is concerned that their son might also be at risk of colon cancer when he is older, and she wants him to be tested to see if he is at risk.

Questions
- Should parents be allowed to have their children tested for adult-onset genetic conditions?
- Do children have a right to know/not to know about their genetic risks?

ANSWER 39

Legal issues

Janice is requesting genetic testing for her son. As he is so young he clearly lacks capacity to understand and give consent for tests himself. Janice could give consent for testing if it is in his best interests. But information provided by the test would not benefit the child now because he will remain pre-symptomatic for decades to come, there is no therapeutic intervention, and there are no steps he can take to reduce the potential risk.

How far are Janice's interests intertwined with her son's? Does the fact that she may be an overly concerned mother if she does not know whether he is at future risk affect his best interests? It is hard to conceive a situation where the mother's distress caused by the uncertainty would so affect her parenting to impact on his best interests. The only benefit for testing the child now is to give Janice possible peace of mind if the test is negative.

The assessment of best interests should also include consideration of the burden of knowledge if the test proves positive. The child is too young to be told now and there is no control over when and how Janice will tell him in the future and whether counselling would be sought. If the test is positive when he is told, he is likely to find the information burdensome and upsetting.

A positive test does not necessarily indicate certainty of developing cancer, nor does it provide information about the time of onset and severity of the condition. A positive test result far from clarifying the position may actually harm the child. The potential for genetic discrimination and the possibility that insurance will be denied also need to be considered for some genetic conditions.

Ethical issues

Janice's interest in knowing could be set against her son's right not to know of his genetic inheritance. Usually availability of information is considered a good thing because it allows informed choices about healthcare options. Patient autonomy is based on the ability to understand relevant information, but Janice's son cannot make autonomous choices now. Joel Feinberg considered that children have anticipatory autonomy rights. These are respected if a child's future options are kept open. Children should be sent into the adult world with as many open opportunities as possible – children have a right to an open future so that they can make decisions for themselves based on their own rational choices. Parents *are* allowed to make decisions which limit the future choices for their child, e.g. neonatal circumcision. However, this is only where it is in the child's best interests, i.e. the benefits outweigh the burdens of the intervention.

 KEY POINTS

- In the future Janice's son may choose to be tested himself when he can make an autonomous choice.
- Genetic testing now would limit the child's open future without any commensurate benefit as no treatment can be offered at present and no steps can be taken to ameliorate the risk of developing the condition.

For discussion of the ethical issues of neonatal circumcision, *See* Case 91: Neonatal male circumcision, page 227.

NEGLIGENCE

Joe is on a busy ward round with his consultant. The round is post-take and he has seen 23 patients so far. One of his patients is septic and needs a prescription for intravenous antibiotics. The consultant tells Joe to put him on cefuroxime. However, Joe is aware that the hospital protocol has changed and that cefuroxime is no longer the first-line antibiotic due to the increasing incidence of *Clostridium difficile* infection after its use. He suggests giving intravenous co-amoxiclav instead. The consultant agrees and appears impressed that Joe is up to date with the antibiotic guidelines. Joe prescribes the antibiotic. A few hours later he is called to the ward urgently as the septic patient is having difficulty breathing and is covered in urticaria. He has had an allergic reaction to co-amoxiclav. Joe realizes that the allergies box on the drug chart states that the patient is allergic to antibiotics. He calls the anaesthetist who intubates the patient and gives him adrenaline. After 24 hours on the intensive care unit the patient returns to the ward. No permanent damage has occurred.

Questions
- What is clinical negligence?
- Has Joe been negligent?
- What can he do to protect himself against a claim in negligence?

ANSWER 40

Legal issues

Three elements are necessary to establish negligence. The patient (claimant) must prove that the healthcare professional owed the patient a duty of care, that there has been a breach of that duty, i.e. the care fell below acceptable professional standards, and that the breach of duty caused the harm. Some examples of clinical negligence are: making a wrong diagnosis, performing a procedure badly or giving a patient the wrong treatment.

Healthcare professionals owe a duty of care to their patients. In practice usually there is no problem in establishing this duty. The General Medical Council (2006) guidance *Good Medical Practice* sets out the duties of doctors practising in the UK, and all doctors are expected to adhere to this. Duties include: providing a good standard of practice and care; keeping professional knowledge and skills up to date; and working within the limits of competence.

The standard of care expected of a doctor was set out in the case of *Bolam* v. *Friern Hospital Management Committee*, over 50 years ago.

> 'a doctor is not guilty of negligence if he has acted in accordance with practice accepted as proper by a responsible body of medical men skilled in that particular art'.
>
> *Bolam v. Friern Hospital Management Committee*

The standard is that of the responsible and reasonable professional and includes a reasonable expectation that they will keep abreast of new developments. If the care provided by healthcare professionals falls below the required standard while a patient is under their care, and causes the patient harm, they may be called to account through disciplinary procedures of the relevant professional body and/or through the courts in an action of clinical negligence. In the later case of *Bolitho* v. *City and Hackney HA* (1992) the court ruled that some medical practices could be considered negligent by a court of law, even if other doctors would have done the same. Whereas previously it was acceptable for a responsible body of doctors to set the standard for clinical practice, the courts have now intervened to say that clinical practice must be defensible and logical.

A doctor who holds himself out as a specialist will be expected to reach the standard of a reasonably skilful doctor of that specialty. A junior doctor is expected to reach a minimum standard of care and cannot plead lack of experience as an excuse for substandard practice. They will not be considered negligent provided that they act within their competence and seek help where appropriate. The circumstances of treatment will affect the standard of care expected. A doctor working in an emergency, under pressure, will not be expected to perform to the same standard as in 'non-emergency' conditions.

The last element in proving negligence is causation. The patient has to prove that, but for the breach of duty, the harm would not have occurred. For example, a patient who is diagnosed with cancer several months after their initial presentation would have to prove that the delay in diagnosis has affected their treatment options and chances of survival. One or more healthcare professionals treating the patient may have caused a medical injury. In practice it may be difficult to establish who caused the harm, but this is necessary to establish legal liability. If the patient establishes negligence then they are entitled to financial compensation to restore them back to the condition they would otherwise have been in had the incident not occurred. Whether this will ever be adequate to compensate physical harm caused by the negligence is questionable.

Legal liability – clinical negligence

National Health Service (NHS) employers are liable for the negligent acts of their employees where these occur in the course of NHS employment. Costs of negligence litigation are carried by the NHS and the NHS Litigation Authority is responsible for handling negligence claims made against NHS bodies in England and Wales.

In 2008–09, 6,080 claims of clinical negligence and 3,743 claims of non-clinical negligence against NHS bodies were received by the NHSLA, up from 5,470 claims of clinical negligence and 3,380 claims of non-clinical negligence in 2007–08.

£769 million was paid out in connection with clinical negligence claims in 2008–09, up from £633 million in 2007–08. This figure includes both damages paid to patients and the legal costs borne by the NHS…

96% of the NHSLA's cases are settled out of court through a variety of methods of 'alternative dispute resolution' analysis of all clinical claims handled by the NHSLA over the past ten years shows that 41% were abandoned by the claimant, 41% settled out of court [and] 4% settled in court… Fewer than 50 clinical negligence cases a year are contested in court.

www.nhsla.com

Moves have been made to reduce the costs of litigation through the NHS Redress Act 2006. Medical negligence claims valued under £20 000 will be dealt with through this redress scheme avoiding litigation in the courts. It applies to claims arising from NHS hospital care.

Clinical issues

If a claim of negligence is brought against a doctor the details of the events will be scrutinized by the claimant's lawyers. It is imperative to document all notes clearly. Medical records are legal documents. Each entry should be dated, timed and signed. They should highlight any discussions with the patient or their relatives and what was explained to them about their diagnosis, treatment and possible options. In difficult situations it is worth considering what your seniors would do, and, if in any doubt, you should seek senior help.

In this scenario it was Joe's responsibility to check before prescribing medication that the patient did not have any allergies. However, the nurse who gave the drug also has a responsibility to check allergies. Although Joe failed in his care to the patient, because there was no long-term harm, it is unlikely that a claim for negligence will be pursued.

 KEY POINTS

A patient has to prove that a doctor is negligent by demonstrating:

- that the doctor owed the patient a duty of care
- that the doctor failed to give an appropriate standard of care
- that, but for the failure of care, the harm would not have occurred.

CASE 41: PROVISION OF INFORMATION

Richard is 68 years old and not in very good health. Five years ago he underwent a quadruple heart bypass due to a myocardial infarction. He also suffers from moderate chronic obstructive pulmonary disease (COPD) and has an exercise tolerance of about 100 m. He is seen in your consultant's clinic because he is part of the national aneurysm screening programme. His latest ultrasound scan has shown that he has a 6.2 cm abdominal aortic aneurysm, which has a 10 per cent risk of rupture. This figure rises with an increase in the size of the aneurysm and the age of the patient. The risks of the operation to repair the aneurysm include a 1–2 per cent mortality rate, postoperative leaking, infection and deep vein thrombosis/pulmonary embolism. Usually your consultant would opt to repair the aneurysm electively. However, because of Richard's multiple comorbidities he poses a high anaesthetic risk. You decide to discuss the options with him to enable him to make the decision about whether he wants to go ahead with the surgery.

Questions
- What inherent risks of a procedure/treatment must be disclosed to a patient?
- Who is responsible for disclosing these risks?
- What documentation is required?

ANSWER 41

Legal issues

Consent must be obtained from a competent, adequately informed patient before any medical procedure. Information must be provided about inherent risks and alternative treatments. The General Medical Council (GMC) in its guidance *Consent: Patients and Doctors Making Decisions Together* (GMC, 2008) states that 'As the law relating to decision-making and consent, particularly for patients who lack capacity, varies across the UK, doctors need to understand the law as it applies where they work'. A failure to disclose legally required information may give rise to a claim in negligence or referral to the GMC for disciplinary action.

Historically the courts have considered that the standard of disclosure is based on the practice of disclosure of a 'responsible body of medical opinion', although some risks are considered 'so obviously necessary to an informed choice on the part of the patient' that they must always be disclosed, for example a 1–2 per cent risk of paralysis (*Chester* v. *Afshar* [2004]). More recently, courts have moved away from the 'reasonable doctor' standard and focused on disclosure of information that is significant to the patient.

> 'If there is a significant risk which would affect the judgment of a reasonable patient, then in the normal course it is the responsibility of a doctor to inform the patient of that significant risk.'
>
> *Pearce* v. *United Bristol Healthcare NHS Trust* (1999)

The amount of information discussed will depend on factors such as 'the nature of the condition, the complexity of the treatment, the risks associated with the treatment or procedure, and the patient's own wishes' (GMC, paragraph 4). Guidance from Royal Colleges will give information about what risks must be discussed with a patient, in particular specialties.

Information should be given in a manner that is readily understandable by the patient and consideration should be given to issues of language, cognitive ability and stress of the patient. It is the responsibility of the person performing the procedure to gain consent from the patient. If the patient asks questions they must be answered fully and truthfully. The information discussed should be documented both on the consent form and in the medical notes.

Ethical issues

Respect for patient autonomy requires that patients are enabled to make informed choices which reflect their aims and values. The virtue of trust in the doctor–patient relationship depends on open frank dialogue. This also allows the doctor to discuss with the patient which specific risks may be important to them. A consequentialist may argue that better outcomes are achieved by advancing patient choices in healthcare decision making. It is important to be aware that for some patients, discussion about a large number of serious risks can be so overwhelming that the patient becomes too scared to make any decision. Time should be given for reflection and discussion of these fears.

KEY POINTS

- Dialogue with patients is key to gain some understanding of the issues that are important to them.
- The setting and manner of providing information are important factors.
- The discussion and outcome must be clearly documented in the medical notes and on the consent form.

For more information on consent to treatment and capacity, *see* Case 27: Valid consent to treatment, page 67 and Case 28: Adult capacity to consent to treatment, page 71.

CASE 42: DISCLOSURE OF PROGNOSIS

Geoffrey, a 68-year-old retired accountant, self-referred himself to accident and emergency with a 3-day history of jaundice and abdominal discomfort. He has no history of liver disease and does not drink alcohol. Two years ago he had part of his large bowel resected following the diagnosis of Dukes' B colonic carcinoma. He has been well since, other than general malaise. On examination he appears jaundiced. His blood pressure, pulse and oxygen saturations are normal, and he is apyrexial. His abdomen is diffusely tender with a 3 cm craggy liver edge. There is also some evidence of ascites. Blood test results are unremarkable, apart from liver function tests, which show increased levels of alkaline phosphatase, aspartate aminotransferase and bilirubin. The following day an abdominal ultrasound scan shows diffuse hepatocellular carcinoma, probably secondary to Geoffrey's previous colonic carcinoma. It is decided that the most appropriate short-term management would be to perform an endoscopic retrograde cholangiopancreatography (ERCP) to relieve the acute obstruction. However, after three unsuccessful attempts at ERCP it is decided that no further treatment can be offered to the patient. During the ward round Geoffrey asks you, the house officer, what is his prognosis. What do you tell him?

Questions

- Do patients have a right to know their prognosis?
- Is it fair to guess how long a patient has left to live based on previous experiences of similar cases?
- How should bad news be broken?
- Should an F1 doctor ever break bad news?

ANSWER 42

Ethical issues

A doctor has a legal and professional obligation to answer direct questions honestly. However, it is difficult to accurately predict a patient's prognosis. Studies have shown that doctors often overestimate the length of time of survival, even in terminally ill patients.

When informing a patient that they have a terminal illness – and in some cases that they may only have a matter of days or weeks left – it is often difficult for a doctor to feel like they are acting in the patient's best interest to tell them such devastating news. It could be argued that withholding information about poor prognosis is a form of benevolent paternalism. That is, the doctor feels that it is better for the patient not to know. Most people, however, would not be able to justify this course of action as it impinges on patient autonomy. It is also difficult for doctors to know what they feel the patient would want to know. Bad news is not always a bad thing as some patients may often suspect far worse. Knowing what the future holds empowers the patient to make decisions which best reflect their own personal beliefs, e.g. it enables them to stop pointless treatment such as chemotherapy before death. It also gives them the opportunity to say goodbye to loved ones and do things they would otherwise 'put off until tomorrow'.

Clinical issues

It should not be the responsibility of the F1 doctor to break bad news. They do not have the experience or knowledge to answer questions about what happens next. In this case the junior doctor should say that the results of the test are back and that a more senior member of the team will be around later to discuss future options with the patient. Geoffrey should be asked whether he would like a relative or friend to be present. The F1 should then accompany the consultant to experience breaking bad news and provide additional support. If possible specialist nurses should be present too or be aware that a diagnosis or prognosis is being given so they can see Geoffrey later. Palliative care nurses are important members of the multidisciplinary team. They are experienced in discussing end-of-life issues and will often have more time to spend with a patient once the terminal prognosis has been given.

Information should be given to the patient in a simple manner, and not too much information should be given at once. Contact details should be given in case the patient wants to ask more questions once the initial shock has passed.

 KEY POINTS

- Patients have a right to know their prognosis; however, in clinical practice this can be very hard to give accurately and doctors often avoid giving a definite answer.
- A senior member of the team who is qualified to answer questions about what happens next should break bad news. Where possible a specialist palliative care nurse should be present.

CASE 43: THERAPEUTIC PRIVILEGE

Scenario 1
Sabrieh is 65 years old and has been brought into hospital with unstable angina. She is clearly worried about why she feels so poorly and what is going 'to be done' to her. An angiogram is considered the next useful investigation, but the clinician is concerned that if Sabrieh is told about the risks she may become very anxious, thus precipitating a fatal myocardial infarction.

Scenario 2
John has schizophrenia and is convinced that worms are crawling over his skin. He finds this extremely distressing. One treatment that could be tried for him is a new antipsychotic drug, but this carries an 8 per cent risk of permanent eye damage. Should John be informed of this risk?

Scenario 3
Jane has asthma. She is being treated with fluticasone. Her general practitioner is aware that a new study has conclusively proved that there is a small risk of osteoporosis with this treatment. He is concerned that if he informs Jane of this risk she will decide to come off the treatment – which he considers is the best option to control her asthma.

Questions
- Is it lawful to withhold information about risks from a patient in their 'best interests'?
- Is it ever ethically justifiable?

ANSWER 43

Legal issues

Therapeutic privilege is a legal principle, which has been used to justify the deliberate withholding of information from a competent patient by the clinician during the consent process, when the clinician considers that disclosure of that information may 'harm' the patient. Therapeutic privilege has been recognized by the courts as an exception to the legal standard of disclosure.

In the case of *Chester* v. *Afshar* (2004) the House of Lords stated that 'there may be wholly exceptional cases where objectively in the best interests of the patient the surgeon may be excused from giving a warning'. However, clearly information of significant risks may not be brushed aside merely because the patient appears 'anxious'. There is no justification to invoke therapeutic privilege where clinicians consider that patients would make an 'inappropriate' choice by refusing treatment that is objectively considered to be in their best interests (*Consent: Patients and Doctors Making Decisions Together,* GMC 2008). This effectively allows the clinician to substitute their view of what is in the patient's best interests. A competent adult patient can exercise autonomy in healthcare decisions, but the exercise of autonomy requires adequate information.

Ethical issues

An evaluation of the consequences of risk disclosure requires that the benefits of disclosure be balanced against the harms of disclosure. The likelihood of causing the patient severe harm from disclosure of serious side-effects may be difficult to predict with any certainty. Although it may seem ethically justifiable to deceive an individual patient to prevent a particular harm, this must be weighed against the effect of cumulative deceptions. A long-term consequence of withholding information from patients is that they feel excluded from the decision making. From a rule-based perspective, the moral worth of an action does not depend on the result expected from it and truth telling is the 'right' thing to do, regardless of circumstances and consequences. A virtuous clinician may value honesty and trust, but do such virtues mandate that side-effects are disclosed where it would seem insensitive to do so?

The case scenarios

- *Sabrieh*: It is clinically unlikely that informing Sabrieh of the need to do an angiogram would lead to a myocardial infarction. Without sufficient evidence that this could happen, therapeutic privilege cannot be justified.
- *John*: It is likely that John lacks the capacity to make informed decisions regarding the possible treatment options for his schizophrenia. If so, the decisions must be made in his best interests, and therapeutic privilege is not strictly relevant (as it applies to the consenting process). Since the risks are relatively high the treatment should probably not be commenced.
- *Jane*: Jane is a competent adult and has the right to make treatment decisions based on all the facts. The risks of all treatment options must be given to her so she can make an informed choice.

 KEY POINTS

- Therapeutic privilege is a legal loophole, which enables doctors to withhold information from a patient so as to prevent causing them serious harm.
- In clinical practice, situations that would ethically justify implementing therapeutic privilege are rare.

CASE 44: TREATMENT AND LIES

Camilla is admitted with high blood sugar. It has been a few weeks since you have seen her and she is looking extremely thin and unkempt. She has bruises on her face and she tells you she was in a fight with another girl. She asks you why she is losing so much weight and whether there are any tablets that she can take to make her gain weight. You explain to her that the reason she is losing weight is because of diabetes. You tell her the weight loss is linked with her high blood sugar, and that is also why she feels tired and thirsty all the time. Camilla says you must be wrong since she does not have diabetes. You reluctantly agree, and then you say that there is a tablet that will help her gain weight if she stays in hospital and takes it and starts eating properly. Camilla enthusiastically agrees and is happy to stay as an inpatient while you prescribe her insulin and gliclazide.

Question

- Is it ethical to lie to Camilla about the reason why she is taking medication?

ANSWER 44

The concept of honesty in medical ethics has evolved along with the changes in modern medical practice. When paternalistic medicine was practised more widely, on many occasions doctors would not disclose information about patients' diagnosis or prognosis in the belief that they were acting in their patients' best interests. However, respect for patient autonomy is now at the core of ethical guidance. This has led to an environment where patients are better informed because they are expected to be involved in their healthcare decisions. Honesty, openness and truth telling are now essential qualities of a virtuous doctor.

This case scenario, however, has a slightly different emphasis. The doctor has honestly told Camilla the reason for her weight loss, the underlying diagnosis and treatment options and that if she fails to adhere to the medication she is at risk of long-term complications and possibly even death. But she refuses to believe the information. Does this render Camilla incompetent or suggest that she has a psychiatric illness? There were no other signs of psychiatric illness and Camilla was capable of making all other decisions affecting her health. A psychiatric assessment also concluded that there was no evidence of mental disorder and that Camilla merely refused to believe the diagnosis.

The doctor is lying in order to give the treatment he believes is in Camilla's best interests. It is difficult to apply a moral theory that can justify this action. He could argue that he is acting in Camilla's best interests and that in this situation beneficence trumps autonomy. Arguably he could justify his actions by saying that he is not lying to his patient; that the medication he is giving will make her gain weight as a secondary response to treating the diabetes.

Another interesting concept is that of care ethics. This theory was developed in the 1980s and initially coined by Carol Gilligan. Care ethics has five central ideas: moral attention, sympathetic understanding, relationship awareness, accommodation and response. To apply these ideas to this specific case we could say that because it was a complex situation and we have investigated different possibilities behind the patient's beliefs about her illness, we have given the situation its due moral attention. We have a sympathetic understanding of the patient in that we appreciate the impact that her diagnosis will have on her health especially in the situation she is in. We are aware of the relationship between the doctor and the patient and the imbalance of power in this specific case, and we have attempted to address this imbalance by involving the patient in her care. Finally, we have discussed what best to do in the situation with other healthcare workers and decided on a response which we feel is best and with the patient's best interests at heart.

 KEY POINTS

- Complex cases may benefit from consideration from different viewpoints.
- Care ethics provides a framework to explore a patient's beliefs in depth and requires the doctor to consider all the different possibilities.

CASE 45: MAKING MISTAKES AND INCIDENT FORMS

During an evening on-call, you are bleeped to one of the rehabilitation wards to assess a patient who has had a fall. The patient is an elderly man who was admitted to hospital 3 months ago with a perforated duodenal ulcer, which was surgically treated. Following the operation he developed hospital-acquired pneumonia. It took him almost 2 months to recover and he was left with a lack of confidence. He was assessed by a physiotherapist who felt he would benefit from a period of rehabilitation before returning to his sheltered accommodation. That evening he had been attempting to mobilize to the bathroom when the healthcare assistant who was assisting him stumbled over an abandoned Zimmer frame. The patient fell heavily on to his hip. Fortunately, he did not seem to have suffered any injuries although he was very shaken by the experience. The staff nurse in charge asks you to fill in an incident form to assess what had occurred.

Questions
- Can you think of instances where you have seen incident forms being completed?
- What is the main point of an incident form?
- Who evaluates the forms once they have been completed?

ANSWER 45

The principle behind the use of clinical incident forms is to identify, manage, record and prevent recurrence of any adverse incident, accident or near-miss that occurs in the workplace. They are used to minimize harm to patients, visitors and hospital staff. Some incidents that require filing an incident form are: dangerous occurrences, visitor accidents, patient accidents or near-misses, defects or failures of medical devices, giving the wrong medication and violence and abuse of patients or staff. There is a legal duty for all employers to comply with the 'Reporting of Injuries, Diseases and Dangerous Occurrences Regulations' (RIDDOR) 1995 and for employers to provide incident forms, which should be available to all staff.

In 2001, the National Patient Safety Agency (NPSA) was established to co-ordinate the reporting of clinical incidents and to ensure patient safety within the National Health Service (NHS). In practice, the majority of clinical incidents are analysed and dealt with at a local level. Each hospital will have a nominated person who has overall responsibility for ensuring that incident forms are recorded, graded and discussed with the relevant individuals.

An incident form can be completed by anyone involved in the incident. Only clear, concise and factual information should be documented. Subjective experiences and conjecture are not permissible. They should be completed legibly, dated and signed. All incidents need to be graded. The grade can be changed as new information comes to light:

- *Serious incident*: where any person on hospital grounds suffers injury or unexpected death and where actions of healthcare staff are likely to attract public concern.
- *Other incidents*: where an individual suffers injury, unexpected death or is placed at unnecessary risk.
- *Near-misses*: an action or omission that may have caused avoidable harm to an individual.

Submitting an incident form is not an admission of liability. The NPSA encourages an open 'no blame' culture. No action is taken against the person complained about unless the incident occurred due to maliciousness, was criminal or was about an individual who has had repeatedly poor performance. Forms are also completely confidential and are reviewed only by the relevant personnel.

 KEY POINTS

- The aim of an incident form is to identify, document and manage incidents and potential incidents.
- Incident forms are not an admission of liability.

CASE 46: COMPLAINTS MADE AGAINST A DOCTOR

You are an F2 on a 4-month general practice placement. One of your patients, John, has come for a check-up after a prolonged hospital admission. He underwent elective laparoscopic cholecystectomy 4 months ago for recurrent biliary colic. During the procedure his large bowel was perforated and subsequently repaired. Following the operation John became acutely septic and was found to have a leak from his large bowel where it had been repaired. He underwent emergency surgery to repair the leak but ended up having an extended right hemicolectomy with a defunctioning ileostomy. He is still distressed by the events and is now suffering from depression. He feels he was not adequately warned about the complications of abdominal surgery and says that if he had known this could happen he would have 'put up' with his bouts of biliary colic. John tells you he wants to make a complaint against the surgeon who performed the operation because he wants an apology. He asks you how he can go about doing this.

Questions
- What should you say to John?
- How can patients make complaints against doctors?
- What should you do, as a doctor, if a complaint is made against you?

ANSWER 46

In the National Health Service (NHS), most complaints are made following a breakdown in communication between the doctor and the patient. Patients can suddenly find themselves in a situation where they come face to face with their own mortality. Becoming ill can be frightening, and hospitals, medical investigations and procedures are often mysterious to lay people. Complaints are not always against specific individuals. Waiting lists and funding issues often mean patients do not receive the quality of care they feel they are entitled to.

It is the responsibility of the local health area to make information available to patients about how to make a complaint against a doctor or a hospital. All patients have the right to make a complaint about the care they have received, and all complaints should be answered. The initial complaint should be handled sensitively and thoroughly, as this can prevent the complaint being taken higher than local level.

Most complaints are resolved at a local level by providing the patient with a full explanation of what happened or an apology. The second stage of the complaints procedure involves the Healthcare Commission. This service was set up in 2004 and reviews all NHS complaints that have not been resolved by the NHS trust involved. The Healthcare Commission also provides guidance for trusts on how to handle complaints effectively. The third stage of the complaints procedure involves the Health Service Ombudsman. This is an impartial review organization, independent of the NHS and government. A complaint must be registered within a year of the incident. Patients can also complain to the General Medical Council, which regulates all doctors practising in the UK.

In the first instance, doctors who receive a complaint against themselves should seek advice from their consultant and the complaints department. They will have to send a response to the complaint, which should include objective details of what happened. Apologizing to the patient is not seen as an admission of liability but is important and should be given whenever appropriate. Medical defence organizations review responses from doctors to complaints and provide advice on the complaints process.

In the case scenario, John should receive an apology. He should be offered a meeting with his consultant if he wishes to discuss in person what has occurred. All his concerns should be addressed by the complaints department. If he is not happy that his concerns have been resolved at a local level, he should be advised about what he can do next.

 KEY POINTS

- Most complaints are due to a breakdown in communication, and can be resolved with open and frank discussion and an apology.
- If a doctor receives a complaint about themselves, they should initially contact their consultant and the complaints department of the hospital.
- Medical defence organizations provide advice to doctors about how to handle complaints procedures.

MENTAL HEALTH

CASE 47: WHEN TO SECTION A PATIENT UNDER THE MENTAL HEALTH ACT

A 23-year-old artist, Jenny, lives with her parents and her 2-year-old daughter. You have received a phone call from Jenny's mother saying that she is worried that her daughter is acting 'oddly'. She asks if you would make a home visit to see Jenny as she is refusing to leave the house. You agree to go after your afternoon clinic. When you get to the house, Jenny's mother takes you upstairs. Jenny is hiding under her duvet in the dark with a torch, which she is turning on and off. She is unwashed and wearing dirty clothes. Her arms are covered with fingernail scratches. As you enter, Jenny asks you to stay very quiet as she is trying to intercept a message from the people who live in her sock drawer. The torch is helping to reflect their thoughts into Jenny's head. On further questioning you discover that Jenny has several abnormal beliefs. She believes that she has been sent as a spy from the government and has a microchip inserted under her skin so that the prime minister can track her actions. Your first impressions are that Jenny has schizophrenia. You feel she should be admitted to a psychiatric hospital for further assessment and possible treatment.

Questions
- What is a mental disorder?
- What are the criteria for detention for assessment and treatment under mental health legislation?
- Who can section an individual?
- Can Jenny be forced to have treatment for her mental disorder?

ANSWER 47

Legal issues

The main purpose of mental health legislation is to ensure that those with serious mental disorders who are at risk of harming themselves or others can be treated irrespective of their consent. The Mental Health Act 1983 (which applies in England and Wales) set out the framework for compulsory treatment of people who have a mental disorder. This Act has now been significantly amended by the Mental Health Act 2007 (MHA 2007). A statement of principles will be included in the Code of Practice to the MHA 2007. These will highlight the importance of: keeping patient restrictions to the minimum necessary to protect the health and safety of the patient and other people; the need for minimum restrictions on liberty; the effectiveness of treatment or care; and the views of the patient. The MHA 2007 also introduces Supervised Community Treatment Orders, which allow compulsory treatment in the community after discharge from detention in hospital.

Mental disorder

The legislation allows detention for assessment and treatment of those with a mental disorder only when certain criteria apply. Clinically recognized mental disorders include schizophrenia, bipolar disorder, anxiety and depression. Also included are personality disorders, eating disorders, autistic spectrum disorders and learning disabilities. Disorders of the brain are not mental disorders unless they give rise to disorder of the mind as well. People with learning disabilities are not considered to have a mental disorder unless the disability is associated with abnormally aggressive or seriously irresponsible conduct.

If Jenny's beliefs and behaviours are not a result of schizophrenia (or other disorder of the mind), she cannot be sectioned even if her behaviour causes alarm or distress to others.

Criteria for detention

People can be compulsorily admitted for assessment when they have a mental disorder which is of a nature or degree warranting detention and when they should be detained in the interests of their own health or safety or for the protection of others. This allows detention for up to 28 days for a psychiatric assessment. As Jenny has not come into contact with mental health services before, she can be admitted for assessment of her mental disorder *if* it is considered that she presents sufficient risk to herself (there seems to be no risk to others). The degree of risk should be weighed against the infringement of liberty.

Following a psychiatric assessment there may then be a medical recommendation that detention is continued for up to 6 months (which is renewable) where 'appropriate medical treatment' is available. Treatment must be appropriate, taking into account the nature and degree of the mental disorder and all other circumstances. Medical treatment includes nursing care and is now defined to include psychological interventions (such as cognitive therapy, behaviour therapy and counselling) and specialist mental health habilitation, rehabilitation and care. The purpose of medical treatment must be to alleviate or prevent a worsening of the disorder or one or more of its symptoms or manifestations.

The MHA 2007 removes the 'treatability' test and there is the possibility that detention could be used as a means of social control. Could the new Act authorize detention to provide day-to-day care to prevent a threat of violence that is a manifestation of a psychiatric condition? Could/should Jenny be denied her liberty so that she can receive counselling or day-to-day care to prevent a worsening of her bizarre beliefs? If care cannot treat the condition can detention be justified?

Who can section an individual?

The initial detention requires two medical recommendations. However, 'sections' may now be renewed by a 'responsible clinician', who may not be a doctor. A patient must be discharged if the grounds for detention are no longer met, i.e. if Jenny was no longer a threat to herself or others. Patients can apply for discharge from detention to the mental health review tribunal or a panel of associate hospital managers.

Medical treatment without consent

A patient may remain competent notwithstanding detention under the Mental Health Act and, unless and until rebutted, must be presumed to be competent to make informed decisions about treatment for medical conditions. It is important to remember that a patient can be detained only to treat a psychiatric illness. However, the MHA 2007 does not require consideration to be given to whether the patient is capable of choosing to refuse treatment. Therefore compulsory treatment can be given for the mental disorder even if a patient refusing treatment has capacity. This distinguishes legislation for treatment of mental disorders from the legal principles concerning the treatment of physical illness.

Ethical issues

Those suffering from a mental disorder are particularly vulnerable. Compulsory detention, assessment and treatment threaten their rights to liberty, dignity, physical integrity and respect for autonomy. The justification for such erosion of freedoms is to prevent harms, to the individuals themselves and to others, but compulsory detention must be proportionate to the harms to be avoided. Another aim of detention must be to enable treatment. Unless the aim is to gain benefit for the patient by seeking an improvement or preventing deterioration of their condition, detention could amount to social control. Failure to provide adequate checks on the use of powers of control and detention may mean that those in need of care are deterred from seeking it, thus increasing the risk to the individual and the public.

 KEY POINTS

- Compulsory detention in hospital is permitted where the person has a mental disorder.
- The mental disorder must be of a nature or degree to warrant detention.
- A person can be detained in the interests of his or her own health or safety or for the protection of others.
- Appropriate medical treatment must be available for the patient.
- If the criteria no longer apply the patient must be discharged.

CASE 48: MEDICAL TREATMENT FOR PATIENTS WITH A MENTAL DISORDER

Scenario 1

A 24-year-old woman has a long history of anorexia nervosa. She has been admitted to hospital under the provisions of the Mental Health Act. Her weight is dangerously low and she is refusing to eat.

Scenario 2

A woman with schizophrenia is 33 weeks pregnant. She has been sectioned under the Mental Health Act. The obstetrician considers that there is a high risk of placenta-abruption and she would like to carry out a caesarean section. However, the woman is violent and aggressive and is refusing all antenatal interventions.

Scenario 3

A 67-year-old man has been referred for semi-urgent (within a week) coronary artery bypass surgery. He is known to suffer from schizophrenia, which is well controlled with medication. From the notes it is apparent that the referring hospital doctors felt that he lacked the capacity to sign the consent form for his coronary angiography.

Questions

- Does mental disorder equate to lack of capacity?
- Can a person with a mental disorder be treated without consent?

ANSWER 48

Although mental disorder does not of itself render a person incapable of making the relevant healthcare decision, mental health legislation provides that people detained under the Mental Health Act may be treated for their mental disorder *despite* their capacity to refuse. Mental illness may of course affect capacity but the question is: has the patient's capacity been so reduced by mental disorder that they do not understand the purpose and nature of the intervention, the risks of the intervention and the risks of not having the intervention?

In *Re C* (1994) a 68-year-old man detained under the Mental Health Act 1983 was considered to have capacity to refuse amputation of a gangrenous foot. Although he had schizophrenia, the court found that he had capacity to refuse the medical treatment because he could comprehend, take in and retain information, believe it, and weigh it up in order to make a choice (the test for capacity now set out in the Mental Capacity Act 2005 is broadly the same). Because he was refusing treatment for a physical disorder, rather than his mental condition, this had to be respected. In comparison, Ian Brady, who went on hunger strike while detained under the Mental Health Act, was found to lack capacity because he had a severe personality disorder. This meant that he was engaged in a battle of wills and was unable to weigh information and balance the risks of refusing food.

The Mental Health Act permits compulsory medical treatment of competent detained patients for their mental disorder. However, medical treatment for a mental disorder has been interpreted widely to include treatment to alleviate the symptoms of the mental disorder. The courts have considered force feeding of an anorexic patient to be medical treatment for the mental disorder because it relieves the symptoms of anorexia. Controversially an induced labour or caesarean section was considered to be medical treatment for the patient's mental disorder – paranoid schizophrenia. The court found that an ancillary reason for the induction/caesarean section was to prevent deterioration in the patient's mental state. Effective treatment required that the woman give birth to a live baby and restart her antipsychotic medication (*Tameside and Glossop* v. *CH* 1996).

Beneficence and public protection take precedence over respect for autonomy of individuals with mental disorders. Paternalism could perhaps be justified where mental disorder is equated with lack of judgement but the law allows even a competent person to be treated without consent for their mental disorder. If beneficence is allowed to trump autonomy then there should be clear demarcation between treatment without consent for a mental disorder (permitted) and a physical disorder (not permitted). If the former is interpreted widely individuals may be forced to have treatment which has only a tenuous link to their mental state.

KEY POINTS

- A competent, mentally ill individual can be treated without consent for their mental disorder but not for any physical illness.
- Mental disorder may affect the patient's capacity to make treatment decisions *about the mental disorder* itself, as the patient could lack insight and therefore be unable to weigh and balance the need for treatment for the mental disorder.
- Assessing capacity is not a neat calculation and the application of the test for capacity by judges and doctors may give rise to a difference of opinion.

Assessment of capacity is dealt with in Case 28: Adult capacity to consent to treatment, page 71.

CASE 49: PERSONAL IDENTITY

Melissa, a 30-year-old woman, had always been hard-working and conscientious, but had often doubted her abilities and worried about her performance at school, university and at work. She was shy and nervous in new situations. She had suffered from depressive episodes since her final year at university and had counselling on various occasions, which she found helpful. Recently, in the space of a few months, she was promoted to a stressful position at work, her mother died unexpectedly, and her boyfriend of 4 years left her having met someone else. She felt permanently tired, lacking in motivation and enthusiasm, and was apt to burst into tears at the slightest provocation. She sought psychiatric help, was diagnosed with depression and was prescribed a course of antidepressant medication. Melissa responded well to the medication, and stopped feeling tired and unhappy and unable to cope. She stopped worrying about her abilities and her performance at work, and found her job much more enjoyable. Where previously she had felt shy or nervous in new situations, she felt more confident and convinced of her own ability to contribute.

Sometime after the course of medication finished, Melissa found herself returning to her previous state. She was less self-confident and more concerned about whether her abilities were adequate for the job she had to do. She was not prone to crying or permanently tired as she had been when the medication was prescribed, but she felt shy and nervous and unable to express herself as fully as she had done when on the medication. She felt lacking in motivation and 'flat'.

Eventually, Melissa asked her psychiatrist whether she could be prescribed the medication again, saying that it was only when on the medication that she had felt her true self. She now realized that the shy, nervous, worrier she had previously been was not really her at all, and she wanted to give her real self the chance to come through again.

Questions
- Should Melissa have been given medication in the first instance, given that she had previously found non-pharmacological treatment for her depressive episodes to be successful?
- Should she be prescribed the medication again?
- What does it mean to say that one has a 'true' or 'real' self, and to say that one's real self can only be expressed with the aid of medication?

ANSWER 49

The simple answer to this case is that antidepressant medication should be prescribed when someone meets the clinical requirements for a diagnosis of depression, and not otherwise. Clearly there are degrees of depression and scope for differences of opinion between health professionals about when treatment is required, and what type of treatment should be given. If the medication does more than simply relieve the psychiatric condition, by improving Melissa's normal functioning, is it fair to deprive her of this additional effect which she sees as essential?

This case raises difficult and fundamental questions about the nature of personal identity. The idea of a real or true self is one that we are all familiar with, but is hard to explain:

- Are there some core personality traits that define us?
- What happens if they change?
- Do I become a different person?
- Who decides what is our 'real' self?
- Is it something that only we can know or is it something that other people could decide?
- Would Melissa's friends and family say that she had become a different person when on medication, or would they say that she was still Melissa, just more outgoing and self-confident than she had previously been?

The question of who decides what is an individual's real self is clearly important in clinical decision making. On what moral basis can a health professional override someone's personal view of themselves? Is an integral part of respect for autonomy an acceptance that all individuals should be able to determine what kind of a person they are, or should be?

Another important point that could affect the way an individual is judged is whether it matters what means are used to change personality. Some people may instinctively feel that changing personality traits using chemical means is wrong. It might seem that although Melissa thinks she is her true self when on medication, this cannot be correct. The medication is creating an artificial effect, which masks Melissa's true self. But now imagine that Melissa gets a new boyfriend, achieves success at work, and makes use of behavioural therapies aimed at improving self-esteem. She might end up feeling the same as she did on medication. How is it different from taking the medication if the end result is the same? If it is possible for Melissa to be her true self without medication, why should she be made to take a longer, harder route, which might have less chance of succeeding? The potential for changing personality through medication also has implications for cases where individuals make decisions about their future treatment. If Melissa would make a different decision on medication than off it, which of these decisions should be respected?

There are no straightforward answers to any of the myriad questions raised by this case. Nor does recourse to generic ethical principles assist. In considering the problems identified, readers should be alert to their intuitive response, attempt to analyse the basis for it, and monitor it for inconsistency.

 KEY POINTS

- Personal identity can be affected by many different things, e.g. medication and alcohol. It can also change throughout life.
- It can be difficult to assess whether a person's 'true' self changes with psychiatric illness.

CASE 50: PSYCHIATRIC ADVANCE DIRECTIVES

Sophie, 32 years, is due to be discharged from a psychiatric ward where you are an F2. She has a diagnosis of bipolar disorder, and this has been her eighth admission under a section of the Mental Health Act in the past 11 years. Her discharge plan contains an advance directive, written and signed by her with the consultant yesterday. This describes 'warning signs' of a relapse: she will seem elated, very confident and disinhibited, and say that her medication is unnecessary or stop taking it. It then gives her consent to treatment in hospital at such a time in the future when she has these symptoms.

You go to discharge Sophie, and ask her about the advance directive. She hopes it will ensure that she gets help more quickly in future. She tells you that during the last episode of mania she ran up unmanageable debts, lost her job and eventually stopped eating and sleeping altogether before she was finally admitted to hospital. Such episodes, she says, have been invariably followed by severe depression – 'the worst kind of hell'. She says that her only doubts regarding the directive are that as she is a painter, she regrets that when she is on the medication she loses the inspiration to paint. Coming off the medication, however, is not worth the risk of 'going though that again'.

Two months later you see Sophie at a follow-up appointment. She tells you immediately that she has come to tell you it was a mistake to agree to take medication, and she does not need it. She says she feels fantastic without it and can paint beautifully again. She seems elated and talks rapidly about her paintings. You remind her of her written request to be kept on the mood stabilizer and she says, 'Ignore it. I wrote that under the influence of those drugs. You don't know how wonderful it is to be able to paint again. If I hadn't had that suppressed by the psychiatrists I would never have written those words.'

Questions
- Is the psychiatric advance directive valid?
- Is the request to revoke the advance directive valid?
- What are the limitations of advance directives in psychiatry?
- What is the legal status of the advance directive?

ANSWER 50

Psychiatric advance directives (PAD) allow competent individuals to express preferences about how mental health treatment decisions should be made in the future if they become incompetent, e.g. if they refuse treatment during an episode of acute psychiatric illness. For a PAD to be considered valid, it must have been written at a time when the author had sufficient mental capacity. This requires at least that they understood the implications of what they were writing, and that they had made their decision without coercion.

If a PAD is to be made in negotiation with health professionals, it is recommended that an advocate should be present to witness that the patient's involvement is voluntary. The PAD might not be valid if the patient's mental capacity was significantly reduced by a mental disorder. However, this is only if the mental disorder specifically affected the patient's ability to make the decision in question. For example, a patient with delusional beliefs about a certain treatment may not have the capacity to make decisions concerning that treatment. However, if the patient's delusional beliefs are unrelated to the treatment they may well retain the capacity to make the decision. It must not be assumed that any patient lacks capacity.

When should a PAD be applied? First, the PAD must describe the present situation with sufficient accuracy. It cannot refer to mental health crises 'in general', nor be applied in a situation which is significantly different from the one specified. New information, such as the availability of new treatments, or a more severe crisis than the one anticipated also call the validity of a PAD into question. Second, the PAD can only be applied to situations in which the patient loses the mental capacity to make treatment decisions at the time. As in analogous medical cases, it is of the highest importance that people who retain capacity are allowed to change their minds.

A PAD can be revoked or changed where the person has capacity. Sufficient reason to suppose that Sophie lacks capacity has not been given. The doctor would need to know more about that Sophie's mental state and factors leading her to revoke the PAD. Difficult situations may arise if it is not easy to assess whether the patient has capacity. The PAD may still be helpful in discussion with the patient and as a reminder of her previous wishes.

As with medical advance directives, a PAD cannot dictate that the patient is to be given a treatment that is considered therapeutically inappropriate by the treatment provider. However, a PAD may be seen as a way for the patient to state their preferences and to consent in advance to a treatment plan created in negotiation with healthcare professionals. A PAD does not have the effect of refusing treatment which can be given compulsorily under the Mental Health Act.

 KEY POINTS

- Efforts to reduce coercion and promote patient involvement in psychiatry have been prominent in recent reviews of mental health legislation and have motivated development of PADs.
- The greatest value of PADs is to help to shift the balance in the making of treatment decisions towards the patient's own choices.

For information about advance decisions refusing medical treatment, *see* Case 67: Advance decisions, page 167.

CASE 51: SELF-HARM

While you are working in accident and emergency (A&E) on a Sunday afternoon you are asked to see Naomi, a 15-year-old 'regular attendee'. No one else wants to see her. Naomi is very subdued and has a deep cut along the top of her thigh. Her legs and arms are criss-crossed with scars. She asks you to just hurry up and 'practise your suturing' so that she can get home in time for *EastEnders*. You are concerned about her blasé attitude to her injuries. Looking through the notes you discover this is her eighteenth attendance to A&E in the past 6 months for similar treatment. You try to talk to Naomi about why she self-harms. Naomi is surprised, as no one has asked her this before.

Questions
- How should patients who self-harm be managed?
- What can be done to prevent a 'revolving door' system of hospital admissions?

ANSWER 51

Hospital records have shown that over 140 000 young people are admitted to A&E every year following deliberate self-harm. The prevalence is actually estimated to be much higher since many patients will not require medical treatment for the harm caused. Self-harm is different from suicide in that there is no desire to die. It is a phenomenon found mainly among 12–25-year-olds and is often an indication of underlying mental illness or emotional instability. It is regarded as a maladaptive coping mechanism. The tangible physical pain is often easier to cope with than emotional distress. As a junior doctor it may be difficult to know how to effectively help young people who present to A&E or their general practitioner with self-inflicted wounds. Many injuries will be superficial and require only minimal medical input, yet these patients will often become regular attendees at hospital. The most recent research suggests that 1 in 15 young people self-harm but that when they have asked for help from professionals they have encountered ridicule and hostility. Self-harm is a reflection of the pressurized society in which young people find themselves growing up.

> **! Examples of self-harm**
>
> - Cutting and scratching
> - Burning and scalding
> - Hair pulling
> - Ingestion of toxic substances

There is a wide range of services across the UK for young people who self-harm, but there are no data on how effective these services are. Patients should be spoken to sensitively and in confidence. If possible, the same doctor should see the patient each time to build up rapport. The patient should be encouraged to tell their family and school teacher about the difficulties they are having with coping.

Ethical and legal issues

Health professionals need to have a greater understanding of the cause and prevalence of self-harm to prevent a revolving door entry system into A&E. Promoting a strong doctor–patient relationship can help the patient make autonomous decisions regarding their own health and will help them feel more in control of their emotions. Listening to them empathetically can help them feel that they are understood and so prevent the need to release their psychological pain through physical outlets.

The 2-year self-harm inquiry launched by the House of Commons in 2004 recommended that health professionals should 're-connect to their core professional skills and values: empathy, understanding, non-judgemental listening and respect for individuals'. Since many people who self-harm are under 16, doctors need to ensure they are Gillick competent before they treat them for any injuries. Just because a person is injuring herself does not mean she is incompetent.

> **KEY POINTS**
>
> - Patients who self-harm need to be treated sensitively. They are vulnerable patients who require understanding, confidentiality and care.
> - Autonomy should be encouraged in people who self-harm.
> - Gillick competence should be assessed.

CASE 52: TREATMENT OF SUICIDE ATTEMPTS

Jane is a 58-year-old woman in the final stages of multiple myeloma. Prior to her diagnosis 5 years ago she was sporty and active, and enjoyed great success as the director of one of London's most prestigious insurance firms. Jane's general practitioner became suspicious after she had a serious of unexplained fractures from seemingly innocuous causes such as playing tennis. A forceful and energetic woman, she resolved to put all her strength into fighting the disease. However, 3 years later and after several rounds of chemotherapy it became apparent that the myeloma was incurable and that Jane had little time left. With lesions present in most of her bones she became unable to walk following vertebral collapse. She is now wheelchair bound. Her deteriorating physical condition has been accompanied by severe depression. She cannot work any more and has no close family, having dedicated much of her life to her career. One evening, she asks her carer not to visit the following day, but he does so anyhow, suspicious of her reasons. He finds Jane drowsy beside a bottle of paracetamol and calls an ambulance. By the time she arrives in hospital she is unconscious. The nurses find a suicide note to her friends and her carer and a letter to the 'staff at the hospital'. The attending doctor reads the letter. It states that Jane wants to die and that this is a serious suicide attempt, she refuses all forms of treatment and she will take legal action against anyone who attempts to save her life.

Questions
- If you were the attending doctor how would you proceed?
- Should a suicide note be respected in such circumstances?
- Is it lawful to provide medical assistance?
- Is it ethical to provide medical assistance?

ANSWER 52

Legal issues

The first issue to consider is whether this suicide note amounts to a valid advance decision. It does not specify the treatment to be refused, rather it is a general desire not to be treated. As this amounts to a refusal of life-sustaining treatment, an advance decision would have to be witnessed and state that the refusal applies even though 'life is at risk'.

If the patient lacks capacity and there is no valid advance decision the patient must be treated in their best interests. Jane's statement is an expression of her wishes and must be considered in assessing her best interests. Relevant features in the story that may influence her best interests include her attempt not to be discovered, her debilitating physical condition, her lack of family support network and her current lack of enjoyment in life. Can it ever be in a person's best interests to allow them to die by failing to treat? Here Jane seems to have assessed her quality of life as not being worth living. A competent patient is considered to be the best judge of her best interests, including the decision whether to refuse life-sustaining treatment. Without dialogue with a competent patient, and given the irreversibility of non-treatment, there is an onus to be sure that the patient did have capacity and that the patient had properly judged the outcome of her actions.

Ethical issues

Do individuals have a moral right to decide about the acceptability of suicide and not to be hampered in acting on their beliefs? If the answer is yes, there is no legitimate basis on which to interfere with an autonomous choice to commit suicide. John Stuart Mill stated that an intervention is justified to establish the quality of a person's autonomy but once it is decided that their actions are substantially autonomous further intervention is not justified to prevent harm to them.

It could be argued that suicide is the ultimate exercise of autonomy. But many who attempt suicide are not acting autonomously perhaps because of mental disorder. Intervention after attempted suicide may be a justified paternalistic intervention to protect patients against harmful consequences of their own choices. Should the burden of proof in justifying interference lie on those who argue that it was not a substantially autonomous choice? Suicide can be considered morally unacceptable because it goes against the principle of sanctity of life. Many religions believe that life should only be taken by God. From a consequentialist perspective, it could be argued that failure to intervene sends out a message of lack of societal concern for those who have expressed such deep distress.

 KEY POINTS

- In emergencies it will almost always be in the person's best interests to give urgent treatment without delay.
- The attending doctor should demonstrate reasonable and objective grounds for his decision.
- All decisions should be documented in the medical records: how they were made, what were the reasons and who was consulted.

For further discussion of some of the issues covered in this case scenario, *see* Case 29: Refusal of treatment, page 73, and Case 67: Advance decisions, page 167.

CASE 53: COVERT MEDICATION

Paul is 35 years old and lives with his parents, his younger sister and her child. He has a long-standing diagnosis of paranoid schizophrenia, and in the past has had formal and informal admissions to hospital under the Mental Health Act. He has experienced persecutory delusions that his parents want to harm him and occasionally he has acted violently towards them. He has no insight into his illness. In the past he has agreed to take risperidone although apparently he believed it was to help him sleep.

Six months ago Paul's mother went to his general practice, concerned that recently he had started to refuse all medication, and this made it very hard to manage him. As she was Paul's main carer and ensured that he took his medication, she was given a prescription for risperidone for him. She now returns to the surgery for another prescription. You find out that Paul's family have been giving him risperidone covertly in his food. Paul is not aware of this. They feel that although his psychotic symptoms remain he is less agitated, and without the risperidone they believe they could not manage him at home. They would like the support of psychiatric services to monitor him but do not wish him to be made aware that he has been given medication.

Questions
- Is covert medication ever justifiable?
- Should Paul be told that he has been given medication with a view to negotiating informed consent?

ANSWER 53

Legal issues

Covert medication may be justifiable for a patient who lacks capacity if it is in his best interests and it is *necessary* either to prevent a risk to others or deterioration in the patient's health. The Mental Capacity Act 2005 emphasizes the need for facilitation and enhancement of capacity, and covert medication might be seen to impede those object-ives. Neither the Royal College of Psychiatrists nor the Nursing and Midwifery Council rules out covert medication as an option.

Ethical issues

Covert medication of patients who have the capacity to make healthcare decisions is a breach of their autonomy. It deprives them of the ability to decide whether or not to take the medication and is unjustifiably paternalistic. Although Paul lacks insight, the issue of whether he has capacity needs to be further explored. The fact that Paul is unaware that he is taking risperidone inevitably compromises the assessment of his capacity because the purpose, relative benefits and harms of either taking medication or refusing it cannot be explored adequately. To assess his capacity properly necessitates disclosure that he is already taking risperidone. In considering Paul's best interests the benefits and harms of disclosing to him that he is receiving medication should be considered.

The *benefits* of disclosing include:

- Maximizing Paul's autonomy. Healthcare professionals have a duty to empower patients to make informed decisions about their care. While Paul may not be able to make an informed, competent decision at present, efforts should be made to enable a return to capacity, and disclosure would be necessary for more thorough discussion of the risks and benefits.
- Continuing with covert medication may be denying Paul the opportunity for better treatment, e.g. with alternative medication for treatment resistance.
- The side-effects of Paul's medication could be monitored.
- Continuing with covert medication may compromise his relationship with professionals in the future if his family cannot continue to take care of him.
- Consider the role of healthcare professionals and the potential damage to their integrity in continuing with the collusion.

The *harms* of disclosing include:

- Disclosure may lead to his refusal of medication with detrimental consequences to his mental state and possible risk of harm to others.
- Disclosure would potentially put the family in conflict with services, and/or lead to distrust by the family of mental health services, which is unlikely to be in Paul's best interests.
- The upset and disruption of a situation that is being managed at present, albeit imperfectly. For example, if he refused medication and deteriorated this may lead to hospital admission, taking him away from his family and further alienating him from mental health services.

KEY POINTS

- Honesty is the basis of an effective therapeutic relationship.
- Engagement with Paul's family and exploration of their understanding of his illness, the treatment options and his future may be a more productive way forward.
- Paul's best interests should be considered separately from the interests of the family.

For further discussion of some of the issues covered in this case scenario, *see* Case 30: Assessment of best interests, page 75, and Case 44: Treatment and lies, page 111.

GENERAL PRACTICE

CASE 54: PATIENTS' RESPONSIBILITY FOR HEALTH AND RESOURCE ALLOCATION

Imagine there are three patients in your clinic. They all need coronary artery bypass surgery. But only one of them can have it due to limited resources.

Patient 1
Aziz is a fellow doctor with special skills in neonatology. He is 50 years old and has a wife and three small children. He has been taking his medication sensibly for the past 5 years. However, he is still a heavy smoker and has two pints of Guinness a day.

Patient 2
Bertie is an 80-year-old man who served in the second world war and was commended for his bravery. His wife recently died and he does not have any children. He has also been compliant with his medication. He has never smoked and only has the occasional whisky.

Patient 3
Chloe is a 30-year-old woman with a genetic disorder that has caused learning disability and early heart disease. She lives in a care home and is visited often by her family. She is much loved by everyone who knows her and is often seen in her local village selling cakes for charity.

Questions
- Who should you prioritize to receive the surgery?
- What are the ethics behind resource allocation in the National Health Service (NHS)?
- Should priority be given to patients who are not to blame for their illness?

ANSWER 54

With ever-increasing frequency the media are highlighting inequalities in the modern-day NHS: newly licensed drugs are available according to a postcode lottery, waiting lists for hip operations vary from area to area and potential life-prolonging treatments are being denied on the basis that they are not cost effective. When the NHS was created in 1948, the Beveridge Report stated that the ideal plan would be 'a health service providing full preventative and curative treatment of every kind to every citizen without exceptions, without remuneration limit and without an economic barrier at any point to delay recourse to it'. In an ideal world access to healthcare would be available to everyone and it would be free. As this is not the case there has to be a compromise between providing an adequate level of healthcare at a cost that consumers find acceptable, and therefore 'rationing' has to be implemented. Rationing has been defined as when 'anyone is denied an intervention that everyone would agree would do them good and which they would like to have'.

The way in which healthcare resources should be rationed is a topic of constant debate and multiple theories. It is an extremely complex area of medical ethics and this answer shall only address the basics. The NHS is continuously under-funded and hospital managers have to find ways of implementing money-saving strategies. Deciding who should receive medical treatment is a difficult ethical quandary. Doctors take an oath to do the best they can for the patients they care for. Healthcare, as with most things in life, is not inexhaustible. How then is it best to judge who should receive healthcare and who must wait? Which illnesses are more deserving of the newest drugs? Which patients? There are several ethical theories regarding resource allocation and healthcare funding.

Ethical issues

Consequentialism advocates the provision of medical treatment which produces the best overall consequences, and perhaps this would include taking into account the benefits that an individual would give to society by having treatment. In this case, Aziz may go on to save the lives of lots of babies and he also has a wife and children to support. On the other hand, it could be argued that Bertie is most deserving of the surgery since he has looked after his health, has been a responsible member of the public and has previously risked his life to save his country. But he is 80 and unlikely to live much longer even with the operation.

The most common way of rationing is based on whether treatment is more or less beneficial to the person receiving it – QALY theory.

> **! Quality adjusted life-years (QALYs)**
>
> The QALY is a measurement designed to assess the number of years and the quality of those years that a treatment would give a patient.
>
> A year of life with perfect health is given the value 1, and years of life with imperfect health are given a value between 0 and 1.
>
> Treatment is considered beneficial if it improves the number of good-quality life-years a person or population has. Each given treatment will have a financial cost which can then be calculated as cost per quality life-years gained.

QALY theory has several problems. QALYs can be inherently ageist since an older person will have fewer quality life-years to gain. They do not take multiple comorbidities into account. A QALY is extremely subjective – what one person may experience as an increase in quality of life, another person will not. It also denies treatment to people who are suffering greatly but in whom treatment will only marginally improve suffering. It denies good-quality care for terminally ill people since they will not have any years left to bene-fit from the treatment. In the scenarios, Bertie would not be favoured for treatment due to his age. John Harris would say that this patient has had his 'fair innings'.

Another theory of how to allocate medical treatment is based on taking the patient's lifestyle and social worth into consideration. This implies that a patient who is respon-sible for their own ill health is less worthy of receiving treatment than someone who is blameless. Suggested ideas include denying operations to patients who are clinically obese or who are still smoking; factors that some consider patients should be able to con-trol. Aziz would therefore be less likely to be allocated the surgery since his need for it stems from his drinking and smoking. Chloe, in contrast, requires the surgery due to her genetic make-up, which is no fault of her own.

But is it justifiable to limit resource allocation based on patient-related factors? Should the obese patient who has not dieted or taken exercise be entitled to their new hips and knees on the NHS? Is the smoker with cardiac disease entitled to his angioplasty and should former alcoholics be allowed new livers? To what extent should patients be held responsible for their own health and be made to be morally responsible for the mistakes they make? Should a doctor continue to treat the patient who misses hospital appoint-ments and is non-compliant with medication? The General Medical Council (GMC) has stated that it is unethical to withhold or otherwise change the treatment a patient receives as a result of their 'lifestyle'.

Is it fair to ask doctors to assess a patient's 'social worth'? Many argue that doctors should assess patients merely on clinical need. There is an argument about whether it is justifi-able to treat the identifiable patient rather than reserving resources for potential future patients. Certainly for doctors it is easier to prescribe expensive medication to the person in pain and suffering sitting in front of them than to refuse them treatment on the prem-ise that another unidentifiable individual will require it.

'Whether you have a management role or not, your primary duty is to your patients. Their case and safety must be your first concern. You also have a duty to the health of the wider community, your profession, your colleagues, and the organisation in which you work.'

General Medical Council. *Management for Doctors*. London: GMC, 2006

 KEY POINTS

- Need, benefit and justice may lead to different results as to which patient should be prioritized for treatment.
- A QALY is one of the most commonly used methods of assessing whether treatment is cost effective. It compares the improvement in quality of life and the number of life years gained after giving a specific treatment.
- More often patients are expected to take responsibility for their own health.

CASE 55: REQUESTS FOR EXPENSIVE MEDICAL TREATMENT

Holly, a 45-year-old nursery school teacher with two young children, has ovarian cancer. She has had two courses of chemotherapy and a total hysterectomy and bilateral oophorectomy. She found the chemotherapy really tiring and had a lot of side-effects. Since she was diagnosed 18 months ago she has not been able to work. A follow-up positron emission tomography (PET) scan demonstrated that she had a further lesion in her breast. A biopsy confirmed this to be a primary breast cancer. Her oncologist suggests a third course of chemotherapy. Holly has heard about a new wonder drug which has been discussed on the news. The drug is reported to increase the curative rates of ovarian cancer in woman under 50. However, there are few randomized drug trial data on the drug. It is also extremely expensive. Holly wants to know more about it and whether or not her doctor will prescribe it for her.

Questions
- Is there a legal requirement to provide treatment on the National Health Service (NHS)?
- How is the NHS funded?
- What is the role of the National Institute for Health and Clinical Excellence (NICE)?
- Should doctors be the gatekeepers of resource allocation?

ANSWER 55

On 5 July 1948, the NHS changed from a vision into a reality. The founding principles were that it would provide free healthcare to everyone resident in the UK: from preventive to curative to palliative medicine. The NHS was, and still is, financed from central taxation. However, with the increase in life expectancy, advances in medical technologies and increase in the cost of drugs, the NHS is struggling to fulfil its original principles. To what extent, however, is the NHS obliged by law to provide healthcare?

> There is a duty to 'continue the promotion in England and Wales of a comprehensive health service designed to secure improvement in (a) the physical and mental health of the people of those countries, and (b) in the prevention, diagnosis and treatment of illness'.
>
> National Health Service Act 1977

The Act implies that there is no absolute duty to provide healthcare – only to continue to *promote* a comprehensive health service.

With the introduction of the Human Rights Act 1998, there have been several high-profile law cases which have sought to declare that the NHS contravenes patients' human rights by not providing them with a specific treatment or by making them wait too long for a treatment. It seems as if there is little chance of the European Court of Human Rights dictating which treatment should or should not be available under the NHS.

The National Institute for Health and Clinical Excellence (NICE) was founded in 1999. Its role, as an independent organization, is to give guidance to the public and to healthcare professionals on the use of new and existing treatments and procedures within the NHS. It examines the clinical benefits of new and expensive treatments and advises NHS funding bodies under what conditions and in which circumstances these drugs should be prescribed. In the case of *R (Rogers)* v. *Swindon NHS PCT* (2006) the claimant argued that it was unlawful for Swindon primary care trust (PCT) to refuse to pay for her to receive the (then) unlicensed breast cancer drug, Herceptin. When refusing treatment to a patient, PCTs are required to make decisions based on a transparent process and should consider relevant factors such as the cost effectiveness of the treatment.

Deciding which patients should be provided with expensive treatment is an ethical minefield. In contrast, the law provides that a treatment does not have to be prescribed if it can be rationally argued that it is not cost effective or of proven clinical benefit.

 KEY POINTS

- Healthcare rationing is a given in the NHS.
- Treatment and medication prescribed should be cost effective.
- NICE is an organization which provides information about the cost effectiveness of new and existing medication.

CASE 56: PATIENT ADDICTION

A young man in his early thirties uses a variety of drugs including crack cocaine and heroin. His habit costs him about £60 a day. To support his habit he deals drugs in the local community and steals from the local shopkeepers. Some of his clients are patients at the practice, and a few of them are school children registered with the practice. He regularly boasts how easy it is to steal from certain shopkeepers who are also patients. He also confides in his doctor how he cuts his crack cocaine with heroin and gives free 'starter samples' to young people to get them hooked.

The surgery has a comprehensive drug-prescribing programme. Patients with drug dependency are seen by a counsellor and prescribed drugs by a doctor after consultation. One day after a patient has left his room a doctor realizes his bag is missing. He suspects, but cannot prove, that the theft was committed by one of the drug users. Two weeks later the counsellor reports that one of his clients admitted stealing a bag from a doctor.

Questions
- What should you do if a patient admits to committing a crime?
- What should you do if a patient steals from you?
- Should patients be prescribed drug substitutions, e.g. methadone, if they are still admitting to taking drugs?

ANSWER 56

Legal issues

The Mental Health Act states clearly that drug and alcohol addiction are not classified as psychiatric disorders. A patient with drug addiction cannot be involuntarily detained to treat their addiction and to ensure that they do not continue to take drugs while receiving substitution treatment. Treating patients with addiction can be frustrating for doctors because there is a high rate of relapse.

Doctors have a duty of confidentiality to their patients; however, this duty is not limitless. The courts have ruled that confidentiality can be broken to prevent the public from being put at danger by criminals. In *W* v. *Egdell* (1990) the courts ruled that confidentiality could be breached if there is a 'real, immediate and serious risk' to public safety. In this case scenario, the patient has confided that he is selling drugs to children. This risk could potentially legally justify breaking patient confidentiality. Although it is advisable for the doctor to report the theft of his bag to the police it would be difficult to justify informing the police of his suspicions about who stole it, if that person is a patient. It would also be difficult to justify giving the police the names of all patients who were present at the time of the theft, since this would break patient confidentiality without there being any identifiable serious risk to the general public.

Ethical issues

Trust is an integral part of a doctor–patient relationship. When patients come to see a doctor they expect the doctor to believe what they are telling them, make an accurate diagnosis and treat them in the best way possible. They also expect sensitive information to remain confidential. But should the same principles apply the other way round? Is there a moral obligation for patients to be honest with their doctor? Trust and respect is a two-way street and is present in every healthy relationship; this should extend to a doctor–patient relationship. Dealing with difficult patients is a skill that a good doctor develops with time and experience, and doctors should not let their personal feelings towards a patient impinge on the care that the patient receives.

There are two issues regarding confidentiality in the above scenario. The first involves the doctor's bag having been stolen. Although this may have detrimental effects on the relationship with that patient, it is difficult to ethically justify informing the police of suspicions about an individual since this would jeopardize the doctor–patient relationship by destroying one of its basic tenets (confidentiality). The second is that the patient has confided in the doctor that he is dealing drugs to children. Although there is no specifically identifiable individual at risk here, the General Medical Council (2009) advises in its guidance *Confidentiality* that doctors can use their discretion to break confidentiality when there is a risk of serious harm to others. In the case scenario, vulnerable children are at risk from the patient's actions.

If you know that the patient is also continuing to take heroin it is questionable whether he should be allowed to continue on the rehabilitation programme. There is an increased risk of overdose if he is taking two different opiate-based drugs and he is also taking up a place on a programme that may benefit another member of the community.

KEY POINTS

- Treating patients with addiction can be frustrating but maintaining a good doctor–patient rapport will help establish a trusting relationship.
- Confidentiality can be broken to prevent serious harm to others.

For further consideration of the duty of confidentiality, *see* Case 36: Confidentiality with regard to Human Immonodeficiency Virus infection and disclosure of risk to known partners, page 89.

CASE 57: ALTERNATIVE THERAPIES

Jason, a 36-year-old businessman, leads an extremely busy and stressful life. Recently he has begun to feel tired and lethargic. He is not enjoying life as much as he used to and often finds himself declining invitations so that he can get home and go to bed early. He has lost his appetite and is losing weight. He went to see his doctor because he was concerned that he may have a serious problem. Fortunately, all his blood test results have ruled out an organic cause for his tiredness and anhedonia. The doctor suggests that Jason might have depression and would like to give him a course of antidepressants. Jason is unhappy about the thought of taking pharmaceutical products to treat a condition he is not sure he has. He tells the doctor he will think about it. The following week Jason decides to go and see a herbalist about his symptoms. She makes the same suggestions that the doctor did. However, instead of offering him medication, she takes a more holistic approach and suggests some lifestyle changes he can make, as well as some dietary changes. She also gives him some St John's wort to try. Over the next few months he goes to see the herbalist again. He slowly begins to feel better and returns to his normal active self.

Questions
- What other alternative therapies are popular in the UK?
- How are these therapies regulated?
- Should doctors and alternative therapists work more closely together?

ANSWER 57

Complementary and alternative medicine (CAM) is an umbrella term for any method of treating disease which is not considered orthodox. Over the past few decades there has been an increase in the popularity of CAM and in 2000, the House of Lords Science and Technology Committee discussed the role of alternative therapies, the training and regulation of therapists, and the need for the National Health Service (NHS) to provide access to these therapies. It split the different specialties into three groups: group 1 consisted of organized professions, group 2 consisted of therapies that complemented traditional medicine, and group 3 consisted of therapies that would not be supported by the NHS until research had shown them to have some proved efficacy. Table 57.1 shows examples of each category.

Table 57.1 Examples of complementary and alternative therapies

Group 1	Group 2	Group 3
Acupuncture	Aromatherapy	Ayurvedic medicine
Chiropractic	Massage	Chinese herbal medicine
Herbal medicine	Hypnotherapy	Eastern medicine
Homeopathy	Reflexology	Crystal therapy
Osteopathy	Meditation and yoga	
	Shiatsu	
	Nutritional medicine	

In 2006 the British Medical Association (BMA) produced guidance for general practitioners (GPs) about when and how to refer patients to alternative therapists. It advises that healthcare professionals gain an understanding of the role of different therapies and the effect they can have on disease. A GP has a legal duty to refer patients only for treatment that is available under the NHS. Most alternative therapies are not available under the NHS, and so there is no legal duty to refer a patient. However, a GP *can* refer a patient to a recommended alternative therapist. Osteopathy and chiropractic are the only therapies that have statutory regulatory bodies, but the therapies in group 1 have voluntary regulatory bodies. A GP should always ensure that they recommend a therapist who has appropriate qualifications and is a member of a regulatory body. The BMA also advises that follow-up appointments should be organized to monitor the efficacy of the treatment and to ensure that there are no harmful side-effects.

Many general practices now have associated alternative therapy clinics. This is beneficial because it aids better communication between the different healthcare professions and provides for a more holistic approach to patient care. Doctors and nurses can also take postgraduate courses in alternative therapies.

If a GP does not believe that alternative therapy will benefit a patient they do not have to recommend a therapist. They should, however, inform the patient that they have the right to seek treatment elsewhere if they wish and not criticize the patient.

 KEY POINTS

- Alternative therapies are increasing in popularity and doctors should have some knowledge of their role in medicine.
- When referring a patient to an alternative therapist a GP should ensure the therapist is appropriately qualified and a member of a regulatory body.
- Patients should not be belittled for wanting to seek an alternative method of treatment.

CASE 58: PRESCRIBING ANTIBIOTICS

Jane is a first-time mother who comes to see you in your morning clinic with Jack, her 3-year-old son. Jane has had to take time off her demanding job as Jack has been asked not to come to the nursery for a few days because he has a very bad cold and the childminders are worried that the other children will pick up his bugs. He does not look very well. He is listless and irritable and cries throughout the consultation. On examination he is slightly pyrexic and has a runny nose. His throat is not red and his tonsils are not enlarged. He has a dry cough. Jane tells you that he has not been sleeping well and has been off his food although he has been drinking more than usual. She says this is the third time he has been unwell since starting nursery 3 months ago. She demands that you prescribe some antibiotics for Jack to help expedite his recovery as her boss will not give her any more time off work to stay at home and look after him. She also criticizes your colleague, who saw him last time, for failing to give him any antibiotics. She is convinced that this is a recurrent infection with the same bug. You suspect that Jack has yet another viral illness and that antibiotics will not help.

Questions
- What should you do in this situation?
- Can you justify prescribing antibiotics?

ANSWER 58

Professional guidance

The General Medical Council (GMC) advises that 'when prescribing medicines you must ensure that your prescribing is appropriate and responsible and in the patient's best interests' (GMC, *Keeping up to date and prescribing in patients' best interests*. London: GMC, 2006). This means being aware of the reasons for prescribing the medication, how to take it and any side-effects or contraindications. Guidance on all of these is given in the *British National Formulary* (*BNF*), which is published every 6 months and contains information on all licensed drugs in the UK.

Communication skills are essential in this case. The doctor needs to elucidate whether Jane understands the role of antibiotics in illness. Does she understand the difference between bacterial infection and viral infection? What does she think antibiotics will do? Does she understand the risk of poor antibiotic prescribing? If she does not, these things should be explained to her and reasons for not prescribing antibiotics should be given. Simply refusing to give her child medication may give the impression that the doctor does not care or that he is trying to cut costs. It can also be useful to give her information on what medication may help. The doctor could explain that antibiotics will not help her child get better any quicker but that simple things such as paracetamol and cough linctus can be given to provide symptom relief. This is also a good opportunity for the doctor to ensure that Jack's immunizations are up to date.

Although viral infections are common, especially in children attending nursery, if a patient continues to attend the surgery, it may be worth investigating further to ensure that they are not immunocompromised.

Ethical issues

Several voices should be listened to and examined in this scenario. The first is that of the mother who is concerned about the health of her child. Although she is demanding unnecessary, and potentially harmful, treatment for her son, she will have his best interests at heart. The doctor needs to show that she appreciates this by listening to her ideas, concerns and expectations and empathizing with her. The voice of the child also needs to be acknowledged; the doctor has to act in his best interests, including his future interests. Although antibiotic therapy may cause antibiotic resistance and is unlikely to confer any direct benefit to him now, prescribing them may prevent a breakdown in the relationship that the doctor has with his mother.

 KEY POINTS

- Medications should be prescribed for therapeutic reasons only and should be based on clinical evidence.
- Listening to the concerns of worried parents may prevent a deterioration in the doctor–patient relationship.

ORGAN DONATION

Debbie, 38 years old, is a trained nurse and married with a young family. Fifteen years ago she was diagnosed with polycystic kidney disease. Unfortunately she had rapid disease progression and 3 years ago she was started on dialysis for end-stage renal failure. At the moment her life revolves around her dialysis. She has to attend hospital three times a week, often for over 4 hours. She has never been on holiday with her family and she has had to give up work. She often misses out on seeing her children perform in school plays or sports days, as she cannot miss her hospital appointments. As well as this inconvenience she has continual pain, which is not easily relieved. She suffers from fluid overload, which affects her breathing and consequently her exercise tolerance. She is anaemic and some days she cannot find the energy or motivation to get up. She is gradually becoming depressed. A year ago Debbie was placed on the UK transplant list. Apart from one false alarm, she has heard nothing. Her family have discussed the situation among themselves and her sister and brother have decided they would like to donate a kidney to her if one or other was found to be a potential match.

Questions
- What are the laws regarding organ transplantation?
- Who regulates organ transplantation?
- Can a stranger donate an organ?

ANSWER 59

During the 1980s, it was discovered that a clinic in Harley Street was buying kidneys from poor Turkish immigrants and transplanting them into wealthy private patients with end-stage renal disease. There was an immediate public outcry about the legality and ethics of this practice. As a result the Human Organ Transplants Act 1989 was quickly passed to prohibit the commercial market in human organs. More recently all the laws governing the use of human tissue have been repealed and replaced by the Human Tissue Act 2004. This Act provides 'a legal framework for the storage and use of tissue from the living and for the removal, storage and use of tissue from the dead'. The Human Tissue Authority has been set up to oversee the removal, storage and use of all human tissue in both the living and the dead. It has six main codes of practice which give guidance on issues such as consent, organ donation and examination of a body after death.

Throughout the Act the emphasis is on the issue of consent. Consent to donate an organ or tissue is considered valid if the person has capacity, consent is given voluntarily and the potential donor is fully aware of the short- and long-term risks of donation. The actual removal of an organ or tissue is still governed by common law.

The majority of live organ donations are between relatives. All potential living organ donations must be assessed by an independent assessor who is trained to examine whether all the conditions of the Act have been met. They have detailed discussions with both the donor and the donee to ensure that consent is valid, that there is no element of coercion, that they are aware of the risks associated with transplantation and to ensure that the donor is not getting any financial compensation. The Act highlights the importance of communication and an open and honest continuous dialogue between all parties involved. Consent should be sought in advance of any procedures to give both donor and donee time for reflection and time for any of their questions to be answered. The donor should also be reassured that they can withdraw their consent at any time, and that if there is any evidence of coercion the transplantation will not be performed.

The Act discusses several new types of organ donation: pooled/paired donation describes organ donation between more than two people due to relatives not being compatible, and non-directed altruistic donation (which is the donation of an organ to a stranger). These cases must be assessed by a panel of three members of the Human Tissue Authority (HTA). Anonymity is paramount to protect individuals from coercion. Where the potential donor is an adult who lacks capacity or a child, the donation must be approved by a court of law first to ensure that it is in the best interests of the donor to donate an organ. As well as this, the case must be assessed by a panel of three members of the HTA.

The Act reiterates that it is illegal to advertise, buy or sell, or have any commercial dealings whatsoever in the sale of human organs, whether they are from living or dead donors.

 KEY POINTS

- The Human Tissue Act 2004 regulates all organ and tissue donation in the UK.
- Live organ donation is permissible, even between strangers, as long as the donor has capacity to consent and there is no element of coercion involved, including financial compensation.

CASE 60: POSTHUMOUS ORGAN DONATION

Mike is a 36-year-old banker with a passion for motorbikes. One winter evening when he is travelling back from a conference down the M1 his bike skids on a patch of black ice. He was driving at 90 mph (145 km/h). He hits the windscreen of an oncoming car and his helmet splits in half. An ambulance arrives at the scene within minutes and Mike is intubated and rushed to hospital. He has sustained severe injuries – he has fractured his pelvis and several vertebrae. At hospital he is assessed in the intensive care unit. Attempts to resuscitate him are unsuccessful and when he is weaned off the ventilator he does not make any respiratory effort. Tests performed by two different consultants confirm that he has had massive brainstem injuries, and he is declared brainstem dead despite the ventilator continuing to keep his heart and lungs working and consequently the rest of his organs perfused. A nurse discovers that Mike is registered on the national organ donation database and so it is decided to keep him ventilated until his next of kin are traced and contacted, so that they can be asked for their permission to use Mike's organs.

Questions
- How can someone donate his or her organs after death?
- Can the next of kin prevent organ donation?

ANSWER 60

Legal issues

The Human Tissue Act 2004 sets out guidelines on the legality of obtaining organs after death. After someone has died, a healthcare professional should endeavour to find out whether the patient had expressed a wish as to what should happen to their organs after death. This can be done by checking medical records, looking for a donor card or checking the Organ Donor Register (ODR). If there is evidence of consent to organ donation by a competent adult then legally organ donation can proceed. The relatives of the patient should be informed of the patient's prior consent to donation. If they object, every effort should be made to ask them to respect the wishes of the deceased and they should sensitively be informed that they cannot legally veto the consent. However, in practice where there is real objection to organ donation, it would be unusual for donation to go ahead.

When no consent prior to death has been given, a person in a 'qualifying relationship' can give consent. The Human Tissue Act ranks persons in a qualifying relationship. Children can consent to posthumous organ donation if they are Gillick competent. It is essential that their decision is discussed with the person who has parental responsibility and to take their wishes into account before proceeding. Where a child lacked capacity or no prior consent had been expressed, consent should be sought from the person with parental responsibility for the child. The easiest way to consent to organ donation after death is to register on the ODR. It is also possible to carry a donor card, inform the general practitioner or express such wishes with the DVLA or passport office.

Ethical issues

Despite consent and respect for the individual being at the heart of the Human Tissue Act, it has a slightly utilitarian flavour by allowing the recently deceased to be preserved while consent to donation can be established or refused. This Act makes it permissible to ventilate a patient after death has been confirmed, e.g. after a cardiac arrest, to continue to perfuse organs. The concept that proxy-consent to posthumous organ donation can be given has interesting ethical arguments. In every other aspect of medicine consent to 'treatment' cannot be made by another adult, unless they have a lasting power of attorney. A dead person lacks capacity – which leads us to the ethical decision of whether 'treatment' can be given in the patient's best interests. Does a dead person have any interests? Can any harm be caused to a dead patient? If the answer to these questions is no it could be ethically justified that consent should not be an issue in posthumous organ donation and, therefore, all healthy organs should be removed and donated to a living person to maximize utility. Deontological theory would consider this morally unacceptable as no person should be used solely as a means to an end.

 KEY POINTS

- Relatives can no longer veto posthumous organ donation if the deceased has given pre-mortem consent. However, in practice, the beliefs and views of the relatives will still be respected.
- It is legal to preserve bodies after confirmation of death to perfuse organs while consent is being established.
- There are complex ethical arguments about the need for consent for posthumous organ donation.

CASE 61: IS THERE A MARKET FOR LIVING ORGAN DONARS?

Dave, a 35-year-old healthy man, has been made redundant by the factory he used to work in. His wife has recently left him as he cannot support her and he has become depressed due to losing her respect. He is also still grieving the death of his son who died from leukaemia at the age of 5. As he is wandering the streets, he notices an advertisement in a shop window.

One functioning kidney to save the life of a 15-year-old girl!
Potential donors will be morally and financially rewarded.

The advertisement makes Dave think. He has two kidneys and he is healthy. He knows that donating one of his kidneys will not be without risk, but he also knows that it could potentially save the life of a young child and ease some of the guilt he feels following the death of his own son. It would also give him enough money to get back on his feet, try to win his wife back and set up a business of his own. It seems that all parties in the transaction would benefit.

Questions
- What are the ethical implications of creating a market in organ donation?
- What other methods could be introduced to increase the availability of organs for transplant in the UK?

ANSWER 61

Despite a marked increase in living donations, as of mid January 2010 there were still 7994 people actively waiting for a transplant organ (www.uktransplant.org.uk). This number continues to rise every year due to advances in medical technology extending life and the number of potential donors declining.

The UK needs to re-examine its current 'opt-in' protocol for organ donation and establish a method to increase the number of available organs, whether they are from living or dead donors. Various possibilities have been discussed and some are more feasible than others, such as making organ donation an 'opt-out' system, or forcing all prisoners to donate organs. Another option is to reconsider the possibility of a 'market' in organ donation.

Ethical issues

For many people the idea of buying, or selling, an organ is repulsive. Yet, on closer examination, the ethical reasons behind this typical 'gut' reaction cannot be substantiated. It is often argued that to buy a kidney is to deny that person the natural dignity that should be given to all individuals. Cohen argues that, 'to sell an integral human body part is to corrupt the very meaning of human dignity' (Selling bits and pieces of humans to make babies: the gift of the magi revisited. *Med Philos* 1999;24:288–306). The most common ethical principle usually ascribed to such sentiment is the Kantian philosophy of not using an individual as a means to an end. Yet what if it was your loved one who could have their life saved for a small financial cost?

Another argument is that the promise of financial reward results in exploitation of the poor and vulnerable, and that the gift of donation should only have a purely altruistic motive. This is an imposition of others' moral sensibilities. Surely if a person can benefit the life of another from donating an organ and can better their own life as a result of it, they should be allowed. People should have a right to sell whatever is theirs. Denying them this infringes their autonomy.

In 1994 Charles Erin and John Harris proposed a model for a market in organ donation that they argued met with all ethical standards.

> 'The market would be confined to a self governing geopolitical area such as a nation state … Only citizens resident within the union or state could sell into the system and they and their families would be equally eligible to receive organs. … There would be only one purchaser, an agency like the National Health Service (NHS), which would buy all organs and distribute according to some fair conception of medical priority. There would be no direct sales or purchases, no exploitation of low-income countries and their populations … There would be strict controls and penalties to prevent abuse'
>
> Erin CA, Harris J. An ethical market in human organs.
> *J Med Ethics* 2003;29:137–8

This concept does, in theory, protect all individuals from the harms associated with the traditional concept of a commercial market in organ donation.

KEY POINTS

- The current organ donation system is 'opt in'. Due to shortage of donors this needs to be reviewed by the government.
- The most acceptable change would be to make organ donation 'opt out'. This was proposed by the British Medical Association in 2006.

CASE 62: A FATHER DOES NOT WANT TO DONATE A KIDNEY

Sometimes the future appears in black and white. A decision that must be made has a logical path to follow. Would you help your dying child to live by donating an organ? For most people the answer would be yes. Many fathers would readily donate a kidney so that their child could live; they would donate a kidney, a segment of their liver, their heart. My story is not black and white but a palette of shades of grey, of heartbreaking decisions and soul-destroying consequences. I have just been told that I am a potential donor for my 5-year-old daughter. If I agree, my kidney can be harvested from my body and put into her tiny abdomen so that she can continue to live. But I cannot do it. I am scared. What if it doesn't work? Will my family hold me responsible for that failure? What will happen in 10 years' time when she will need a new kidney? Am I to donate my remaining kidney or are we then to watch the inevitable, slow death of my beloved daughter. I cannot go through with this. I cannot reveal to my wife how scared I am. Will you lie for me doctor? Will you tell them that I was not a compatible match?

Questions
- To whom does the doctor owe a duty of care in this scenario?
- To whom does the doctor owe a duty of confidentiality?
- Could the father be forced to donate a kidney since he agreed to undergo compatibility testing?

ANSWER 62

This extraordinary case highlights important issues. It is unusual for a healthy person to visit a doctor and undergo tests to benefit a third party. Having had a consultation and blood tests, the father and the doctor have entered into a doctor–patient relationship. The doctor owes his patient a duty of care since it can be reasonably foreseeable that the doctor's actions could harm the patient, that the doctor and patient are in a sufficiently proximate relationship and that it is fair, just and reasonable to owe a duty of care.

As it can be established that the doctor owes a duty of care to the father, it follows that the doctor owes him a duty of confidentiality. Confidentiality can only be broken in specific situations, e.g. where there is risk of serious harm to another individual. Although the doctor's other patient, the daughter, is at risk of dying if her father does not donate his kidney, this would not justify breaking his confidence because the father is not presenting a risk of harm to her.

The law surrounding organ donation is tightly regulated and both the donor and the recipient receive support throughout the decision-making process. The donor is assessed to ensure that any decision to donate is completely voluntary. Donation between unrelated individuals is more closely regulated to ensure that there is no coercion and that the donor is not being taken advantage of or financially compensated. However, it is worth considering that donation between relatives can be fraught with emotional coercion and pressure from other members of the family. There is pressure to donate from the father himself. How can a parent say no to organ donation for their child? Love and loyalty are powerful emotions that remove an element of independence from an individual. But can they be considered so coercive as to make valid consent impossible?

Undergoing compatibility testing does not mean that the father has agreed to donate a kidney if he is found to be a suitable match. This point was highlighted in an American case *McFall* v. *Shrimp* (1978) in which a cousin refused to undergo bone marrow transplantation after agreeing to undergo the first test to establish tissue compatibility. The judge ruled that although his actions were morally indefensible, there was no legal requirement to take part in such an act of positive beneficence.

In practice, the father should be reassured that any decision he makes will be confidential and that the details of his compatibility will not be disclosed to the rest of his family. However, it may also be worth addressing his fears and the reasons he does not want to donate, and encourage open and honest communication within the entire family.

 KEY POINTS

- Close relationships may impose a moral obligation of beneficence on a person to donate a kidney.
- Legally, a person cannot be forced to donate a kidney, and indeed, donation may not be allowed if there is any evidence of coercion from other family members.

END OF LIFE

Tony, a 79-year-old man with a history of hypertension and type 2 diabetes, collapses while playing golf and is taken to the local accident and emergency unit, still unconscious. A computed tomography (CT) scan reveals a large haemorrhagic stroke and he is transferred to the neurosurgical unit. Here he fails to regain consciousness, although he does not require ventilatory support. He receives fluids and parenteral nutrition for 11 days and is regularly visited by his wife and two children.

Eventually, senior medical staff discuss with Tony's family the extensive nature of damage to his brain and the likelihood that he will never regain consciousness. The family are asked to consider the possibility of withdrawing nutritional and fluid support and allowing Tony to die 'naturally'. They are warned that this may take some time, as much as a couple of weeks, but that Tony will not be in any pain.

His son approaches you, the F1 doctor on the ward, during visiting hours and tells you that watching her husband die is becoming increasingly distressing for his mother and that, if this is to be the inevitable result, why is it not possible to offer a quicker end to the family's suffering, such as an injection which would stop Tony's heart.

Questions
- What does an 'act' and an 'omission' mean in relation to end-of-life decisions?
- What are the ethical arguments for and against the distinction between the two?
- What is the legal position regarding acts and omissions?

ANSWER 63

Acts and omissions

Is there any moral difference between acting to achieve a goal and omitting to act, knowing it will produce the same result? The distinction between acts and omissions underpins treatment options which are lawful, and those which are unlawful, at the end of life. Passive euthanasia describes the withholding or withdrawal of life-prolonging treatment (i.e. involves an *omission*) while active euthanasia involves an *act* that will inevitably result in someone's death. The clinical team has proposed the former for the patient in this case scenario, and the latter has been requested by his son.

The ethical case for a distinction between acts and omissions

For many, passive euthanasia is deemed the more morally acceptable of the two, supporting the idea that there is an ethical distinction between acts and omissions.

> 'in certain contexts, failure to perform an act, with certain foreseen bad consequences of that failure, is morally less bad than to perform a different act which has the identical foreseen bad circumstances.'
> Glover J. *Causing Death and Saving Lives*. Harmondsworth: Penguin, 1977

Many explanations have been offered for this distinction. Some argue that to act is less morally acceptable because it 'interferes' with the natural course of events, i.e. Tony will eventually die, but to give him a lethal injection is to disrupt this natural process. Others argue that in medicine, an omission provides a safeguard against wrong diagnosis whereas an action does not. That is to say, in the unlikely event that a patient can recover, to allow them to die gives the opportunity for this to become apparent. If a lethal injection is given, any chance of recovery (albeit minute) is obliterated.

The ethical case against a distinction between acts and omissions

Tony's son clearly has a different view of acts and omissions, as he thinks an act to end his father's life would be preferable. Many would find it hard to disagree with him on compassionate grounds – surely it is preferable for both Tony and his family that he has a quick resolution to his current situation rather than a long-drawn-out death.

Yet there is the problematic idea of what constitutes an 'act' or an 'omission'. After all, in the patient's case even the 'omission' involves the physical *act* of stopping his intravenous fluids. In addition, the argument that acts interfere with natural events is flawed as it can be extrapolated to all interventionist medicine – the patient would have died anyway if it were not for doctors intervening with intravenous fluids and nutrition. As doctors, we are in the business of disrupting nature if its course happens to be disease or death.

A thought experiment can be used to illustrate that often those who act and omit to act can be seen as equally morally reprehensible if their intention and the result is the same. James Rachels, a philosopher, famously gives the example of Smith and Jones. Both stand to inherit a lot of money if their 6-year-old cousin dies. If Smith were to sneak up on the cousin's bathtime, with the intention of holding his head underwater until he drowned, and succeeded in this, thus inheriting the money, would it be any more morally reprehensible than if Jones went with the same intention, witnessed the boy accidentally trip, knock himself unconscious and drown and did nothing to prevent the death, with the same financially desirable result?

As doctors support the distinction, it could reflect that they are conditioned throughout their training to act – to prescribe the right medicine, to recognize conditions at an early, treatable stage. It could also be a result of the difference in the daily work of bioethicists and doctors – while ethicists use hypothetical thought experiments and moral philosophy, doctors are faced with difficult and very real decisions which need some resolution. As is often the case, it is left to the legal system to try to bridge this divide between complex ethical arguments and practical, real dilemmas.

The legal position

Active euthanasia is not legal in the UK under any circumstances. However, passive euthanasia is, in certain circumstances, permitted. It is obvious therefore that the law *does* draw a distinction between acts and omissions.

Two cases occurred within a year of each other in the 1990s which illustrate this. In *R* v. *Cox* (1992), Dr Cox was convicted of attempted murder for administering a lethal injection of potassium chloride to Mrs Boyes, a 70-year-old woman suffering from intractable pain secondary to rheumatoid arthritis. Here Dr Cox's *act* was unmistakable – the potassium chloride had no possible therapeutic benefit and his intention in administering it, however compassionate, was to end Mrs Boyes' life. A year later the case of *Airedale NHS Trust* v. *Bland* concerned a young man left in a persistent vegetative state following the Hillsborough Football Stadium disaster. The House of Lords established that an *omission* to treat, with the same intention of ending life, *was* acceptable in law. Not all the Lords in the case supported the distinction; in fact one stated that to make such a distinction made the law 'morally and intellectually misshapen'. However, in the Bland case, the key issue was how to act in the best interests of a patient who cannot and has never expressed his wishes. This gives us some insight into why the law maintains a distinction between acts and omissions in the face of many arguments to the contrary – it highly values the individual's right to choose (autonomy) and where this cannot be expressed, the need to act in the patient's best interests. To allow active euthanasia, e.g. to find Dr Cox not guilty of murder, sanctions action which is, it is feared, open to misuse by those who intend to act dispassionately and without the patient's consent. Although it can be argued that omitting to act by withholding treatment could be exploited in the same way, the idea that people who would have died will die is clearly more palatable in our society than the idea of an act to end the life of a person who otherwise would have lived.

The doctrine of double effect

This doctrine states that an action which has a good objective may be performed although this can only be achieved at the expense of a corresponding harmful effect. The doctrine permits the administration of high dosage of medication for pain relief where the doctor is aware that death may be an adverse effect of adequate pain relief, but where there is no intention to kill. The British Medical Association has advised that 'if the intention is clearly to relieve pain and distress and the dosage provided is commensurate with that aim, the action will not be unlawful' (BMA Ethics Department, *Medical Ethics Today*, 2004). However, misunderstanding about the application of the doctrine of double effect sometimes leads to inadequate pain relief for patients amid fears that if the patient dies it will be suggested that the person relieving the patient's pain had the intention of hastening death as well as relieving pain.

Baby doctor cleared of misconduct

A doctor who admitted hastening the deaths of two dying babies by injecting them with a paralysing drug has been cleared of misconduct. The consultant neonatologist gave 23 times the normal dose of a paralysing muscle relaxant in the final moments before one baby's death. The GMC said he intended to relieve suffering rather than hasten their deaths.

BBC News, Health, 11 July 2007

 KEY POINTS

- The law distinguishes between acts and omissions to act.
- This distinction can seem ethically contentious.
- The acts/omission distinction can be seen to allow inroads into the principle of sanctity of life.

CASE 64: QUALITY OF LIFE AND SANCTITY OF LIFE JUDGEMENTS

Nora is 62 years old and has had multiple sclerosis for 25 years. Initially the disease followed a relapsing and remitting course and Nora would have long periods of good health in between months of various disabling side-effects, such as temporary paralysis and visual problems. For the past 10 years, however, her condition has become more disabling and Nora has had to move into a nursing home. The staff are friendly and she is well cared for. However, as a result of the insidious effect of her illness most of her bodily functions have ceased to work. She is doubly incontinent. On the days when she is well enough to be aware of her surroundings she finds her condition extremely distressing. She is embarrassed by her lack of bodily control and the fact that she has to have 24-hour nursing care. Her swallowing is unsafe and the decision was made a year ago to feed her via percutaneous endoscopic gastrostomy (PEG). She gets no pleasure from eating or drinking and rarely gets visitors. Some days she is described as being barely conscious.

Questions
- Is there a *moral* obligation to maintain life at all cost, irrespective of the quality of that life?
- Is there a *legal* obligation to maintain life at all cost, irrespective of the quality of that life?

ANSWER 64

A decision about the provision of medical treatment to an incompetent patient centres on whether it is in the person's best interests, and judgements about the patient's quality of life may become relevant.

Ethical issues

The doctrine of sanctity of life states that human life has intrinsic value, and therefore it is always wrong to intentionally deprive a person of their life, even to avoid extreme suffering. A religious version of the doctrine states that as life is God given, only God has power to take life away. A secular version of the doctrine provides that all humans are equal and therefore no one has the authority to determine that another's life is not worth living. But even if human life has infinite value this does not mean that other values such as beneficence, non-maleficence and justice are irrelevant. Where the continuance of medical treatment to preserve life comes at such cost in terms of suffering of the patient, is there an ethical obligation to continue to provide such treatment? Quality of life judgements *are* relevant to healthcare decision making but the threshold at which sanctity of life yields to quality of life can be notoriously difficult to assess – how can a 'minimum' quality of life, such as to justify withholding/withdrawing treatment, be defined and measured? The assessment of quality of life goes beyond purely medical factors and includes reference to social, emotional and physical wellbeing. The ability to carry out tasks and intellectual capacity should also be taken into consideration. Therefore an acceptable quality of life depends from whose perspective it is viewed – the decision maker or the patient. Concepts such as 'dignity' and 'meaningful life' are vague and difficult to delineate.

Legal issues

The courts have recognized that although the starting point is that there is a strong presumption in favour of a course of action which will prolong life, this is not an absolute principle: 'important as the sanctity of life is, it may have to take second place to human dignity' (*R (Burke)* v. *General Medical Council* [2005]).

It is relevant to consider the quality of life which the patient will experience, from the patient's perspective. The courts have stated that there is a heavy burden on those who are advocating a course which would lead inevitably to death. Ultimately, the lead clinician is responsible for the decision that it is not in the patient's best interests to continue treatment which imposes an intolerable burden, with no commensurate benefits. However, what views that patient may have had and, in the case of children, the views of the parents, should be considered in the decision.

 KEY POINTS

- Sanctity of life is not absolute; human dignity must also be considered.
- Quality of life assessments are highly fact sensitive.
- A person's quality of life may be suboptimal but still be worth living from the patient's perspective.
- It is lawful to withhold or withdraw treatment when it is not in the best interest of the patient to continue with life-prolonging treatments.

CASE 65: BASIC CARE AND MEDICAL TREATMENT AT THE END OF LIFE

Gerald, a 52-year-old man, has been diagnosed with muscular dystrophy. He has recently spent a lot of time nursing his mother who had dementia. Following a recent hospital admission for pneumonia his mother passed away. Gerald comes to see you, his general practitioner, because he is very distressed about some of the things he saw while visiting his mother in hospital. He is an intelligent person and is aware that his muscular dystrophy will probably mean that towards the end of his life he will become reliant on others. He wants reassurance now that when this happens he will be cared for properly; to him this includes receiving all possible medical treatment, feeding and hydration. He is adamant that he does not want his life to be curtailed because he is not being fed properly.

Questions
- What is the difference between medical treatment and basic medical care?
- Can hydration and nutrition legally be withdrawn?
- Can a patient insist in an advance decision that medical treatment is *not* withdrawn?

ANSWER 65

Nutrition and hydration provided by usual means such as a cup or a spoon form part of the basic care of the patient. Basic care is a necessity of life and should always be offered. It cannot be refused in an advance decision.

If the supply of food is a basic human requirement then does it make a difference if it is provided through a tube? Surely it serves the same function. In *Airedale NHS Trust* v. *Bland* (1993) the House of Lords decided that provision of artificial feeding by means of a naso-gastric tube amounted to 'medical treatment'. Tony Bland was in a persistent vegetative state but he was not dying. He could breathe unaided but he could not swallow and was fed by nasogastric tube. The House of Lords considered that nutrition and hydration provided by artificial means amounted to medical treatment. Medical treatment can be withdrawn if it is not in the patient's best interests to continue with it. The principle of sanctity of life is not infringed by ceasing to give invasive treatment that confers no benefit on the patient.

> 'How can it be lawful to allow a patient to die slowly, though painlessly, over a period of weeks from lack of food but unlawful to produce his immediate death by a lethal injection, thereby saving his family from yet another ordeal to add to the tragedy that has already struck them? I find it difficult to find a moral answer to that question. But it is undoubtedly the law.'
>
> *Airedale NHS Trust* v. *Bland* [1993] AC 789 at p. 885 per Lord Browne-Wilkinson

If artificial nutrition and hydration (ANH) can be withheld or withdrawn from an incompetent patient where it is not in his best interests to continue to provide it (this being different from saying that it is in a patient's best interests to die) what about the situation where a competent patient wants reassurance that ANH will not be withdrawn? Leslie Burke has cerebellar ataxia, a degenerative brain condition which does not affect mental faculties but which leads to loss of speech and control of limbs and eventually the need to receive ANH. He was concerned that doctors could withdraw this 'treatment' even though he still wished to live. The Court of Appeal found that a clinical decision cannot lawfully be taken to withdraw/withhold ANH in the case of a competent patient who expresses the wish to remain alive (*R (Burke)* v. GMC (2005)).

A patient cannot make an advance decision *requesting* the provision of ANH in the event of loss of capacity but nevertheless such a wish would be taken into account in assessing the best interest of the patient.

 KEY POINTS

- Basic care, including oral provision of nutrition and hydration, should always be offered.
- Nutrition and hydration provided by artificial means, i.e. by nasogastric tube is considered a medical treatment.
- Medical treatments can be withdrawn where it is not considered to be in the best interests of an incompetent patient to continue to provide them.
- ANH cannot be withdrawn from a competent patient who wishes it to be continued.

CASE 66: A REQUEST FOR ASSISTED SUICIDE

Enid, a widow, lives alone in a rather dilapidated council block in a rough area of London and is often too scared to leave her flat. As her doctor you are the only person with whom she has regular contact, and as such she has developed a soft spot for you. She often sends little gifts of chocolates and socks to your surgery and is always pleased to spend a few minutes chatting about your family after her consultation. Although she is 73, she is in good health other than being troubled by attacks of gout and annual bronchitis. You have noticed, however, that over the past year she has become increasingly breathless and often struggles to fight off chest infections. She is finding it harder and harder to leave her home and since she is always so appreciative of your visits you often make home visits to check on her. On a routine visit you realize that the bed looks as if it has not been slept in and you discover that she has taken to sleeping in an armchair, as she gets too breathless to lie flat. After some persuasion, she agrees to go to hospital for some tests. Enid is diagnosed as having inoperable lung carcinoma with bone metastases. The next time you see her, she is very angry with you. Her eyes are stony and she looks at you with fear and mistrust.

'You are all to blame for this,' she tells you. 'I was doing just fine before you came along and interfered and sent me to hospital. Now what is to become of me? I'm all alone and have nothing to live for other than the promise of a lingering, painful death. Well I shan't stand for that. You are to blame so you must help me to end this nonsense now. I know you can help me.'

Questions
- What is Enid asking you to do?
- What would you do?
- What are the legal considerations?

ANSWER 66

At first glance it would seem that Enid is asking the doctor to help her to end her life. However, is this really what she wants? Is she actually just scared of uncontrollable pain and loss of autonomy? How can her doctor restore her autonomy and provide her with reassurance without resorting to assisted suicide?

Legal issues

Although suicide was legalized in the UK in 1961 it is still illegal to assist someone to die. Guidance from the Department of Public Prosecutions as to when someone may be prosecuted for assisted suicide is available at www.cps.gov.uk.

> 'a person who aids, abets, counsels or procures the suicide of another or an attempt by another to commit suicide, shall be liable on conviction on indictment to imprisonment.'
> Section 2 of the Suicide Act 1961

If the doctor were to supply Enid with a method to end her own life, or were to aid her to do it, he could be found guilty of assisted suicide, despite any moral justifications. This case is comparable with the case of Dianne Pretty. Mrs Pretty had motor neurone disease and asked the courts' permission for her husband to help her to commit suicide. The courts found that the right to life protected by Article 2 of the European Court of Human Rights did not confer the diametrically opposed right to die.

Physician-assisted suicide (PAS) is a controversial ethical dilemma, which has recently been much debated in parliament. In 2006, the House of Lords rejected a proposed bill by Lord Joffe to legalize PAS in the UK. The laws surrounding PAS are more relaxed in some other countries in Europe. In 2003, Reginald Crew travelled to Switzerland to be assisted to die by an organization called Dignitas. Dignitas and similar organizations believe that terminally ill individuals have the right to choose when they wish to die and that they should be allowed help to die with dignity.

Clinical issues

It is not uncommon for patients to ask their doctors to help them end their life. In clinical practice it is always important to ask the patient why they have made this request. Undoubtedly, there are patients who have made a considered request, but the vast majority may ask because they feel that death is the only option they have left. It could be established that the main problem is that they are in pain and sometimes addressing their pain control can rectify this. Or it could be that they are scared and lonely. Palliative care services in the NHS are improving and patients who are terminally ill should be referred to these specialist services as they have more time and experience to address individual concerns and patient-specific symptoms. A request for death may only be a cry for help that can be solved without having to resort to assisted suicide.

 KEY POINTS

- Assisted suicide is where another person provides the means for an individual to end his life. By comparison, voluntary active euthanasia is where another person (doctor) takes the life of an individual at his request.
- Both of the above are illegal in the UK.

CASE 67: ADVANCE DECISIONS

Marjorie is a 70-year-old widow. She was diagnosed with multi-infarct dementia 7 years ago. She was once an intellectual and successful woman but over the past 7 years her memory has declined to the extent that she no longer recognizes her family. Six months ago Marjorie had a much larger stroke due to infarction of the middle cerebral artery. Consequently she is now bed bound, doubly incontinent and has difficulty swallowing. Over the past 3 months there has been minimal improvement in her condition and she has had to remain in hospital.

As an F1 doctor, you are just starting your third rotation. On your first ward round you find that Marjorie's condition has deteriorated overnight. She is tachycardic and tachypnoeic with a temperature of 38°C. You suspect she has developed bronchopneumonia. This is confirmed by a chest X-ray and you decide that it would be best to start intravenous antibiotics and fluids. You discuss this with Marjorie's family but they are adamant that she would not wish to continue living in her current state as she would not consider her quality of life acceptable. Her daughter says that her mother had felt so strongly about this that she had made an advance decision. She gives you a two-sided piece of paper which states 'If, as a result of my illness, I become unable to perform any basic tasks myself, then I would not wish to receive any form of life-sustaining treatment.' It is signed 'Marjorie Jenkins' and dated 5 years ago. You tell the family that antibiotic treatment is likely to cure Marjorie's pneumonia but that she is likely to die without it. However, they say that you should respect their mother's wishes and that all treatment should be withheld except for pain relief.

Questions
- What is an advance decision?
- Is this advance decision valid?
- If it is, do you have to follow it even if you do not think it is in the patient's best interests?

ANSWER 67

Legal issues

An advance decision (AD) is a statement made by an adult with capacity about the treatments they would wish to refuse in the event of loss of capacity. An AD cannot dictate that treatments are given, although a request for specific forms of treatment should be taken into account in deciding what treatment would be in that person's best interests. Basic care, including oral food and water, warmth and hygiene measures may not be refused by an AD.

The Mental Capacity Act 2005 sets out a framework for ADs. At present there is no particular format for an AD, although where it refers to a refusal of life-sustaining treatment, the AD must be in writing and witnessed. The treatment to be refused must be specified although this can be in layman language. If a person makes a valid AD which applies to the circumstances of the situation then it must be followed, even though the doctor may not consider the course of action to be in the patient's best interests. To treat in the face of a valid and applicable AD would render the doctor liable to a claim of battery.

Is Marjorie's AD valid and applicable? Marjorie made her AD 5 years ago, 2 years after onset of dementia. There is a presumption of capacity so healthcare professionals should assume the person had capacity to make it unless they are aware of reasonable grounds to doubt it. There is no legal requirement that an AD must be recently made or reviewed, although the more recently it was made the more likely it is to be a valid representation of the patient's views.

An AD to refuse treatment must state precisely what treatment is to be refused. A statement giving a general desire not to be treated is not enough so Marjorie's AD is not specific enough about the treatments which she wants to refuse to be valid. However, it does guide the clinician about what she would have wanted in these circumstances, and this is supported by the views of her family. If there is reasonable doubt about the validity or applicability of the AD then an application should be made to the Court of Protection for a decision, and in the meantime it would be lawful to continue to provide treatment to save the patient's life or prevent serious deterioration in health.

Ethical issues

It may be easy to second guess the authority of an AD and thus fail to give effect to the values that the person has stated would be relevant to them in future circumstances. Alternatively, it could be presumed that they reflect a high degree of commitment to choices they express. One of the ethical dilemmas is that personal identity, and therefore values, may change with the onset of dementia. Can an AD, written 5 years ago by a healthy person, still reflect the interests of Marjorie now?

 KEY POINTS

- If an advance decision is valid and applicable it must be respected even if healthcare professionals do not think that it represents the patient's best interests.
- They reflect the autonomy of a person expressed at an earlier point in time.

For a discussion of refusals of blood for religious reasons, see Case 88: Jehovah's Witnesses and blood transfusions, page 219.

CASE 68: DO NOT ATTEMPT RESUSCITATION FORMS

During the night you admit an elderly man who has fallen over and fractured his hip. He is 93 years old and lives in a residential home because he has difficulty mobilizing and caring for himself. His medical history includes ischaemic heart disease, polymyalgia rheumatica, large bowel carcinoma and recurrent small bowel obstruction secondary to adhesions. He is also partially sighted. While you are clerking him in he tells you about how lonely he has become since his wife died 2 years ago. His children are elderly and cannot visit him that often and his grandchildren have both moved abroad. He feels that he has lived his life and that it is time for him to go and join his wife. He asks you not to treat him and to make him 'not for resuscitation'. Although he is lonely he does not seem depressed and you believe that it is probably a reasonable request. What should you do at this point?

Questions
- When should do not attempt resuscitation (DNAR) forms be used?
- Who should make the decision?
- What should the F1 do immediately?

ANSWER 68

Every person over the age of 18 is presumed to have capacity until proven otherwise. This patient does not show any evidence of dementia or acute confusion and should therefore be deemed competent to make his own healthcare decisions. Anyone who does have capacity has the right to refuse medical treatment, even if by refusing it, this results in their death. In 2001 the British Medical Association, the Royal College of Nursing and the UK Resuscitation Council brought out national guidelines on DNAR orders. They have been updated in 2007. DNAR orders document a decision by the medical team or the patient not to attempt cardiopulmonary resuscitation in the event of cardiac arrest. The guidelines give advice on DNAR orders with competent adults, incompetent adults and children. They also give guidance on when DNAR orders are appropriate and how to involve a patient and their relatives in the decision-making process.

A DNAR decision should be requested by the patient or made by the most senior member of the medical team after discussion with the patient and their relatives. It is the responsibility of the consultant who has overall care of the patient to ensure that a DNAR order is appropriate and has been discussed with other members of the healthcare team. All decisions should be clearly documented. Individual hospital trusts will have a form for this and usually a protocol to follow. The decision should also be documented in the medical notes. It should also be stressed that making a patient not for resuscitation does not mean that the doctors are 'giving up' on them. They would still be for full active treatment.

The form should be completed with the patient's full name, date of birth and hospital number. It should be documented whether or not the patient is competent, the people who were involved in the decision and the reason for the decision. It should be signed and dated by the person completing the form and countersigned by the consultant. A review date should also be added in case the patient's circumstances change and the DNAR order may be removed.

The reasons behind making a DNAR order are usually multifactorial. Each case should be considered by itself and blanket decisions about DNAR should not be made, e.g. making all patients over the age of 80 'not for resuscitation'. Some examples of when a decision is appropriate are: when cardiopulmonary resuscitation (CPR) is unlikely to restart the patient's heart; when the patient is in the terminal stages of an illness; or where it is believed that the patient's quality of life is such that the benefit of CPR would not improve their quality of life.

In the above scenario it would be appropriate to inform the nursing staff of the patient's request and to document the conversation in the notes. The following morning the request should be discussed with the consultant and a DNAR form should be completed.

 KEY POINTS

- All DNAR forms should be discussed with the patient, where possible, and their relatives before they are implemented.
- The patient, the consultant and other members of the healthcare team should be involved in making DNAR decisions.
- A DNAR form is a legal document and should be completed accurately and fully. It should be signed by the consultant in overall charge of the patient's care.

CASE 69: CONFIRMING BRAINSTEM DEATH

Jimmy is bought into accident and emergency following a motorbike accident. On examination he has multiple injuries, and a Glasgow Coma Scale score of 3. His airway is clear but he has a fractured mandible. His oxygen saturation is 82 per cent and he is only making sporadic respiratory effort. His pulse is 50 per minute. He also has a fractured left femur and has fractured ribs three to six on the left. He is immediately ventilated and transferred to intensive care. A chest X-ray confirms that he has a pneumothorax on the left. A chest drain is inserted and his saturation improves to 90 per cent. A computed tomography (CT) scan shows a massive intracranial haemorrhage. Jimmy makes no improvement over the next 24 hours and a decision is made by your consultant to perform the necessary tests to confirm brain death. Later that day brainstem death is confirmed and you decide that he should be removed from the ventilator. His parents are furious. They want to know how he can still be breathing and still have his heart beating, yet be confirmed dead.

Questions
- What tests are performed to diagnose brainstem death?
- What would you say to the parents?

ANSWER 69

With advances in medical technology the way in which death is confirmed has had to change. Historically death was confirmed when there had been cardiac and respiratory arrest. The ability to mechanically ventilate someone has meant that a different method of confirming death has been introduced. Brainstem death is confirmed by establishing that the cerebral cortex is no longer active and that without ventilation the patient would not be able to breathe spontaneously or regain consciousness. It is the 'irreversible loss of the capacity for consciousness combined with the irreversible loss of the capacity to breathe' (Kumar P, Clark M. *Clinical Medicine*, 5th edn. Edinburgh: Elsevier Saunders, 2005).

Before attempting to diagnose brainstem death it is essential to exclude other causes of coma such as drug overdose, a change in metabolic state, hypothermia, hypoxia, infection and structural lesions.

! **Confirmation of brainstem death**

The examination must be performed by two senior doctors:

- Absent oculocephalic reflexes (doll's eye movements).
- Absent corneal reflexes.
- Pupils fixed bilaterally and unresponsive to light.
- Absent vestibulo-ocular reflexes (normally ice cold water inserted into the ear canal will cause nystagmus. This is absent in brainstem death).
- Absence of any motor response to painful stimuli.
- Absent gag and cough reflex.
- Absence of spontaneous respiration (a trial off the ventilator will be needed to establish this).

Although it would be legally permissible to switch of the ventilator since continued ventilation is futile, in practice, agreement should be sought from the next of kin. Good communication is essential and it will be necessary to explain about the different types of death and that it is simply machines keeping the patient alive. It can sometimes be an opportunity to discuss whether the patient had thought about being an organ donor.

 KEY POINTS

- Brainstem death is a clinical assessment.
- Before turning off a ventilator relatives should be informed of the differences between brainstem death and the ability of a machine to keep someone artificially alive.

CASE 70: COMPLETION OF A DEATH CERTIFICATE

Priya, a 79-year-old woman, is admitted to the medical assessment unit from her nursing home. She presents with a 4-day history of increasing shortness of breath. She has a history of chronic obstructive pulmonary disease and has had decreased exercise tolerance for the past 3 years. On examination she is tachycardic and febrile. There is generalized decreased air entry and bi-basal crackles. Her chest X-ray shows bilateral blunting of the costophrenic angles, cardiomegaly and upper lobe blood diversion. There is also some patchy consolidation at the left base. Her white cell count and C-reactive protein (CRP) levels are raised. Her medical history includes a myocardial infarction a year ago, osteoarthritis and polymyalgia rheumatica. Despite starting intravenous antibiotics and intravenous furosemide Priya continues to deteriorate and dies 3 days later. You are asked to complete her death certificate.

Questions
- What would you put as cause of death of this patient?
- How do you fill in a death certificate?

ANSWER 70

To complete a medical certificate of cause of death (MCCD) the doctor has to be sure of the cause of death. If they are not sure of the medical cause of death or in other specific circumstances, the death must be referred to the coroner. The doctor must also have seen the patient within the past 14 days. The body should either be viewed by the person issuing the death certificate or by another medically qualified person.

In this example the clinical, biochemical and radiological findings are all in keeping with bronchopneumonia. This is an acceptable cause of death for certification. Since Priya had known chronic obstructive pulmonary disease, this would lead to an increased risk of pneumonia so it should also be put on the certificate. Her myocardial infarction last year and continuing angina are significant medical conditions, but in this case did not lead directly or indirectly to her death.

The death certificate has several sections:

- Patient details: Name, age, date of death and place of death
- When you last saw the patient alive
- Whether or not the patient underwent a post-mortem or was reported to the coroner
- Who saw the patient after death
- Cause of death.

The disease that led directly to the patient's death is entered in 1a. Any conditions that directly resulted in 1a are put in 1b and 1c. Other significant diseases that the patient suffered from but did not die from are put in 2. It is not possible to put modes of death such as heart failure or renal failure as these are not specific enough. Causes of death that should be reported to the coroner such as fractured femur or asbestosis should also not be put unless the coroner has been informed as the registrar of deaths will reject the death certificate. The form must then be dated and signed and the doctor's medical qualifications given. The consultant in overall care of the patient must also be named. The form is then given to a relative of the deceased who registers the death of the patient with the registrar of deaths.

Some patients with human immunodeficiency virus (HIV) infection have expressed concerns that their illness will be disclosed on a death certificate and cause distress to relatives who may have been unaware of the diagnosis. A doctor does not have to record that a patient had HIV infection as it is not a notifiable disease. It is also rarely the actual cause of death. A patient may die of an acquired immune deficiency syndrome (AIDS)-defining illness but the actual illness can be documented, for example *Cryptococcus* meningitis or *Pneumocystis* pneumonia (PCP) without alluding to the fact that the patient had AIDS.

CASE 71: COMPLETION OF A CREMATION FORM

Priya's relatives come to speak to you after the death of their mother. They want to ask you about cremation and what it involves. After a lengthy discussion they decide that they would like Priya to be cremated. You fill in a cremation form.

Questions
- What are the different sections of the cremation form and how do you fill them in?
- How has the law surrounding cremation changed since the Shipman inquiry?
- Is it ethical to be paid for cremation forms?

ANSWER 71

The main reason for extra precautions being taken before a cremation is that any evidence that may suggest an unnatural cause of death is destroyed.

Clinical issues

There are two different forms which must be completed by medical professionals before a request for cremation can be accepted by the medical referee of a crematorium. The Certificate of Medical Attendant (Form B) must be completed by a medical practitioner who has attended the deceased before death and has seen and identified the deceased's body after death. This form asks a number of questions about the circumstances and cause of the death and about the certifying doctor's involvement with the deceased before death. The date, time and place of death must be given. The doctor must state any personal relationship with the patient or any pecuniary interest in their death. It also asks whether the doctor suspects any violence, poisoning or neglect. The form also asks whether the deceased underwent any operation in the year before their death, and if they did what was the nature of the operation and who was the surgeon. The doctor completing Form B also has to inspect the body for any cardiac pacemaker or radioactive implant as these may explode in a body which is cremated.

The Confirmatory Medical Certificate (Form C) must be completed by a doctor who has been registered for more than 5 years and is not related in any way to the patient or the doctor completing Form B. They too must view the body of the deceased and they must discuss the case with the doctor completing Form B. In addition they must also speak to either another doctor or a nurse who looked after the deceased or a relative of the deceased.

Legal issues

The Shipman inquiry was held as a result of a general practitioner from Manchester, Harold Shipman, being found guilty of murdering 15 of his patients. Its aims were to investigate how this could have happened and what measures could be implemented to prevent something similar happening in the future. It looked at several areas of medical practice, death and cremation certification, controlled drugs and monitoring and disciplinary systems and complaints. Dame Janet Smith, who chaired the inquiry, came to several conclusions regarding the current practice of cremation in the UK and proposed several changes. Some of these overlap with the current reform of the Coroners Act and will be discussed in the corresponding case scenario. The main change she recommended in relation to completion of cremation forms is that the doctor completing Form C should speak with a relative of the deceased to ascertain whether they had any concerns surrounding the death of the patient or the cause of death of the patient. She also recommended that cremation forms should be standardized throughout the UK.

Ethical issues

Doctors are paid for filling in cremation forms and the fee is colloquially known as 'ash cash'. It is worth considering whether this is ethical. Doctors can often charge patients fees for services that go beyond those of caring for a sick patient, e.g. signing passport photographs or providing letters for insurance companies. Is assessing a patient posthumously for any evidence of an unnatural death or any cardiac implants a continuation of that care or an extra duty for which doctors should be reimbursed?

CASE 72: WHEN TO REPORT A DEATH TO THE CORONER

A 65-year-old man presents to accident and emergency with a 3-day history of abdominal pain which suddenly worsened 4 hours ago. He has had decreased appetite and some nausea and vomiting over the past 24 hours. There is nil of note in his medical history. On examination he is most tender in the right hypochondrium. He has some guarding and some rebound tenderness. Bowels were last open normally 2 days ago. He is pyrexial and tachycardic. On rectal examination he has an empty rectum. His blood test results show an increased white cell count and increased levels of C-reactive protein (CRP). His liver function tests and renal function are normal. An abdominal X-ray is unremarkable, but there is air under the diaphragm on an erect chest X-ray. He is taken straight to theatre where a laparoscopy shows a perforated appendix with intra-abdominal sepsis. He has a appendicectomy and is started on intravenous cefuroxime and metronidazole. Postoperatively he does well and 2 days later he is pain free and eating and drinking. His blood test results are normalizing. You are called to see him one evening as his blood pressure has dropped to 90/65 mmHg. His pulse is 130/minute and regular, temperature 37.6°C and oxygen saturation 93 per cent. He is tachypnoeic and has non-specific pain. An electrocardiogram shows some T-wave depression. Bloods show acute renal failure and sepsis. Despite intensive resuscitation he dies 3 hours later. The cause of death is unknown and could be intra-abdominal pathology, pulmonary embolism or myocardial infarction to name but a few. The case is referred to the coroner for a post-mortem.

Questions
- What is the role of the coroner?
- When should deaths be referred to the coroner?
- How do you refer to the coroner?

ANSWER 72

The office of the coroner is one of the oldest in English history and possibly dates back to the Saxon times. The primary function of the medieval coroner was to keep records of all events leading up to a court case. However, these days the coroner has the much simpler job of investigating death. Most coroners are lawyers although in London some are doctors and a few are dual qualified.

! When to report a death to the coroner

- Infant death
- Traffic accidents
- Alcoholism
- Industrial disease
- Drugs and poisons
- Suicide

- Sudden death
- Murder
- Deaths in custody
- Domestic accidents
- Perioperative deaths
- Cause of death unknown

In practice, if a doctor is in any doubt about whether a death needs to be reported to the coroner, it is advisable to first discuss the case with senior members of the team that has been looking after the patient prior to his death. If a decision cannot be made about the exact cause of death, it should be discussed with one of the coroner's officers who can decide whether a post-mortem should be performed. Sixty per cent of cases reported to the coroner result in a post-mortem being ordered to determine the exact cause of death. When a post-mortem has not fully confirmed the cause of death or where there are still doubts, the coroner can hold an inquest into the death.

Legal issues

In 2000, the murders committed by Harold Shipman caused public outrage. How was it possible for a doctor to kill people without anyone noticing? His conviction led to a complete overhaul of the death certification, cremation and coroner services in England and Wales. 'The Coroner Reform: The Governments Draft Bill', published in June 2006, makes five main recommendations:

- that bereaved relatives will be able to make a larger contribution to any investigations surrounding the death of their loved ones
- a chief coroner will be appointed to oversee the role of coroners throughout the UK and will be supported by an advisory coronial council
- all coroners will be employed on a full-time basis
- all coroners will have new powers to request information or investigations when trying to determine cause of death at an inquest
- coroners will be provided with better medical advice.

There is also still a common law duty for any member of the public to report a suspicious death to a coroner. However, there is no statutory duty for doctors to report a death. The registrar of births, deaths and marriages undertakes this responsibility. Section 28(2) of the Coroners Act 1988 requires information on the number of deaths reported to the coroner and the number of inquests held. The information is published in an annual Home Office statistical bulletin.

Section 3
DUTIES OF A DOCTOR

CASE 73: GOOD SAMARITAN ACTS

You are enjoying a well-deserved holiday from your schedule as an overworked F1 doctor, sipping cocktails, overlooking a warm sunny beach. Suddenly you become aware of a commotion on the road beside the bar, with people waving and shouting. A man is lying on the road and several people nearby are loudly calling for help. Your first reaction is to run over to the man who is lying motionless, having been struck by a car. There seems to be a lot of blood on the road and a woman screams at you to 'please help, please do something'. You tell her you are a doctor and begin to assess the man, frantically trying to remember your immediate life support course details. You ask someone to get an ambulance as you perform basic first aid, doing all you can in the street to stabilize the casualty until the ambulance arrives to take him away.

The local policeman wants to take down your details. By this point you feel a little bit shaky yourself, but you tell him your name and where you are staying. You return to the hotel and find your friends waiting for you, worried about where you have been. When you tell them what has happened they are instantly concerned, wondering if you could end up in trouble for any of your actions and whether you should have got involved. One of them suggests that in a similar situation she would not have gone to help, for fear of being sued.

On the last day as you are about to leave, you find a letter waiting for you at the hotel reception. You are instantly worried about what it contains. With some trepidation you open it to discover that it contains a letter from the woman at the scene. It was her husband you had helped, she writes, and although he is still in hospital he is recovering well. She wanted to thank you for all that you had done and she feels sure you saved his life, so she asked the local policeman to forward the letter to you. Smiling, you head back out into the sun.

Questions
- What is a 'Good Samaritan' act?
- What is the legal position for doctors acting outside of their working environment?
- To what standard would the Good Samaritan doctor be held?
- What are the ethical considerations?

ANSWER 73

A Good Samaritan act is usually understood to be where medical assistance is provided in an emergency situation, free of charge and where the doctor is present in a personal rather than a professional capacity. This is a common situation that healthcare workers can find themselves in. Someone might be in need of medical treatment in situations as diverse as an aeroplane or a supermarket. Assistance is most often offered with minor problems – it is estimated that only 0.1 per cent of flights are diverted because of a serious medical problem. Most incidents are less serious, such as sprains or faints. Despite the relatively common nature of Good Samaritan acts, the concern of the doctors' friends is misplaced, as they rarely result in legal action. Neither the Medical Defence Union (MDU) nor the Medical Protection Society (MPs) know of a case at the time of writing.

Legal issues

In the UK it is generally accepted that a doctor who comes across an emergency in the working environment would have a duty of care to the injured party. In addition, some general practitioners are also required to act if the accident occurs within their practice area, provided that they are not relieved of this responsibility, for example, because there is already another doctor present. Where there is no such duty of care, there is no legal obligation to provide assistance in the UK. A doctor would be perfectly within the law to walk past a person in need of medical help without intervening, although there may be a professional obligation to provide assistance.

Some countries have Good Samaritan laws. In some areas such as the USA and most Canadian provinces these laws are designed to protect the 'Samaritan' from legal claims for damages, but in others there is actually a requirement to assist in an emergency unless doing so would endanger you. This is the case in Quebec in Canada, and in Japan and many European countries, e.g. France and Germany.

Standard of care provided by a Good Samaritan act

Once a doctor has become involved in the care of a patient, a duty of care is established. This raises the issue as to what standard he would be held to. In this situation the standard of care he can realistically deliver on the street, with no equipment, is going to differ greatly from that which would be available in hospital. Of course, the doctor should not make the victim's condition worse but the likely standard of care would be higher than this. The General Medical Council (GMC) suggests the standard is that which could 'reasonably' be expected to be provided in the circumstances. In this scenario, the doctor would not be expected to measure up to a trauma surgeon who receives the patient in a hospital.

It is also important to note that a doctor may not be in the best position to provide care. For example, he may have been drinking alcohol. Tiredness or language barriers may also impair performance. The GMC requires that doctors recognize and work within their competencies. However, it may be that they are still the best person at the scene to provide help. In such a situation the MDU advises explaining the situation to the patient if possible. It is also essential to document events accurately as one would with any other clinical situation, to provide a record of one's actions as well as providing contact details to the authorities.

Medical defence organizations offer worldwide protection to their members against the unlikely event of legal action. In addition, some airlines offer indemnity to Good Samaritan doctors. However, if a doctor was acting as part of an expedition, or working at an event, they would not come under the definition of a Good Samaritan as they would be present in a 'work' capacity, which would likely result in a duty of care.

Ethical issues

Ethically it would be difficult to justify non-intervention in an emergency, unless there was an actual risk to the individual offering help. The GMC guidance on this area is unequivocal.

> 'In an emergency, wherever it arises, you must offer assistance, taking account of your own safety, your competence, and the availability of other options for care.'
> General Medical Council. *Good Medical Practice*. London: GMC, 2006

It could be argued that the risk of legal action and potential subsequent loss of livelihood presents a risk of harm to the doctor. These consequences are so rare that it seems ethically difficult to justify this as an excuse. A doctor might also consider the risk of coming into contact with bodily fluids and the risk of infection, although again, this is not common. The principle of beneficence would strongly support intervention.

KEY POINTS

- Off duty, a doctor in the UK does not owe a passer-by a duty of care.
- In some countries this is not the case and Good Samaritan laws require that medical assistance should be given to those who are in need.
- The standard of care required of a doctor providing assistance on the streets is not as high as the standard of care that would be given in a hospital setting.

CASE 74: RECEIVING A BLEEP JUST BEFORE FINISHING AN ON-CALL

It is Friday night and you have almost finished admitting your patient. You are just waiting for his blood test results. The locum doctor taking over your shift is running late and you are getting a bit stressed as you have a train to catch back to London so that you can make it home in time for your cousin's birthday party. Just as you are about to leave your bleep goes off. A nurse informs you that one of your patients, Eric, is having some chest pain. He was admitted 2 days ago with pneumonia and you suspect that the pain is related to the infection. You ask the nurse to do a set of observations and an electrocardiogram (ECG) and say you will ask the doctor taking over to assess him. You then receive an incoming call. It is your cousin, who is very drunk and urging you to hurry up as you are missing out on all the fun. You tell her you are on your way. The locum arrives 20 minutes later and you rush off straight away. Later that night you remember that you completely forgot to hand over the patient who was having chest pain. You decide to ring the hospital and find that he is now a patient on the coronary care unit, having had a massive heart attack only an hour ago.

Questions
- Who has a duty of care to this patient?
- Did you, as the F1 who received the call, have a duty of care to a patient you have not seen since the onset of new symptoms?
- Should hospitals have systems in place to ensure that ill patients are handed over to night staff?

ANSWER 74

Legal issues

The question, 'When does a doctor owe a duty of care to a patient?', has often been discussed in the courts. Duty of care can be established if it was *reasonably foreseeable* that the doctor's actions (or lack of) could harm the patient, that the doctor and patient were in a sufficiently proximate relationship and if it would be *fair, just and reasonable* to owe a duty of care. The hospital also has a duty of care to its patients. There are two types of liability.

! Types of liability

- *Direct liability*: this includes a failure of the hospital to provide competent and qualified employees, a failure to provide the necessary equipment and failure to provide safe communication systems in the hospital.
- *Vicarious liability*: an employer would be vicariously liable for negligent acts performed by an employee during the course of employment.

Professional guidance

The General Medical Council (GMC) states that a duty of care exists when there has been doctor–patient interaction in a professional capacity. This particular case is fairly straightforward. The on-call hospital doctor had a duty of responsibility to the patient having chest pain. As an inpatient the hospital is also deemed to have a duty of care to that patient. Consequently, if a claim were to arise it could be brought against the hospital under National Health Service (NHS) indemnity. The doctor involved in the case would probably be subject to investigation, either internally or via the GMC. Medical defence organizations provide support and advice for any investigations or disciplinary actions held against individual doctors.

Handing over sick patients is an important part of a doctor's job. All hospitals should have a system in place to enable the on-call doctors to be aware of which patients are acutely unwell and may need medical attention or review during the out-of-hours service. Doctors should check with the hospital they are working in, to find out how to hand over patients and how to find out which patients need reviewing on-call. In the scenario the Fl doctor failed in his duty of care because he did not hand over information regarding an ill patient.

'you must be satisfied that, when you are off duty, suitable arrangements have been made for your patients' medical care. These arrangements should include effective hand-over procedures, involving clear communication with healthcare colleagues.'

General Medical Council. *Good Medical Practice*. London: GMC, 2006

 KEY POINTS

- A duty of care is established when there has been interaction between a doctor and a patient in need of medical attention.
- Doctors have a duty to ensure that patients are handed over to the out-of-hours team.

CASE 75: TREATING FRIENDS AND RELATIVES

Since you graduated from medical school you have been bombarded with people asking you about their possible medical problems. When you went home for a weekend to escape from the hospital, your brother-in-law asks you to give him some advice on his hayfever. You felt able to do this so you made some suggestions. Your aunt then asked you about her arthritis and whether you could prescribe her some extra pain relief. Later that day your grandparents come to visit. Your grandma confides in you that she is worried about the number of times your grandpa is getting up to go to the toilet in the night. She wants some reassurance that this is normal.

Questions
- What should a doctor do when a friend or relative asks for medical advice?
- Can a doctor write a prescription for a friend?

ANSWER 75

Professional guidance

Medical training means that a doctor should have extensive knowledge of different medical illnesses. A lot of this knowledge, however, comes with experience. A newly qualified doctor may find that more people begin to ask them about various aches and pains that they have because they assume that the doctor will know the answer. There is, obviously, a broad spectrum of medical illnesses that can be asked about by relatives and friends. If a doctor is asked about symptom relief for a cold or, as in the scenario, hayfever, they may feel confident to give advice.

It is generally not advisable to treat friends and relatives. However, there are two ways in which this could happen. First, relatives and friends can ask for advice and treatment on an informal basis. However, it is hard to diagnose people's problems without the appropriate tests and investigations. Simple things can be suggested, but a doctor should always advise relatives or friends to see their own doctor if they are concerned. Alternatively, in some smaller villages, relatives may be official patients. This should be avoided if possible. In smaller hospitals it can raise issues of confidentiality and it may make either the doctor or the patient feel uncomfortable. Doctors may find it hard to give impartial advice and it may be possible to miss signs or symptoms that an impartial doctor would see.

A doctor treating friends or relatives also risks being accused of nepotism if the patient gets seen quicker or gets referred for urgent investigations. Conversely, a doctor could be accused of negligence or neglect if they stand to benefit from a relative's death.

Writing prescriptions

Fully registered doctors are allowed to write private prescriptions. Again, it is advised that this does not happen too frequently. A course of antibiotics would be considered an acceptable use of this privilege. However, long courses of medication should be monitored by doctors and consequently prescribed by a general practitioner.

 KEY POINTS

- Treating friends and relatives is not advisable because it raises important issues regarding confidentiality and the nature of the doctor–patient relationship.
- Doctors could be accused of giving preferential treatment to their relatives. Or they could be accused of negligence if they were to benefit from a relative's death.

CASE 76: WHISTLE BLOWING

You are a surgical house officer on call over the bank holiday weekend. It has been extremely busy and so far you have admitted 24 patients. You are covering accident and emergency because your registrar and senior house officer are scrubbed in theatre operating on a woman with critical small bowel obstruction. They have been in theatre for the past 2 hours and you assume that it must be a complicated operation with multiple adhesions. You are fast bleeped to the ward where one of your recently admitted patients has had a drop in his blood pressure. You suspect a ruptured abdominal aortic aneurysm. You prepare the patient for theatre and call the vascular consultant. He arrives in 15 minutes but when he does you can smell alcohol on his breath. You ask him if he is safe to operate and he roars at you to not be rude and says he has only had a pint of shandy to celebrate Arsenal's victory. However, in theatre the consultant appears slower and slightly clumsy. The patient cannot be saved in time and dies due to a ventricular fibrillation arrest secondary to massive blood loss. You are convinced that the consultant had had more to drink than he should have but you also believe that it was unlikely that the patient could have been saved anyway.

Questions
- Should you report your concerns to someone even though you suspect that the patient's death was unavoidable?
- Who should you raise your concerns with?
- What are the General Medical Council (GMC) guidelines on 'whistle blowing'?

ANSWER 76

Professional guidance

Whistle blowing is a derogatory term used to describe an action when one person voices their concerns about a colleague or organization to someone in authority. The concept of 'whistle blowing' is something that many doctors used to fear. The stereotypical image is that of doctors looking out for doctors. If a doctor reported concerns about a senior colleague or processes within the hospital it reflected badly on them. Junior staff did not 'grass up' their colleagues for fear of reprisal. Several high-profile cases such as the Bristol Royal Infirmary Inquiry (www.bristol-inquiry.org.uk) and the murders by Harold Shipman have led to a change in this attitude. Medical students, doctors and other healthcare professionals are now taught that any concerns they have regarding a colleague should be discussed openly with the appropriate people.

> 'you must protect patients from risk of harm posed by another colleague's conduct, performance or health. The safety of patients must come first at all times. If you have concerns that a colleague may not be fit to practise, you must take appropriate steps without delay, so that the concerns are investigated and patients protected where necessary. This means you must give an honest explanation of your concerns to an appropriate person from your employing or contracting body, and follow their procedures.'
>
> General Medical Council. *Good Medical Practice*. London: GMC, 2006

In the above case the doctor should first discuss his concerns with another consultant or a designated member of staff.

Legal issues

The Public Interest Disclosure Act 1998 was created to protect individuals from reprisals in the workplace after they have raised concerns about a colleague. It has been nicknamed the 'Whistle-blowing Act'. The Act is supported by the National Health Service (NHS). Doctors who are concerned that they will get in trouble for blowing the whistle can seek advice from their medical defence organization.

 KEY POINTS

- Above all doctors have a duty to protect the patients under their care.
- Doctors have a duty to report any concerns they have about a colleague to someone senior.
- Statutory law is in place to protect 'whistle blowers'.

CASE 77: OUT OF YOUR DEPTH

You are an F1 doctor on an oncology firm in a busy London hospital. Ezra, one of your patients, is a 54-year-old woman who was diagnosed with inoperable ovarian cancer 4 months ago. She has lung and liver metastases and has been receiving palliative chemotherapy. Yesterday she was admitted to hospital with a 2-week history of gradually worsening shortness of breath. On examination she is tachycardic and tachypnoeic. Her oxygen saturation on air is 89 per cent. Her left lung is dull to percussion and on auscultation she has decreased air entry on that side. A chest X-ray confirms that Ezra has Meige's syndrome. On the ward round the consultant tells you that she will need a chest drain to remove the fluid and enable her to breathe more easily. The consultant expects you to do this within the next hour because both she and the senior house officer are in clinic. You have not had much experience of chest drains. You remember seeing a couple as a student and have assisted with one a few months ago. Before you can explain this to the consultant she has moved on to discuss the next patient. You are not sure what to do. You feel you could probably insert the chest drain but are not entirely confident to do so without supervision. But your consultant has a reputation for a fiery temper and you do not want to tell her you cannot perform the procedure without help.

Questions
* What would you do in this situation?
* Who could you turn to for help?
* Who would be held responsible if you inserted the chest drain and there were complications?

ANSWER 77

Clinical issues

This is a common problem for many junior doctors. The ability to gain experience in performing different procedures varies widely from hospital to hospital and can also depend on the specialty a doctor works in. One of the most important skills as a doctor, however, is to understand the level of their own abilities. Everyone has different strengths and weaknesses. In this case it would be important for the doctor to inform someone that he cannot insert a chest drain because he has not inserted one before. It may be useful for him to seek assistance from someone who has the time to assist him in inserting one so that he can do so in future.

Consultants can often seem intimidating but it is useful to remember that they too were once juniors. Doctors should never attempt a procedure they are not confident or competent to perform. The risk of an adverse event causing a patient harm is much more important than the doctor being reprimanded by a consultant. However, it is also not advisable to leave the patient without a chest drain. The doctor could ask for assistance from a senior house officer, a member of the respiratory team or one of the on-call doctors. If no one is available, he must inform the consultant that he cannot insert the chest drain and that he has attempted to find someone else to do so.

With the introduction of the European Working Hours Directive junior doctors are spending less time on call and are consequently having less opportunity to acquire essential skills. Successful completion of the foundation years of training does not depend on the number of hours worked but on attainment of 'core competencies'. Currently, these include being observed performing six different procedures and admitting or managing six different patients, as well as discussing six different cases.

Legal issues

If the doctor performed a procedure he was not competent to perform he would be legally accountable for his actions. He would have to justify why he performed the procedure when he was not experienced enough to do so. The doctor would potentially face disciplinary action either internally or through the General Medical Council (GMC). The patient could also sue the hospital trust for negligence.

 KEY POINTS

- Doctors should only perform procedures that they have the ability and confidence to perform.
- Patient safety is paramount and if a procedure has not been performed before, it should not be performed without supervision and guidance.

CASE 78: DIFFICULTY WITH COLLEAGUES WHICH MAY AFFECT PATIENT CARE

In the pub one evening the conversation turns to politics. You, an F1 doctor, are out with about 20 other doctors and are having a good time. One of the senior house officers (SHOs) is expressing his views very loudly. They are quite extreme, and although you do not want to argue with him you are embarrassed and worried that the other people in the pub may be taking offence at what he is saying. You jokingly ask him to keep his voice down. Rather than doing this he becomes even louder and more antagonistic. You decide to stand up for yourself, but because you have both been drinking the friendly debate turns into a heated argument. The barman eventually comes over and asks you both to either quieten down or leave the premises. At this point you storm off. A few days later you are asked by your consultant to get help with doing an ascitic tap. You realize, then, that the gastro SHO who you need to ask for help is the person you had a big fight with. You do not want to ask for his help and are not sure what to do. You feel slightly embarrassed by what happened at the pub and do not want another confrontation with him at work.

Questions
- What should you do?
- How can you avoid confrontation with colleagues?
- Is it ever acceptable to let personal relationships potentially adversely affect patient care?

ANSWER 78

Hospitals are renowned breeding grounds for inter-professional relationships. The long hours and stressful situations often result in doctors and nurses unwinding with each other. It is also common for personal beliefs to be aired freely and for arguments to brew.

Under no circumstances should a doctor's personal grievances with another member of staff compromise patient care. If personality clashes or previous personal relationships create a problematic working environment the situation could be rectified by attempting to work separately if possible. Previous arguments could be discussed maturely to try to put aside grievances or amend misunderstandings. If this is not possible, both parties involved should ensure that patient care is the main priority.

> 'you must treat your colleagues fairly and with respect. You must not bully or harass them, or unfairly discriminate against them by allowing your personal views to affect adversely your professional relationship with them. You should challenge colleagues if their behaviour does not comply with this guidance.'
> General Medical Council. *Good Medical Practice*. London: GMC, 2006

CASE 79: DOCTORS AND DVLA REGULATIONS

Fabian is a 38-year-old taxi driver, who is admitted to accident and emergency following a collapse. He was at home with his wife and son when he 'fell to the floor and just started shaking'. He has no memory of the event and does not recall feeling strange beforehand. A collateral history is taken from his wife who describes the collapse as sudden with all of his body jerking. She says it lasted about a minute 'but felt like a lifetime'. There is no history of tongue biting or incontinence and he recovered spontaneously, although he felt a little drowsy afterwards. Nothing like this has happened before and there is no history of epilepsy in the family. He did, however, start taking a new drug called Pellidron for his headaches 3 days ago. Fabian has a history of headaches, oesophagitis and mild depression. He does not smoke and drinks about 20 units a week. He is taking omeprazole 20 mg daily and citalopram 20 mg daily, and he says he takes a baby aspirin as his brother, aged 47, recently had a myocardial infarction. He does not have any known allergies.

Questions
- Can Fabian continue to drive because he has only had one unexplained seizure?
- What are the rules surrounding seizures and driving?
- Is there a legal requirement to inform the Driver and Vehicle Licensing Agency (DVLA) of Fabian's seizure?
- Is there a legal requirement to tell his employer?

ANSWER 79

Clinical issues

The DVLA publishes guidelines on medical conditions that disqualify an individual from holding a driving licence. These restrictions vary, depending on the vehicle being driven. It is the responsibility of the patient to inform the DVLA of any medical condition which may affect their licence. In this case it will be prudent to advise Fabian both to abstain from driving due to the risk of having a seizure and losing control of his vehicle, and to inform his employer and the DVLA that he has had a seizure of unknown aetiology and is currently under continued medical investigations. DVLA guidelines state that a vocational driver who has an unprovoked solitary seizure should refrain from driving for 10 years. If they had a seizure thought to be provoked by alcohol, illicit drugs or prescribed medication, they should refrain from driving for 5 years. Information like this can have a severe effect on an individual's livelihood. It is important when breaking the bad news that doctors emphasize why the regulations are so strict.

Other conditions that may affect a patient's ability to drive include:
- Cardiovascular disorders
- Diabetes mellitus
- Psychiatric conditions
- Drug and alcohol misuse
- Visual disorders
- Renal disorders
- Respiratory and sleep disorders.

Legal issues

If a doctor discovers that a patient is continuing to drive against medical advice the General Medical Council (GMC) advises that it is acceptable to break patient confidentiality and inform the DVLA (GMC, *Confidentiality*, FAQs, 2009). The GMC provides guidance on the steps that should be taken. The legal position and the risks should be discussed with the patient again and they should be asked to inform the DVLA. Alternatively it would be appropriate to gain consent to inform the DVLA on the patient's behalf. If the patient refuses, a doctor has a professional obligation to inform the DVLA and the patient should be informed that this will be done. It is important to inform the patient once a disclosure has been made.

There is no absolute legal obligation to inform either the DVLA or the patient's employer. Breaking confidentiality should be on a need-to-know basis only and should only be done to prevent serious harm to others.

Ethical issues

Confidentiality is an important factor in the doctor–patient relationship and as such should only be broken in specific circumstances. Breaking patient confidentiality can be ethically justified using a consequentialist argument; it is done to protect the health of the patient and protect the general public from harm. In this case informing the DVLA that the patient has had a seizure may prevent harm to the patient and the general public by preventing a road traffic accident caused by having a seizure while driving.

 KEY POINTS

- When a patient has a medical condition that may prevent them from driving they should inform the DVLA.
- If a patient refuses to inform the DVLA, a doctor has a professional and moral obligation to do so, but must inform the patient that this has been done.

CASE 80: OVERSEAS VISITORS

Nathalia is a doctor from the Ukraine who has flown to England to help care for her daughter-in-law who has just given birth to Nathalia's first grandchild. She is helping her son carry the pram up a flight of steps when she trips and falls down the stairs, hitting her head on the concrete paving. Unconscious, Nathalia is rushed to hospital. A computed tomography (CT) scan shows an intracerebral haemorrhage. It is uncertain whether this was as a result of the fall or whether the haemorrhage caused the fall. After spending a week on the intensive care unit she regains consciousness and is taken off her ventilator. It becomes apparent that she has suffered permanent brain damage and is completely para-lysed on the right side of her body. She also has difficulty with her speech. The doctors looking after her tell her family she is out of danger but will need an extensive period of neuro-rehabilitation. Unfortunately, although emergency treatment is provided free of charge to anyone visiting the UK, the National Health Service (NHS) is unable to provide funds for Nathalia to have continued care. They explain to the family that this must be paid for privately or they will have to arrange for Nathalia to be transferred back to the Ukraine.

Questions

- What is the role of the healthcare professional in assessing entitlement to NHS care?
- How is the tension between the professional and moral duties of healthcare professionals to assist those in need, and the role of 'gatekeeper' to NHS treatment, resolved?

ANSWER 80

Legal issues

> 'the National Health Service provides healthcare for people who live in the United Kingdom. People who do not normally live in this country are not automatically entitled to use the NHS free of charge – regardless of their nationality or whether they hold a British passport or have lived and paid National Insurance contributions and taxes in this country in the past'
>
> Department of Health. *Implementing the Overseas Visitors Hospital Charging Regulations, Guidance for NHS Trust Hospitals in England.* London: Department of Health, 2004, paragraph 1.1

NHS trusts have a legal obligation to identify and charge those people not entitled to free NHS hospital treatment. This will be done by the trust's overseas visitors manager.

There are reciprocal healthcare arrangements between the UK and some countries which entitle eligible residents of those countries to treatment which becomes *medically necessary* while temporarily staying in the UK. In return, eligible UK residents are entitled to receive free (or reduced cost) medical treatment while visiting these countries. It does not cover situations where individuals come to the UK to access treatment without an explicit referral. These people are colloquially known as 'health tourists'. Emergency treatment given in accident and emergency departments, treatment for some communicable diseases and compulsory psychiatric treatment will not incur a charge.

Ethical issues

The Department of Health considers that 'misuses' are of concern to the NHS and the public. But are there moral justifications for treating those from overseas differently? It could be argued that those who have contributed to the system have a right to receive its benefits, and that others do not have such rights. A nation has a moral obligation to pursue the interests of its citizens. However, the NHS could be said to have a 'duty of rescue' and that treatment should be provided where a delay would have serious effects.

> '" Insiders" have contributed to the welfare system while "outsiders" have not, but the point remains that insiders are able to contribute to the national economy simply because they are on the inside, and they are on the inside through morally arbitrary factors. Outsiders have made no contribution to the economy simply because they happen to have been, up to now, legally outside the national border.'
>
> Cole P. Human rights and the national interest: migrants, healthcare and social justice. *J Med Ethics* 2007;**33**:269–72

Despite the apparent rise in health tourism in the UK and the ever-increasing pressure on the allocation of limited resources it is not ethical to expect a healthcare professional to act as a 'gatekeeper' to medical care. A doctor has a duty of care to any patient who needs treatment irrespective of their ability to pay. This duty would be compromised if a doctor was also charged with the role of deciding who is eligible for free treatment.

 KEY POINTS

- There are legal restrictions on who is entitled to receive free healthcare in the UK.
- The role of gatekeeper to health services should be independent to the individual providing care to prevent a conflict of duty.

CASE 81: SUSPECTED CHILD ABUSE

An 18-month-old girl, Lilly, presents to accident and emergency with vomiting. She is well known to the paediatric department for vomiting and poor feeding. She was born at 29 weeks' gestation and was very ill as a neonate. She spent the next 4 months in hospital with various infections and difficulty tolerating feeds. Since coming home, her mother struggled to feed Lilly and ensure she put on weight. Her mother coped as well as she could but had to give up her job as an office manager, as she felt no one else could spend the time Lilly needed to feed. Lilly's mother also has to look after her 3-year-old son, who is healthy.

Lilly has no defined diagnosis and this makes managing her condition difficult. Her mother has consulted a number of different hospitals in a desperate attempt to help her daughter. Each hospital performed the same tests and came to the same conclusion – that Lilly was malnourished but no firm diagnosis could be made.

At presentation, Lilly looks thin and small. Her mother says she has not been able to keep anything down for days because she has been coughing. You think she looks a little dehydrated but otherwise not too bad. Her chest is clear. You ask for a chest X-ray to rule out a chest infection. The radiologist later alerts you to the multiple rib fractures of differing ages. He also tells you the bones look osteopenic, consistent with chronic metabolic bone disease. You discuss the case with your consultant who is not convinced of any child abuse. He asks you to focus on making the child better and ready for discharge.

Questions
- What are your legal obligations in this case?
- How would you proceed?
- Do you have any ethical obligations to Lilly's mother?

ANSWER 81

Legal issues

The welfare of the child is paramount (Children Act 1989). Lilly's welfare may be compromised if she is suffering as a result of directly inflicted damage (abuse) or as a result of failure to protect her from harm (neglect). The latter includes failing to provide adequate nutrition or appropriate medical care.

Has Lilly's mother failed in these respects? If no, then no further action needs to be taken. If yes, any concerns should be discussed with a consultant. There is still a legal duty to follow up any remaining concerns an individual may have, despite a contrary opinion of the consultant. A doctor may find it useful to discuss the situation with peers, other senior colleagues or even other agencies while preserving patient anonymity. If, after all this, a doctor still suspects child abuse, they have a positive obligation to disclose information promptly (*Confidentiality*. General Medical Council, 2009). After contacting social services on the phone, a doctor should send a written referral within 48 hours. If they have not had a reply within 3 working days the doctor should contact social services again.

There are three outcomes of referral:

- No further action
- The child may need to be assessed
- Urgent action to safeguard the child if there are concerns about the child's immediate safety (e.g. admitting the child into hospital).

It is important that anyone involved in the care of the child accurately documents events and concerns in the patient's notes, including discussion with senior colleagues. It is the duty of the doctor to recognize and follow up child protection concerns. This applies not only to those who have suffered significant harm but also to those at risk of suffering in the future.

When speaking to the child, it is important not to ask any leading questions or attempt to investigate alleged abuse as this may be detrimental to any criminal prosecution. All hospitals will have a protocol which should be observed by every doctor, e.g. some trusts have a policy of referring all unexplained fractures directly to social services.

Ethical issues

The diagnosis and misdiagnosis of non-accidental injury carry obvious ramifications for the parents (or guardians) and of course the child. Perhaps a less apparent consequence may be the subsequent reluctance of the parents to present to medical services in the future. An honest approach by keeping parents informed and discussing one's concerns and the processes involved with them is good medical practice and may help prevent these outcomes. This should be attempted as far as is compatible with the welfare of the child.

 KEY POINTS

- The welfare of the child is the paramount consideration.
- Suspected child abuse cases are complex and should be handled sensitively with advice from senior colleagues and social services.
- NHS trusts should have local protocols, which should be adhered to.

CASE 82: TREATING VICTIMS OF RAPE

You are an F1 doctor working a night shift in accident and emergency when a 23-year-old woman is brought in by one of her friends. The patient, Tammy, is very subdued and tearful. She does not look at you and sits clutching her bag. Her friend is with her. She is very jumpy. Her friend hesitantly tells you that Tammy had been in the pub with her earlier and had been chatting with one of her colleagues from work. Tammy left with the colleague at closing time to share a cab home. She rang her friend at 1 am in tears and confessed that she had gone home with the colleague 'just to talk', but her colleague sexually assaulted her. Tammy had not wanted to call the police as she felt she would not be believed and that she had 'asked for it by going back to his house'. However, she was bleeding quite heavily and had a painful wrist which she thought might be broken from being restrained by her attacker. When you ask Tammy if this is true she just nods.

Questions
- What are the procedures in accident and emergency regarding victims of assault?
- What should you do in this situation?
- Should the police be informed?
- Are there specialist centres for rape victims?

ANSWER 82

Clinical issues

A recent survey reported in the *British Journal of Gynaecology* (2007) found that only eight of 21 medical schools were teaching students how to assess rape victims. As the incidence of sexual assault and rape is increasing and the rates of conviction are low it is important that junior doctors have the necessary skills to sensitively assess patients who are admitted following an assault. It is also important for them to be aware of the closest specialist centre to their hospital. When assessing a patient the doctor should listen and ask only open questions such as 'What happened?' and 'When did it happen?' It is important to be non-judgemental and to reassure the patient that whatever they say will remain confidential. However, the doctor should also ask them if they would like anyone else to be present, such as a relative or a police officer.

Medical needs include discussion about:

- treatment of any injuries
- emergency contraception
- sexually transmitted diseases (STDs) and human immunodeficiency virus (HIV) infection counselling
- STD treatment and possible HIV prophylaxis
- forensic examination
- psychological support.

Legal issues

The Sexual Offences Act 2003 sets out clear definitions of rape, assault by penetration and sexual assault. The common link is that in all of the above the act was performed without the consent of the victim. Consent has to be active and it is now up to the defendant to prove that consent was given.

! Sexual Offences Act: definitions of terms

- *Rape*: vaginal, anal or oral penetration by a penis
- *Assault by penetration*: penetration of the anus or vagina by someone else or a foreign object
- *Sexual assault*: intentional touching in a sexual manner.

It is often difficult to get a conviction as evidence is needed to ensure that the offence was committed beyond all reasonable doubt. Staff at specialist rape centres are trained in how to take samples and package clothes and record medical details so that they can be used in court. Locard's Principle states that every contact leaves a trace. DNA evidence can be collected from an adult up to 7 days after the assault and up to 3 days from a child. There is a protocol for handling evidence specimens and forms must be completed to document the 'journey' of the evidence – saying who handled it, when and for what purpose. The same applies for any bodily fluids that are collected. Written consent must also be obtained to collect samples.

There is no legal duty to inform the police that an assault has taken place. It is up to Tammy to make that decision and she should be allowed to come to a decision in her own time without any pressure from healthcare professionals.

 KEY POINTS

- Consent, confidentiality and sensitivity are necessary when medically assessing rape victims.
- There is no legal duty to report a sexual assault to the police.

CASE 83: DRUG REPRESENTATIVES AND THE ETHICS OF A FREE LUNCH

As I am tucking into my sandwich and looking forward to my chocolate cake I half listen to what the speaker is saying while also mentally running through the list of jobs I have to do this afternoon. I am not sure what drug is being sold this time – so many representatives have come and given their spiel that all the different facts are blurring into one. To be honest I still have a hangover from the firm dinner we had last night. That had been good fun. A three-course meal and an endless supply of alcohol and all I had to do was pretend to listen to the benefits of the latest asthma treatment. As an F1 it is not as if I have any say in which drugs are put on formulary and whether they are considered first line or second line treatment! The best thing about the drug reps, of course, is the endless supply of free pens and tourniquets. It is almost a competition between the house officers to see who can get the pen with the most embarrassing drug on it. Richard had won last week for having one which advertised the latest drug for the menopause. Very childish really.

Questions
- Who makes decisions about which drugs should be used in a hospital?
- Whom should the drug reps really target?
- Is it ethical for drug reps to buy doctors their lunch and dinner and give them free gifts?

ANSWER 83

Historically there has always been a love–hate relationship between doctors and pharmaceutical companies. Huge amounts of money used to be spent entertaining medical professionals in order to educate them about the pharmaceutical company's newest creations. Weekends in Spain and golfing tours in Scotland were considered part of a consultant's working life. Over the past decade, however, there has been a clampdown on the amount of money that can be spent advertising and promoting drugs. This is to prevent doctors from being influenced in their prescribing habits.

Professional guidance

Both the British Medical Association (BMA) and the General Medical Council (GMC) have issued guidance that warns doctors against accepting gifts from pharmaceutical companies as it may seem that their prescribing protocols change as a result of bribery rather than good medical practice. When making decisions about investigations or treatment doctors are advised to consider the most appropriate medication based primarily on clinical suitability, bearing in mind the cost effectiveness of the treatment. Although some treatments may be extremely effective, their price may limit their use since it would be unjust to allocate a large portion of money to one individual.

The BMA states that it is 'unethical for a doctor to receive payment or other reward for prescribing in a way which was not in the patient's best interest' (*Incentives to GPs for Referral or Prescribing.* BMA, 1997). Patients must also feel reassured that their doctor is acting in their medical best interests, rather than being persuaded to trial new medication. If patients feel they are not being treated based solely on their clinical symptoms, it may lead to a breakdown in the doctor–patient relationship.

Furthermore, the GMC states that a doctor must ensure that they are *actively* perceived to be acting solely in the patients' best interests.

> 'You must act in your patients' best interests when making referrals and when providing or arranging treatment or care. You must not ask for or accept any inducement, gift or hospitality, which may affect or be seen to affect the way you prescribe for, treat or refer patients. You must not offer such inducements to colleagues.'
>
> General Medical Council. *Good Medical Practice*. London: GMC, 2006

Ethical issues

The only ethically justifiable reason for accepting small gifts or hospitality is when the meeting between the clinician and drug representative is educational. Prescribing should be evidence based, and drug representatives have up-to-date information on the latest drugs trials and their cost effectiveness in relation to other drugs used for treating a disease. But it may be that the best interests of patients take a back seat if the main aim of the 'free lunch' is to benefit the doctor and promote the interests of the pharmaceutical company. The pharmaceutical industry's code of practice contains strict guidelines on what is acceptable to offer as a gift and what could be construed as bribery or coercion.

 KEY POINTS

- Pharmaceutical companies can be useful at promoting drugs in an educational forum.
- Small gifts and hospitality can be accepted by doctors.
- Doctors must not let drug companies influence their prescribing habits. Treatment must always be given to benefit the patient, not a drug company.

CASE 84: DRUG TRIALS

James is a fourth-year medical student. He has funded himself through medical school with a little bit of financial support from his parents. In 6 months' time he is supposed to be going on elective to experience studying and practising medicine in a different country. James has been excited about this for the past year and has endeavoured to organize an educational placement in a small village in Western Samoa. He has just discovered, however, that the flights are going to be more expensive than anticipated and he cannot afford them. He starts thinking of ways to earn the money. An advertisement in his local general practice catches his eye. A new drug trial is looking for candidates to take part in the research. The new wonder drug is expected to be effective in treating young people with asthma by reducing bronchospasm. James rings up for more information. He discovers that they need healthy men of his age to undergo bronchoscopy. Individuals will be reimbursed £100 for time and travel costs. James signs up and undergoes bronchoscopy. Later that week he signs up to another drug trial and then another. Within 5 weeks he has earned enough money to buy a ticket.

Questions
- What is the role of a research ethics committee?
- What are the ethics of drug trials?

ANSWER 84

In 1946 the Nuremberg Code was written to give guidance on the ethics of using humans in medical research, in response to the atrocities performed by the Nazis during their experimentation on prisoners. Since then all potential research projects involving humans must be submitted to a research ethics committee to gain ethical approval. All NHS trusts are legally required by the Department of Health to have a local research ethics committee (LREC). This consists of doctors, lawyers and lay people. Before any research project can begin, it must be approved by an LREC.

The most important ethical consideration in research is that of autonomy. Generally, all research participants must be able to give valid consent. This means that they must have the capacity to understand the proposed aims of the research, what the research will involve and any associated risks. Some ethical theories would justify that as long as a participant consents to take a risk, it does not matter how large the risk is. However, in reality the World Health Organization has limited the risks that a participant can take. Research can only be given ethical approval if there is a small chance of a minor risk or a rare chance of a serious or life-threatening risk. There are special considerations to protect the interests of incompetent research subjects who cannot give valid consent.

One element of informed consent is that participants must not be coerced. Coercion can take several forms. Patients may feel that if they refuse to participate it will affect any future medical care they receive. Another possible form of coercion is the prospect of financial gain. In the case scenario James received £100 for a bronchoscopy. It is possible that the lure of financial gain has persuaded him to participate in the research against his better judgement. The Department of Health advises that research participants should only be reimbursed for their time and travel expenses.

Throughout any research trial every participant should be treated with respect and care. Patient safety must take priority over research data, and if harmful effects are demonstrated the trial should be stopped immediately. Participants should also be advised that they are free to withdraw from the trial at any time. They must also be treated with dignity. Any information regarding a participant is confidential and where possible all research data should be anonymized.

Research trials also need ethical approval to ensure that the aims of the research are sound and based in scientific fact. Poor-quality research or a poorly thought-out trial is unethical for two reasons. First, if the research is of a low standard the risk to participants cannot be justified as the long-term benefits of the trial will not exist. Second, poor-quality research can have a detrimental effect on people's health in the future, for example, the measles, mumps, rubella (MMR) trial conducted by Andrew Wakefield, which suggested a (false) link between the MMR vaccine and autism.

  KEY POINTS

- Consent to involvement in research must be informed and voluntary.
- All research projects involving humans must be approved by a research ethics committee.

CASE 85: HARMFUL TREATMENT

Sonya is a 32-year-old business executive who presents to hospital with a 4-week history of lethargy. She tells you this has become worse over the past few days and she thinks she is coming down with flu. She has no other medical history and you initially suspect she has glandular fever. You take her blood to test for this and some other routine tests. However, her blood test results show she has a haemoglobin of 82 g/l, white cell count of 283×10^9 and neutrophils of 19×10^9. A haematologist had reviewed the film and 97 per cent of the white blood cells were probable lymphoblasts. She is diagnosed with acute lymphoblast leukaemia and it is advised that she should be admitted for an immediate course of intensive chemotherapy. She is told that the side-effects of the chemotherapy include hair loss, immunosuppression, infertility and an increased likelihood of solid cancers later in life.

Questions
- What are the ethics of giving medical treatment that has associated harmful side-effects?
- Whose decision should it be to initiate treatment?

ANSWER 85

The four principles approach is useful in discussing the dilemmas faced by clinicians when recommending or prescribing treatment with potentially serious side-effects. It could be argued that an autonomous person has the right to make a decision about whether they wish to accept the associated risks of any treatment. If they are competent enough to make an informed decision then the responsibility of that decision should rest with the patient. However, doctors have a *prima facie* duty to 'do no harm', also known as non-maleficence. There is a spectrum of risk associated with drug prescribing. For example, treating a patient with gentamicin for bacterial sepsis carries a risk of deafness and renal failure. However, with careful monitoring of the therapeutic range the risks are minimal. It is justifiable to risk causing the patient harm because the primary role of the gentamicin is to benefit the patient. At the other end of the spectrum are treatments which doctors prescribe which have definite side-effects. Chemotherapy can have serious short- and long-term implications to a patient's health. Yet it is routinely given to attempt to cure or palliate cancer. Can this be ethically justified?

In this situation three of the four ethical principles need to be carefully balanced to reach a conclusion. The doctor must ensure the patient is informed of the potential risks – of having the treatment and not having the treatment. If the patient is incompetent, people close to the patient should be included in discussions to establish what would be in the best interests of the patient. Would the patient have wanted to be treated? The risk–benefit ratio should be analysed. Do the potential benefits of treatment outweigh the associated risks?

Often no definitive answer can be given, and each decision should be analysed on a case-by-case basis. What is important to the individual patient should be established. A young woman may not want to risk becoming infertile if there are other treatment options that could be tried first. Someone with a family to provide for may opt to have the treatment with the highest cure rate, irrespective of the short-term side-effects. In a different scenario the principle of justice may also have a role in determining which treatment should be initiated. Imagine a drug being developed in the future which could cure cancer and which did not have any harmful side-effects. However, the drug is 100 times more expensive than other chemotherapy regimens, which means that only 1 in 100 of your patients with cancer can receive this treatment. Could it be ethically justified to prescribe this wonder drug?

Generally, harmful treatment is justified when its primary aim is to treat disease that carries a greater risk to life than the actual treatment. Beneficence trumps non-maleficence. However, autonomy should never be forgotten.

 KEY POINTS

- Patients should be fully informed about potential harmful side-effects of all treatment in order to make an autonomous choice.
- It can be ethically justified to prescribe harmful treatment if the benefits outweigh the harms.

CASE 86: THE ROLE OF CLINICAL AND RESEARCH ETHICS COMMITTEES

Scenario 1

You are an F1 doctor on your general practice rotation. At medical school you were interested in the law on advance decisions and you now wish to do a research study to look at the prevalence of advance decisions in general practice. You have drafted up a questionnaire which you want to send out to all general practices in the primary care trust.

Scenario 2

You are an F2 doctor on an intensive care rotation. A patient with multiple sclerosis is admitted to the unit and treated for pneumonia. The patient was adamant that she did not want to receive intravenous antibiotics but no specific reasons were given. The patient's condition deteriorated rapidly and she became unconscious. It was considered clinically necessary to give intravenous antibiotics since they were more likely to be effective against her sepsis, and she was no longer able to swallow oral medication. You think that the patient's prior refusal of intravenous antibiotics should be taken into account, and you would like an opportunity to discuss the ethical issues.

Questions
- In what circumstances is research ethics approval required?
- What does a clinical ethics committee do?

ANSWER 86

Clinical ethics committees and research ethics committees have distinct functions.

Research ethics

From 1 April 2007 the National Research Ethics Service (NRES) has taken over the role of Central Organisation of Research Ethics Committees (COREC) to co-ordinate applications for ethics committee approval. It protects the 'rights, safety, dignity and well-being of research participants, whilst facilitating and promoting ethical research'. Prior approval from a research ethics committee is required for any research involving patients and users of the National Health Service (NHS) or NHS resources (including NHS staff). All applications must be made on the standard NRES application form, which is available from the NRES website (www.nres.npsa.nhs.uk). Applications should be booked for review before submission, either to the Central Allocation System or direct to the local research ethics committee in the domain in which the research is to be conducted. The NREC has 60 days in which to provide independent advice about whether the research complies with recognized ethical standards.

Governance approval is required for all research undertaken within the NHS from research and development offices at each site that the research will take place. The application process can begin when the research ethics committee has agreed the validity of the application. An audit or service evaluation does not require ethical review by an NHS research ethics committee, and the NRES will advise if ethical review is needed, and where it may be unclear, advice should be taken. The relevant research and development office should be approached, even where the NRES has stated that no approval is needed.

Clinical ethics

A clinical ethics committee (CEC) considers the ethical implications of the treatment and care of patients. These are multidisciplinary committees and members include clinicians, other healthcare professionals, and religious, legal and lay members. Although the role of CECs varies, many will provide ethics input in trust policy (e.g. limitation of treatment plans), ethics education (e.g. open days for trust staff) and consider the ethical implications in individual cases referred by health professionals (e.g. conflict within the treating team about the best interests of a patient). The role of the CEC is advisory only – it does not direct healthcare professionals. CECs can provide a supportive forum for discussion of difficult ethical issues.

There is no requirement that an NHS trust must have a clinical ethics committee. Currently there are more than 70 CECs in the UK. The UK Clinical Ethics Network provides information and support to developing and existing clinical ethics committees and the website contains ethics education materials (http://www.ethics-network.org.uk).

 KEY POINTS

- In scenario 1 approval by a research ethics committee is not required as this is an audit. However there may be different views about what defines an audit. Advice from the NRES may be required.
- In scenario 2 there is a conflict of views between the priority accorded to the best interests of the patient and respecting her autonomy. These issues can usefully be discussed in a CEC and can provide a good basis for ethics education. However, this does not replace the need for legal advice where necessary, in this case whether there is a valid advance decision that applies in the circumstances.

Section 4
FAITH, VALUES AND CULTURE

CASE 87: FAITH ADVISERS IN HOSPITALS

Judy, a 34-year-old woman, is a non-practising Roman Catholic from Northern Ireland. For the past 7 years she has been married to Zeb, who is a practising Muslim. They have chosen to live in London as they feel more at ease in a diverse multicultural society. Judy has been diagnosed with end-stage liver failure as a result of persistent and ongoing alcoholism. She has been admitted to hospital for analgesia. Her best friend from Ireland has come over to be with her in her last days. The friend has a strong religious faith and now Judy feels the need for spiritual support.

Questions
- Why is it necessary to recognize the spiritual, cultural and/or religious needs of a patient?
- What support is available for the spiritual, cultural and religious needs of patients and healthcare professionals?
- When and how should such support be sought?

ANSWER 87

Patients may feel vulnerable in the unfamiliar setting of hospital particularly when faced with upsetting information and difficult decisions. Religious and spiritual beliefs can provide comfort for patients in such stressful times. Recognizing and meeting such needs is an important part of patient-centred care. However, discussing the religious beliefs and spiritual needs of a patient can present challenges for healthcare professionals, who may feel embarrassed and unprepared, or outside their familiar territory. Healthcare professionals who are not religious, practise a different religion or have different values from the patient may not fully appreciate the importance of religion, spirituality or cultural practices for the patient.

Spiritual healthcare

A trust's spiritual healthcare team (known as chaplaincy) provides information and support regarding the spiritual, religious and pastoral care of patients and their families. Chaplaincy input should not just be considered at the end of life or for serious conditions. Listening to people's stories is also a part of the day-to-day service that chaplaincy provides. Chaplaincy is staffed by Christian ministers and other religious leaders reflecting the local population, and so may, for example, include a rabbi and an imam. The chaplaincy service can provide information to healthcare professionals about religious practices. This can be helpful in understanding a patient's attitude to illness, dietary requirements and religious obligations. It may be particularly important regarding preferences at the end of life. Advice may also be sought on ethical issues.

Ensuring patients have their faith recorded on admission and indicating to them that the chaplaincy service exists can provide reassurance. The chaplaincy service can be accessed directly by patients and their families. The support offered by chaplaincy is often that of reconnecting or maintaining a link with a faith community. In this case scenario the chaplaincy service was able to support Judy's spiritual requirements at the end of her life, despite her previously having rejected her religious beliefs.

Chaplaincy can also support the needs of healthcare professionals and other members of staff through the role of a neutral listener and by providing prayer times and religious services.

 KEY POINTS

- Patients are individuals and stereotypical judgements based on a patient's religion or cultural identity should be avoided.
- Recognition and respect of a patient's religious needs is not only ethically important but may also have legal implications, e.g. disposal of an amputated limb without the consent of a Muslim patient, blood transfusions in the face of refusal by a Jehovah's Witness.
- A patient's request for treatment on the basis of their culture or religion may conflict with the views of those providing care and other patients.

Table 87.1 Religious beliefs and their impact on medical practice

Religion	General beliefs	Diet and medication	Family planning and birth	Blood transfusion and organ donation	Resuscitation and death
Buddhism	A deep respect for all creatures; will always expect to be treated with dignity	Mainly vegetarian; do not drink alcohol; will often refuse sedative drugs as like to be conscious	Do not approve of contraception	No specific rules	Prefer to have prayers said by a Buddhist monk or nun before the body is moved
Christianity	Men were created in the image of God so should be treated with respect	Some observe the period of Lent	Catholics disapprove of contraception	No specific rules	May request confession and Holy Communion before death
Hinduism	Believe in reincarnation and that the soul will pass on after death to be born again in another creature	Beef and pork are not eaten; various other restrictions; may prefer herbal medicines	Women are expected to rest for 40 days after birth	No specific rules but support organ donation as selfless giving	Prefer to be placed on the floor so closer to God. Relatives should be present. The body should always be left covered after death
Islam	Islam means peace and submission – to the will of Allah; prayers said five times a day except by patients with major illnesses	Halal food; no alcohol; strict fasting rules	None	Can donate as long as it does not compromise their own life	Place facing Mecca. Do not allow post-mortems unless legally required
Jehovah's Witnesses	Usually very devout	None, although some may be vegetarian because of constraints on blood products	None	Do not usually accept blood or blood products	Believe that the Bible teaches a resurrection of the dead
Judaism	Following the advice of a medical professional will usually take precedence over other Jewish laws; where life is in danger religious laws can be breached	Kosher food	Baby boys circumcised on the eighth day following birth	A rabbi should be consulted first	A dying person should always have someone sitting with him. No post-mortem unless legally required

CASE 88: JEHOVAH'S WITNESSES AND BLOOD TRANSFUSIONS

A 27-year-old devout Jehovah's Witness, Gemma, is walking home from work one evening when she is attacked. She is mugged and stabbed in the abdomen. A passer-by calls an ambulance and she is rushed to accident and emergency (A&E), where she is found to have a ruptured spleen. Although she is unconscious she is carrying a document that informs doctors that she does not wish to receive a blood transfusion even if the outcome would be death. When Gemma's husband arrives, he informs the doctors that her wishes have not changed since signing the document. Instead the doctors attempt to resuscitate her using fluids and blood salvaging. Tragically these do not work and Gemma dies due to massive haemorrhage.

Questions
• Should Gemma have received a blood transfusion as it could have saved her life?
• What efforts should be made to find out whether a person has an advance decision when they arrive in accident and emergency?

ANSWER 88

If a patient is conscious on arrival at hospital their competent refusal to accept a blood transfusion must be respected. In this case, Gemma was unconscious on arrival at hospital. Therefore, unless she has made a valid advance decision (AD) refusing blood products, she would be treated in her best interests. Is the document she is carrying an effective advance refusal of blood products? The Hospital Information Services for Jehovah's Witnesses have in the past two years produced an updated 'Advance Directive to Refuse Specified Medical Treatment' to reflect the requirements of the Mental Capacity Act 2005 (MCA). It includes the statement: 'I direct that no transfusions of blood or primary blood components (red cells, white cells, plasma or platelets) be administered to me in any circumstances'. However, the use of non-blood fluids, volume expanders and blood salvaging is permitted. The Code of Practice to the MCA provides that an advance decision refusing all treatment in any situation, for example with an explanation of his/her personal or religious beliefs, may be valid and applicable (paragraph 9.13).

Clearly the lack of advance dialogue with Gemma about whether she really understands the nature and effect of her AD presents a real problem. It would be easy to err on the side of caution and treat in her medical best interests irrespective of her AD. This is legally and ethically problematic; treating in the face of a valid and applicable advance refusal may be subject to a claim of battery. In an emergency it is difficult to know whether this is still the wish of the patient and whether she understood the implications of a refusal. But the MCA does not require that there has been a prior discussion with a healthcare professional to render an AD valid. Capacity of a patient should be presumed unless there are reasonable grounds to doubt that the patient lacked capacity at the time of making the AD.

There is protection from liability if a healthcare professional provides treatment when they were unaware of an AD. It is wise to check the clothes of unconscious patients arriving in A&E to see if they are carrying such documents. If somebody tells a healthcare professional that the patient has made an AD reasonable efforts should be made to find out what it says, e.g. speak to relatives, look in clinical notes, contact the general practitioner. Healthcare professionals should not delay emergency treatment to look for an AD if there is no clear indication that one exists. Clearly if no such document is found on an unconscious person, they should be treated in their best interests.

 KEY POINTS

- Jehovah's Witnesses do not accept blood transfusions. They obey the Biblical injunction to abstain from blood (Acts 15:29).
- It is the responsibility of the person who is in charge of the care of the patient when treatment is required to determine whether a valid and applicable advance decision exists.

The issues raised in this scenario are further considered in Case 29: Refusal of treatment, page 73 and Case 67: Advance decisions, page 167.

CASE 89: RAMADAN AND ILLNESS

Ahmed is a devout Muslim. He lives in central London with his family. He is admitted to hospital with a non-healing ulcer on the medial aspect of his calf. Following investigations, he is diagnosed with diabetes. His blood sugar levels are very high and he is initially treated with insulin and metformin. After discussion with his consultant, the diabetes nurse and the dietician it is decided he should attempt to control his diabetes with a mixture of diet and tablets as he is not keen on using insulin every day. Everything seems to be going well. Ahmed is very conscientious and follows a strict sugar-free diet. Several months later he is admitted to hospital with severe dehydration and a decreased Glasgow Coma Scale score. His relatives tell you that he has been fasting during the day as it is Ramadan. After initial resuscitation Ahmed improves medically. You have a conversation with him about what happened. He understands that fasting will have affected his diabetic control and that he is running the risk of long-term complications but he tells you that he is extremely religious and feels he will be disobeying Allah if he does not fast along with the rest of his family.

Questions
- What does the Qur'an say about Ramadan and illness?
- What advice should you give Ahmed?
- Who else can you ask for help in this situation?

ANSWER 89

Ramadan is the month during which Allah revealed the contents of the Qur'an to Muhammad. To commemorate this Allah instructed all devout Muslims to fast from sunrise to sunset during the month of Ramadan. Fasting during Ramadan is one of the five pillars of Islam. It involves abstaining from food, and all medication, to demonstrate obedience and learn sympathy for the poor and hungry. However, this can have health repercussions for Muslims who have diabetes or other chronic illnesses. People who are healthy and intentionally do not fast commit a sin in the eyes of Allah. However, there are exceptions to fasting. Those with chronic illnesses, the acutely unwell, children and people with learning disabilities who would not understand the reason behind fasting, are not expected to fast.

Having diabetes does not necessarily preclude someone from fasting. With careful attention to glycaemic control and good dietary advice, fasting can be possible but there will always be an increased risk of hypoglycaemia and ketoacidosis. Extremely religious Muslims believe that only Allah can cure or control illness and that doctors and medication are merely His tools.

In the above scenario it is worth considering that Ahmed may be able to fast. However, if he is to do this then the doctor should encourage him to closely monitor his blood sugar level and educate him on the early warning symptoms of hypoglycaemia. Pre-Ramadan optimization of glycaemic control can help during the fast. Taking a careful history of what and when the patient plans to eat can help implement a safer insulin regimen. Despite doing all this there may be some Muslims with diabetes who are still at risk of severe deterioration during Ramadan. If this was the case with Ahmed, the doctor should consider asking a hospital faith adviser or the patient's own imam for help. They may be able to talk to Ahmed about his beliefs and reassure him that the Qur'an does have exceptions to fasting. There are other things that Ahmed could do to compensate for not being able to fast, such as providing food for someone else.

 KEY POINTS

- Ramadan is a religious festival during which Muslims fast from sunrise to sunset.
- This can affect the health of people with chronic disease, including diabetes.
- Healthcare professionals should advise patients on how to fast safely.
- An imam can offer help and guidance to Muslims who feel their health is being affected by following their religion.

CASE 90: FEMALE GENITAL MUTILATION

Sayida, 21 years old, has recently arrived in the UK with her husband and two-year-old daughter from their home country, Sierra Leone. The family left Sierra Leone because of war and continuing political unrest and are seeking asylum in the UK. Sayida is 10 weeks pregnant when she attends the antenatal clinic for her first booking appointment, accompanied by her husband and a middle-aged female relative of the husband. The latter explains that she has come along to act as chaperone and interpreter because Sayida speaks no English and her husband very little. During initial assessment it transpires that a friend already living in London has told Sayida about the African Well Woman Clinic (AWWC) and Sayida's husband has telephoned for an appointment. Through the interpreter Sayida explains that she had problems with her first pregnancy and during the birth, and her friend has told her that the AWWC would be able to help her with this and 'difficulties' she has had since the birth of her daughter.

Clinical examination by a female genital mutilation (FGM) public health specialist reveals that Sayida has FGM III and is presenting with symptoms consistent with problems associated with urinary tract infection and the menstrual cycle.

Questions
- What is FGM?
- What are the laws in the UK regarding the practice of FGM?
- Should a competent adult be able to consent to the procedure?
- What is cultural relativism?

ANSWER 90

Across the globe the controversy of FGM has ignited arguments by human rights activists, healthcare professionals and feminists for nearly half a century. In 2000 the World Health Organization (WHO) defined FGM as 'all procedures which involve partial or total removal of the external female genitalia or other injury to the female genital organs whether for cultural or any other non-therapeutic reasons'.

! WHO classification of FGM

- Type I: excision of the prepuce, with or without excision of part, or all, of the clitoris
- Type II: excision of the clitoris with partial or total excision of the labia minora
- Type III: excision of part, or all, of the external genitalia and stitching/narrowing of the vaginal opening, also known as infibulation
- Type IV: unclassified. This includes pricking, piercing or incising of the clitoris and/or labia, stretching of the clitoris and/or labia, cauterization by burning of the clitoris and surrounding tissue.

In many countries, FGM is accepted as the norm – an expected part of the customary practice of many local communities. For many women FGM is a fact of life, a pain that must be borne because they must conform to social expectation. People with little or no knowledge, skill or training in female anatomy and surgical techniques perform FGM. It is usually performed on girls between the ages of 4 and 13 years, but sometimes it is done in newborns or on young women before marriage or pregnancy. It is often performed in unhygienic conditions and without anaesthesia. Despite worldwide attempts to end the ancient tradition, every year millions of women and girls are being 'circumcised'. There are three main arguments against the practice of FGM:

- It is a dangerous tradition with horrific medical consequences.
- It is primarily performed on girls who cannot consent to the procedure.
- It is a misogynistic practice carried out in patriarchal societies to repress female sexuality.

Ethical issues

In a multicultural environment, it is important to respect others' religious and cultural beliefs and value systems. Many of the arguments centred around FGM are tied up in an intricate web of ethical issues with the main conflict arising between cultural and individual rights. Opponents of FGM argue against the practice on the ethical basis that some human rights are fundamental and supersede differences in cultural morality. The counter-argument to this is that different moral codes are applied by different cultures and that these should not be criticized by people who do not have an intimate understanding of that culture. In bioethics this argument is described as cultural relativism.

Relativism is a strain of ethical theory that holds that there are no absolute truths or morals. Mackie, a contemporary philosopher, cites that the proof of this is the existence of diverse moral values, which have changed greatly over time and culture. Cultural relativism argues that morals are merely socially approved habits, and the moral code that one culture follows does not have to be the same as that of another culture. It holds that the morals of other cultures should not be subjected to criticism from the subjective view of an outsider. It encourages diverse cultural expression and harmonious living in pluralistic societies because it fosters an attitude of acceptance of other cultures.

A strong example of the ethical hypocrisy of criticism of FGM and of moral double standards is reflected in the law concerning it. The UK and other countries have legislation making it a crime to 'excise, infibulate or otherwise mutilate the whole or any part of the labia majora or labia minora or clitoris of another person' (Female Genital Mutilation Act 2003, section 1.1). Yet in these same countries, genital cosmetic surgery is rarely criticized.

Legal issues

In 1985 the Prohibition of Female Circumcision Act was introduced due to pressure from global conventions to criminalize the practice amid fears that FGM was occurring in Britain by African immigrants who had fled their own countries to escape from war and poverty. This Act made it a criminal offence to circumcise any girl or woman living in the UK no matter what their nationality, religion or culture. In 2003 this Act was repealed by the Female Genital Mutilation Act 2003, which was introduced to close a loophole in the current law. It prevented British inhabitants from taking their children away on 'holidays' to be circumcised. This is an unusual step to take since crimes usually committed abroad are not liable to prosecution under the British penal system.

Section 6 has some things to note about the legislation. No distinction is made between FGM being performed on minors or competent adults and prosecution can occur no matter in which country FGM is performed. Note that the Act specifically forbids mutilation 'required as a matter of custom or ritual', even if not performing it may have adverse mental health consequences. The Act also extended the prison sentence from 5 years to 14 years, demonstrating once again how serious a crime this is considered to be in the UK.

Child protection issues

Healthcare professionals have an obligation to safeguard girls who are at risk of FGM and must report cases to the child protection team. Refugees, asylum seekers and migrants to the UK need to be given information about their health and the UK legal and child protection issues regarding FGM. Sensitivity is an essential component of any interaction with patients and their families. Wherever possible the aim must be to work in partnership with parents and families to protect children through parents' awareness of the harm caused to the child.

A girl may be considered to be at risk if it is known that older girls in the family have been subjected to the procedure. Pre-pubescent girls aged 7–10 years are the main subjects, although the practice has been reported among babies. If any agency is informed that a girl has been or may be subjected to these practices, a referral must be made to social services in accordance with child protection procedures. In planning any intervention it is important to consider cultural factors because culture and cultural identity are frequently given as the reason that FGM is generally performed, and any intervention is more likely to be successful if it involves workers from, or with a detailed knowledge of, the community concerned.

Female genital mutilation is different from other child protection issues since it is a one-off event of physical abuse (albeit one that may have grave permanent sexual, physical and emotional consequences). A girl who has already been genitally mutilated should not usually be registered on the child protection register, unless additional protection concerns exist, although she should be offered counselling and medical help. Consideration must be given to any other female siblings at risk.

KEY POINTS

- In the UK, FGM is illegal. But despite this it continues to be practised due to the growing number of refugees and asylum seekers from countries where FGM is widespread.
- People who may perform FGM on their children should be educated sensitively about the dangers of the practice and its illegality.
- In a multicultural environment it is important to respect others' religious and cultural beliefs and value systems.

CASE 91: NEONATAL MALE CIRCUMCISION

Four-month-old Jack is brought to his general practitioner (GP) by his father, who is seeking information about having his son circumcised. Although he has no immediate concerns about the health of his son's penis, he feels that, in the long run, his son will be better off circumcised. When asked, he denies any particular religious or cultural background that might grant circumcision special importance. However he explains that he, and all of his family, including Jack's older brother, are circumcised, and that it simply feels right that Jack should be too. He also considers uncircumcised penises as unhygienic and has read several articles on the internet suggesting that circumcision can protect against human immunodeficiency virus (HIV) infection and acquired immune deficiency syndrome (AIDS).

History and general examination give no cause for concern and examination of Jack's penis reveals no obvious phimosis (tight foreskin), balanitis (inflammation of the glans penis) or any other abnormality. The GP explains that what Jack's father is seeking is termed a 'non-therapeutic' circumcision, which is not covered by the National Health Service (NHS) in that area and he refers Jack to a private urologist. The urologist hears the reasons for Jack's father wanting his son circumcised and confirms the GP's findings of a healthy infant with a normal penis. He then offers Jack's father a brief explanation of the procedure and informs him that the risks involved in circumcision are mainly those relevant to all surgery (e.g. bleeding and infection) and that any long-term adverse effects are unlikely when the procedure is carried out properly. Jack's father jokingly agrees that it is hard to see how an experienced surgeon could mess up a 'routine snip'. When asked whether Jack's mother agrees that Jack should be circumcised, he says that she feels that such matters are best decided by a boy's father. An appointment is made within the next month for Jack's circumcision.

Questions
- Following consultation with the urologist, is Jack's father able to give informed consent for the procedure?
- Has the urologist given due consideration to Jack's best interests?
- Why was it pertinent to enquire about Jack's cultural and religious background?

ANSWER 91

Non-therapeutic male circumcision is the excision of the foreskin for reasons other than a clear clinical indication. There are only a few clinical indications and 'therapeutic circumcision' represents a minority of the circumcisions carried out in the UK. Cultural reasons for non-therapeutic male circumcision include religious or cultural traditions (notably Islam and Judaism), 'family tradition' and the concept of the foreskin as being inherently dirty or unhealthy. National Health Service (NHS) provision of neonatal circumcision for religious reasons is variable. Non-therapeutic male circumcision is currently a controversial procedure, and the British Medical Association (BMA) has issued ethical and legal guidelines for doctors on the subject (*The Law and Ethics of Male Circumcision – Guidance for Doctors*. London: BMA, 2006).

Parents can give consent to medical procedures considered to be in the best interests of their child. 'Best interests' encompasses social, religious and cultural issues. However, these best interests would have to be clearly outlined to justify non-therapeutic intervention. The informed consent of both parents is required, as this is an irreversible, non-therapeutic procedure. Where there is parental discord the case should be referred to the courts. The informed consent of Jack's mother should be sought before proceeding with the operation. It is not enough to accept his father's word that she agrees with him on this matter.

The literature on non-therapeutic circumcision is characterized by significant bias, which is reflected in the polarity of attitudes towards the subject among clinicians. This probably leads to a wide variety in the amount and content of information provided to parents and the rigour of best interests assessments carried out by clinicians. It is important to consider whether the potential benefits of the procedure outweigh the harms. Benefits include identification with a religious or cultural group and the possible decrease in the risk of transmission of sexually transmitted diseases. Possible harms include physical and psychological damage and decreased sexual pleasure as an adult. It also limits the infant's future choices.

In the case of *Re J* (1996), 'J' was a 5-year-old boy whose father was a non-practising Muslim and wanted J to be circumcised. J's mother, with whom J lived, was a non-practising Christian and she opposed the circumcision. It was decided that J should not be circumcised as he was not being brought up in the Muslim religion. In this case general anaesthetic was to be used and this was a factor in balancing the harms of the procedure against any benefits, which did not include the benefit of identifying with the tenets of a religious or cultural group. The GP in this case scenario was right to enquire about Jack's cultural and religious background, as this represents an important consideration in assessing best interests, as illustrated in *Re J*.

 KEY POINTS

- The justification for non-therapeutic male circumcision is that the potential non-medical benefits, such as identification with a religious group, outweigh the potential harms.
- Is there is a difference between male and female circumcision if both restrict the future autonomy of the child?

CASE 92: DISCLOSURE OF DIAGNOSIS AND CULTURAL RELATIVISM

An 85-year-old Japanese man, Aiko, who came to the UK 10 years ago to live with his children, is admitted with haematuria. He has known bladder cancer, but has been under surveillance with regular cystoscopy for many years, and has been admitted with haematuria several times before, always dealt with relatively swiftly. After investigation, it appears that this time he is in the terminal stages of his disease and would be best treated with palliation. His son and daughter are insistent that their father should not be informed of his prognosis, since they feel that he will 'give up'. Rather, they ask that 'we should respect him and not directly tell him of his prognosis so that he might enjoy the last part of his life'.

As the junior doctor, you consider the following opinions of your team: the palliative care nurse insists that the patient has a right to informed consent and must be told the whole truth directly; the senior ward nurse takes the view that the team should balance the risks and benefits of telling the truth to this patient; and your registrar mentions in passing that the team could give Aiko the correct information in terms of tumour staging. The situation may be allowed to remain unclear though if his children are strongly against informing their father.

Questions
- Is there a moral obligation to tell Aiko his prognosis?
- To what extent should cultural beliefs and practices influence your decision making?

ANSWER 92

When informing patients of their prognosis, it is appropriate to consider the cultural slant on patient-centred decision making, since it may not be universally endorsed. In contemporary bioethics it is considered that respect for autonomy is best served when individuals make decisions for themselves without influence from others, even on the part of their own families. The dominant view of those involved in Aiko's care is that autonomy should be promoted through openness and truth telling.

In the first instance, it is imperative that informed consent be gained for any treatment course. In the case of palliative nursing, healthcare professionals must ensure that as a team they do not create any medico-legal implications for the nurse or her department. The nurse suggests that the doctor should inform Aiko regardless of his family's views but wider issues should be considered. From an ethical point of view, respect for patient autonomy must take patient values into consideration. If members of the patient's family have informed the doctor that non-disclosure of prognosis to elderly relatives is culturally acceptable this should be taken into account. Disclosing prognosis against the family's advice may inadvertently cause distress to the patient and set up tensions within the family. If, as the ward nurse suggests, the doctors balance the risks and benefits of fully informing the patient, note that this family's expectations in the sphere of Japanese health culture may mean that their interpretation of 'risk' and 'benefit' may be different. Considering the concept of respect for the elderly, it may seem a benefit to fully inform Aiko, yet this is perceived by his family as a potential harm to his dignity. Hence we cannot use the traditional utilitarian way of measuring harm and good in order to dictate the information a doctor gives.

The 'hands off' scenario presented by the registrar may fulfil a doctor's duty now. However this may lead to future problems of obtaining consent. For instance, if, to offer a good standard of care, later a long-term catheter is thought to be appropriate, Aiko requires not only correct information, but that he should be given *all* the information surrounding this treatment option in the light of his prognosis for him to give informed consent. So, while it may be taken for granted that telling patients the truth about terminal illness is always the right thing to do, many cultures assume the opposite. From a legal point of view, patients being treated in the UK are of course subject to UK healthcare laws, and particular informed consent must be gained for any treatment. However, it is important to be culturally sensitive in conveying the truth, and not disrupt family communication patterns.

 KEY POINTS

- Faith, culture and individual values should be taken into account when determining the exercise of healthcare choices.
- The legal requirements for disclosure should be interpreted with consideration of different cultural practices.

CASE 93: CULTURAL ISSUES IN THE DYING PROCESS

Latisha is a 24-year-old woman who has been admitted to hospital after being found drowsy and uncommunicative at home by her younger sister. She is brought in wearing a full burkha. Her family have requested that she is only seen by female staff and that she is treated in a side room since the patient and her family are all strict Muslims. The hospital has tried to do this as well as possible. It is not immediately obvious why Latisha is unwell but her Glasgow Coma Scale score continues to drop. Her younger sister comes to speak to you to tell you that she is worried that Latisha may have attempted to commit suicide since she had had a massive argument with their father who had found out that Latisha had a non-Muslim boyfriend. You decide to test her blood for drug levels. Just after you have done this Latisha has a cardiac arrest. Despite three cycles of cardiopulmonary resuscitation (CPR) she never regains a heartbeat. She is pronounced dead at 20.17 hours, 5 hours after her admission to hospital. You know that a post-mortem is legally required. You go to discuss this with her family.

Questions
- Which religions do not allow post-mortem examinations?
- Can a post-mortem not be performed if there is religious or cultural opposition to it?
- What should you say to Latisha's family in this situation?

ANSWER 93

Post-mortem examinations are a legal requirement in some circumstances because the exact cause of death must be known before a person's death can be registered. However, some religions, such as Judaism and Islam, do not allow post-mortems. Many other individuals also find the concept of a post-mortem distressing, regardless of their religious or cultural beliefs. In this scenario Latisha's death must be referred to the coroner for a post-mortem because the cause of death is unknown, she was in hospital for less than 24 hours and it is possible that she may have committed suicide.

When discussing the need for a post-mortem with the family it is important to be sensitive to their beliefs. Post-mortems are usually legally required when a person has died unexpectedly, so the relatives will often be in shock or denial about what has happened. It is useful for a doctor to be accompanied by another healthcare professional to offer additional support to the family. The family should also be asked if they would like anyone else to be present during the discussion, e.g. a religious leader. The first thing that should be explained is that the post-mortem is a legal requirement. The family cannot refuse a post-mortem and their consent is not needed. But doctors should show that they are aware of the family's religious beliefs and that they appreciate their religious objections to post-mortems.

Discussing sensitive issues with recently bereaved people is one of the hardest things a doctor has to do. It can be upsetting for the doctor as well as the family, and good communication skills are essential. During the discussion the doctor should be as honest and open as possible about the reasons a post-mortem is required. Euphemisms should not be used to protect the family as they can be misconstrued. Before the discussion the doctor should find out when the post-mortem will be done and how this will affect the funeral arrangements, as these are questions that the family will have. The doctor could also ask them if there are any religious or cultural traditions that can be followed to see if these can still occur despite the necessity for the post-mortem. If a doctor is upset about what has happened he may find it useful to talk to other people rather than bottling up the experience.

In general, doctors should be aware that people from different religions and cultures will want to follow certain procedures during the dying process and after death. Being aware of what these are can make the experience less traumatic for the patient and their relatives.

 KEY POINTS

- Some religions do not allow post-mortem examination of the body.
- If there is a legal requirement to have a post-mortem, this takes precedence over religious and cultural beliefs.
- Always be sensitive to religious needs during the dying process. If in doubt ask if there is anything you can or should not do.

For more information on the role of the coroner, *see* Case 72: When to report a death to the coroner, page 177.

CASE 94: REQUESTS TO SEE A 'BRITISH' DOCTOR

You are an Asian F2 doctor working in accident and emergency. During an unusually busy night shift, a patient starts shouting about how the department is too slow and is staffed by lazy foreigners. Various members of staff have tried to diffuse the situation but this encourages him even more. At first, other patients join in his banter. Every time you walk through the waiting area, the patient makes increasingly insulting comments about you and other non-white staff members and patients. Other patients are beginning to feel uncomfortable and the atmosphere in the waiting room is changing. He is next to be seen by you. You call him into the treatment area but he refuses, stating he wants to be seen by a 'British' doctor only.

Questions

- How will you deal with this situation?
- What is your legal duty of care to this patient and the other patients?
- What are your ethical obligations?

ANSWER 94

Legal issues

The doctor, and indeed, the hospital owe this patient a duty of care, which encompasses the provision of adequate and timely treatment. There is no duty to provide a particular doctor to treat a patient. If a patient refuses to be seen by a doctor this raises the practical problem of fulfilling the ongoing duty of care to the patient. The National Health Service (NHS) is under a legal duty, by virtue of race relations legislation, to promote race equality.

Ethical issues

To what extent do we respect the autonomy of patients? Although respect for patient autonomy is given high priority it cannot trump all other interests. The patient's demand for respect for his 'autonomous' choice of the type of doctor he sees is justifiably limited because of the harm to the respect and dignity of the Asian doctor and to healthcare professionals of different ethnicity in general.

'This case occurred when I was an A&E SHO. However, my patient demanded a "home-grown" doctor; this was easy to rebuff as I had been born and raised in London. He claimed there were too many foreign doctors, preventing "proper" doctors from getting jobs. As a young and passionate doctor, I reacted to his jibes. I replied that I believed racism was still rife in the NHS so I had to be better than every other non-white man and woman and every other white man and woman to get my job. So potentially, I am far better than the average doctor. Furthermore, like bus drivers, healthcare professionals have the right to go about their work without fear of abuse or attack. So, he needed to take his seat and wait his turn with a civil tongue in his head. He sat down and remained silent. I got a round of applause from the rest of the waiting area. Later, I treated him for his minor injury and he went on his way, without apologising. Was this the best course of action? Undoubtedly he had shouted his abuse for a reason and I had responded in kind. But what were the options? Ask him to leave without treatment? This allows his racism to go unchallenged. Tackle the situation once he was separated from his audience? This is a more reasoned approach to his bad behaviour, but would not have demonstrated the unacceptability of his actions to the other patients. In effect, I prioritised my needs for justice for me, as an Asian woman, and for my service. The patient's beliefs and any duty of care I owed him came a long way behind.'

KEY POINTS

- The hospital owes the patient a duty of care. However, there is no requirement that a patient must be seen by a particular doctor.
- Racism in the workplace will not be tolerated in the NHS.

CASE 95: VIOLENCE IN ACCIDENT AND EMERGENCY

You are on a night shift in the accident and emergency unit of a city hospital. It is a busy night and you have already clerked five patients. A patient with superficial cuts as a result of a street fight has been waiting for 3 hours. While you are attending a patient who has been admitted as an emergency with chest pain, there is a commotion in the waiting room. Apologizing to your patient you go to find out what is happening. The man with the cuts is shouting and swearing at the nurses. You then see him attempt to punch your colleague, a female F2. It is clear that the other patients waiting are intimidated by his behaviour.

Questions

- Do you have an obligation to treat all patients regardless of their behaviour?
- Can a patient be considered to disentitle him/herself to treatment through bad behaviour?
- To what extent does loyalty to and protection of colleagues have greater weight than the patient's need for treatment?

ANSWER 95

Violence against health professionals has increased. The ultimate sanction against violent and abusive patients is to withhold treatment. In what circumstances could this be considered a justifiable limitation of the doctor's duty of care? A doctor's duty of care is not limitless and may be restricted by competing duties to other patients (time and resource implications), duties to self (not to go beyond boundaries of competence and therefore to be exposed to potential liability, not to undertake obligations where there is a recognized conscientious objection) and duties to colleagues. An aggressive patient, who, having been informed that treatment will not be provided if such behaviour continues, may be regarded as having made an autonomous choice to forfeit treatment in such circumstances. Mentally ill patients and those who are not competent are not considered able to make an autonomous choice to forfeit treatment, and therefore treatment must be provided (and reasonable force can be used to effect necessary treatment).

A doctor's duty to act in the best interests of a patient may be balanced against the harms to others. Except in extreme circumstances, the harms of not providing emergency treatment will outweigh the harms of violence and aggression to healthcare professionals and other patients. This may not be so if there is a serious threat of violence, e.g. a patient carrying a gun or knife.

A National Health Service (NHS) trust has an obligation to provide a safe working environment for its employees, and it may be failing in this duty if it does not have appropriate safeguards against abusive and violent patients. Trusts have policies on treating violent patients and when it may be acceptable to refuse to continue to treat. Professional guidance recognizes that 'in rare circumstances' the relationship of trust between a doctor and patient breaks down, perhaps by the patient's violent behaviour, and it may be necessary to end the relationship (*Good Medical Practice*. London: General Medical Council, 2006).

Ethical issues

The primary aim of medicine is to restore a patient to health, or to at least optimize their wellbeing when disease is incurable. This is undoubtedly easier to achieve when a patient is co-operative and pleasant. However, some patients may not understand the need for treatment – be it through dementia, delirium or drug intoxication. When treating these patients, the virtues of respect and dignity and the needs of other patients and members of the healthcare team are useful to bear in mind. Some patients may be aggressive and difficult to treat through no medical problem. It is more difficult to justify tolerance of these patients. The consequence of non-treatment of a violent patient may not only be harm to that patient but also potential physical harm to others and harm to their dignity. In the long term, healthcare professionals may be unwilling to work in an environment where they feel insufficiently protected.

KEY POINTS

- Doctors should be able to justify their actions and decisions.
- All acts of violence, verbal aggression and physical threats should be reported to security, and if necessary, the police.

CASE 96: CHAPERONES

An attractive 25-year-old woman presents to accident and emergency with a 3-day history of abdominal pain. She has not had her bowels open for 2 days but says she has not been eating either. As part of her investigations you need to perform a digital rectal examination. You explain this to her and she consents but is obviously unhappy about it. She asks you if it can be done by a female doctor. Unfortunately the only female doctor on duty is busy with a trauma call. You decide to go ahead and perform the examination. The patient is diagnosed with constipation and discharged home with senna and lactulose. A few weeks later your consultant calls you into his office. He has received an angry letter from the patient's boyfriend saying that the patient had been distressed by the experience of the rectal examination and felt that you had touched her inappropriately. She wants a written apology.

Questions
- What should you do?
- What should you have done at the time?

ANSWER 96

Practising medicine often requires a doctor to ask personal questions and perform intimate procedures on strangers. When patients are seen in accident and emergency there may often be a period of less than an hour in which a doctor has to ask a patient about their sexual history and personal drug use and perform vaginal and rectal examinations. Although this cannot be prevented, there are protocols that should be followed to make patients feel more at ease, less intimidated and to reduce the risk of complaints against the doctor.

In 2004 the Ayrling Report gave National Health Service (NHS) trusts permission to produce their own chaperone policies. Guidance in most trusts states that patients having an intimate examination should be offered a chaperone. Patients do have a right to decline a chaperone, but if they do, it should be documented in the medical notes. Occasionally it may not be possible for a chaperone to be present. In an emergency the examination should go ahead without a chaperone. If the examination can wait, the doctor should wait until a chaperone is available. The General Medical Council and the Medical Protection Society recommend that chaperones should always be offered when performing examinations of the breast, genitalia or rectum. If no chaperone is available the examination should be delayed until one is available, unless it is a medical emergency.

When asking personal questions, it can help to explain why the questions are relevant, and that the questions being asked are routine and used to exclude different medical problems. Time should be spent building a rapport with the patient before proceeding to external or internal examinations. Again, the doctor should explain what they are doing, why they are doing it and how long it will take. Intimate examinations should be performed with a chaperone present. They should also be performed in a well-lit room or cubicle. If there is a lockable door the doctor should explain that the door is being locked to prevent someone walking in on the patient. There are some people who may be more sensitive to examinations of any kind, e.g. adolescents. Cultural sensitivity is also important. If the doctor is in doubt about what patients are happy for them to do, always ask first.

In the above scenario the doctor should contact his medical indemnity insurer to ask for advice and to let them know a complaint has been made. Since the patient has just asked for a letter of apology it may be worth the doctor writing one saying that he did not mean to make the patient feel uncomfortable and that next time he will ensure that he has a chaperone present.

 KEY POINTS

- A chaperone should always be offered to a patient when a doctor is going to perform intimate examinations or procedures.
- All procedures should be fully explained to ensure the patient knows what to expect.

CASE 97: PRIVATE LIVES OF DOCTORS

I had had a long week at work. Two on-calls meant that I had stayed late in the hospital on Monday and Wednesday. It was finally Friday. The morning had been spent trying to resuscitate a man who had been brought in after a road traffic accident. Breaking the news of his death to his wife and three children had taken its toll on me. And then I had to do a pre-op assessment clinic for patients who were being referred for surgery. It was a difficult clinic. The computers had crashed for 30 minutes so I could not access recent patient results. I was running late; patients were complaining and the paediatric clinic next door was full of screaming children. My head hurt and my shoulders ached. It was with much relief that I finally slung my jacket over my shoulders and headed out into the balmy summer evening.

Despite my exhaustion I had a busy evening ahead – it was my brother's birthday and a big bash had been organized down at our local pub. A curry and a few pints later I was beginning to relax. As I gradually unwound with a whisky and a cigarette in the pub garden, I was accosted by someone who looked familiar. I could not place him though until he started shouting at me. His sentences at first incomprehensible began to penetrate my mind. 'You hypocrite, how dare you patronize me! Call yourself a doctor?'. The man shouting at me was a patient I had seen earlier, an obese man in his late fifties. He needed a new hip. I had told him that in his present state of health he was unsuitable for an operation – particularly a hip replacement – and if he wanted an operation he needed to lose weight, cut down on his drinking and stop smoking. He has caught me doing all the things I had advised him not to do.

Questions
- Should doctors be expected to set an example to their patients?
- Does a patient listen to an obese doctor when they are telling them to lose weight?
- How much does the role of a doctor impinge on someone's private life?

ANSWER 97

Professional guidance

Should patients take advice from a doctor who is telling them 'Do as I say, not do as I do'? It seems that hypocritical advice can work both ways. Some patients may take offence at being told to lose weight by an obese doctor. Conversely, other patients may feel that there is a greater degree of empathy by someone struggling with the same problem that they are – sticking to a diet or giving up smoking.

A doctor does not necessarily have to be a role model for patients; it is a profession and not a way of life. Stereotypically, doctors have a reputation for smoking and drinking too much. However, this is often a reflection of a stressful working environment and a doctor's poor coping strategy. The best way to handle the situation in the case scenario would be for the doctor to try to build a good rapport with the patient and explain to the patient that he is not perfect but that he is only giving him advice on how to live more healthily. It is up to individuals to take control of their own health – a doctor's role is to give information and support while they are doing that.

The General Medical Council (GMC) expects that doctors have a duty to maintain a level of professionalism since they hold a trusted and respected position in society. Doctors who let their activities outside work impinge on their ability to practise medicine safely may have their 'fitness to practise' questioned.

In its 2009 publication *Tomorrow's Doctors* the GMC sets out the knowledge, skills and behaviours that medical students are expected to learn and acquire during their time at UK medical schools. In *Good Medical Practice* (2006) and other publications the GMC sets out the standards expected of good doctors. Registration and fitness to practise procedures have been transformed, and licensing and revalidation support regulation, professional values and lifelong learning.

Ethical issues

It may be difficult to expect a patient to trust the advice of an obese doctor who smokes and drinks. Although doctors should set a good example to their patients it is not a necessity. Other virtues are more important in establishing a trusting doctor–patient relationship, such as honesty, integrity and compassion. If the relationship between the doctor and patient remains strained it may be worth considering that the patient should be referred to another doctor. The patient's health should be a doctor's paramount concern, but doctors cannot be expected to be a role model for society, as long as their actions do not directly affect their ability to care for their patients.

KEY POINTS

- Doctors have a right to a private life.
- Doctors should promote a healthy lifestyle by educating their patients about the risks of smoking, alcohol and obesity while empathizing with them that the things they enjoy can be difficult to give up.

CASE 98: PERSONAL BOUNDARIES

John is admitted to hospital following a car accident. He has multiple injuries and requires full nursing care. During his stay in hospital he becomes very attached to one of the junior doctors. He sees her every day on the ward round and she often stays to talk to him after taking his blood or changing his dressings. As John recovers he starts flirting with the doctor. She is flattered and is finding more and more reason to stay and talk to him. While she is removing the sutures from a scar on his face, he tells her that she is beautiful and tries to kiss her. Uncertain about what to do and her own feelings, the doctor leaves and avoids seeing John for a few days. However, when he is discharged a week later she gives him her number and says they should go out for a drink now that he is no longer an inpatient.

Questions
- Is it appropriate for a doctor to have a relationship with a patient?
- What can a doctor do to avoid undue attention?
- What should a doctor do if she is serious about having a relationship with a patient?

ANSWER 98

Professional guidance

The General Medical Council (GMC) guidance on relationships between doctors and patients is quite straightforward – it does not condone it. As a healthcare professional it undermines the trust that a patient places in them and potentially takes advantage of vulnerable individuals.

> 'you must not use your professional position to establish or pursue a sexual or improper emotional relationship with a patient or someone close to them'
>
> General Medical Council. *Good Medical Practice*. London: GMC, 2006

The same reasoning applies to medical students working in hospitals. As professionals in training they are expected to establish their own professional relationships with patients and must learn the importance of professionalism (*Medical Students: Professional Behaviour and Fitness to Practise*, London: GMC and MSC, 2007).

When caring for patients it is important for doctors to be aware of personal boundaries. They must not engage in intimate conversations with patients about their own personal life, and when performing intimate procedures they should have a chaperone with them so that the purpose of the procedure cannot be misconstrued. All hospitals have a dress code, which should be adhered to. This generally involves not revealing midriff or wearing low-cut tops, not wearing jewellery and keeping make-up to a minimum. The National Health Service (NHS) has a policy which states that all staff must dress smartly, safely and hygienically while at work.

In some small villages it can be very difficult to meet people who are not patients. If it looks like a relationship may be establishing itself then the doctor–patient relationship should be stopped so that the two roles do not overlap.

Ethical issues

There are several ethical arguments in favour of zero tolerance for sexual patient–doctor relationships. These include the premise that sexual relationships will be nearly always harmful to the patient due to the imbalance in power between doctors and their patients. It is, however, worth considering whether this could now be considered true since medical practice has moved away from paternalism and towards a patient-centred approach where doctors no longer have such control over the management of their patients. Virtue ethics argues that a good doctor is one who extols virtues and that a doctor who commences a sexual relationship with a patient would not be adhering to these virtues. Consequentialists could argue that any sexual relationship between patients and doctors would inevitably lead to a breakdown in trust and respect of the medical profession as a whole and as such should not be allowed as it would reflect poorly on the profession.

 KEY POINTS

- Doctors are not allowed to enter into intimate or sexual relationships with patients.
- Medical students should also not enter into relationships since they should behave as young professionals.
- It is unethical to have a relationship with a patient since it jeopardizes the trust that the public has in healthcare professionals.

CASE 99: ETHICAL ISSUES ON ELECTIVE

As a final-year medical student you have just arrived in Western Samoa to undertake an 8-week elective at the local hospital. You have spent the last week getting to know the area and some of the other medical students who are also on attachment with you. Although you were feeling relaxed you are now quite nervous about your first day in the hospital. On arrival the first thing you notice is how busy it is everywhere. Whole families are queuing outside a door, waiting to see the doctor. Everyone is very subdued. Despite seeming exceptionally busy the doctor in charge of paediatrics is extremely pleased to see you. After a brief introductory talk he gives you a list of names and shows you to a big room. On one side a large group of mothers and their children are sitting on benches. On the other side are a desk and an examination couch. He gives you a prescription pad and then waves goodbye. Nervously you call your first patient, a 5-year-old boy. His mother tells you in very stilted English that he has a sore throat and painful knees. Could this be rheumatic fever? You feel out of your depth but do not know what to do about it.

Questions
- Should students follow the ethical guidelines that they would follow in their own country or do these not apply in another country?
- Do medical schools provide guidelines for their students?
- What would you do in this situation?

ANSWER 99

The ethical framework within which an individual practises medicine should not change simply because they are practising in a different country. The Hippocratic Oath and the more contemporary Declaration of Geneva set out ethical principles and the General Medical Council (GMC) echoes these principles in its guidance for medical students and doctors.

Electives offer students the chance to experience medicine in a different country. It enables them to become more self-sufficient and can give them increased confidence. Working in developing countries with severe resource issues and fewer doctors provides an opportunity to gain more experience as there are often more patients to learn on and more procedures which are done by junior members of the team. However, it is essential that students are aware of their own limitations and should not feel pressurized to perform procedures until they have been taught how to do them correctly and safely. Above all a medical student must 'do no harm'. This applies both in the UK and when working abroad. When students are unsure of what to do and do not feel they have the necessary knowledge or experience they should seek help or supervision. Attempting to perform a procedure or treat a patient when a student is not sure of what they are doing is both potentially harmful for the patient and not educational for the student.

Medical treatment is often seen as a privilege in developing countries, and while patients may seem grateful for attention they are still owed the same respect that a patient would receive in the UK. They should be told that you are only a student and not a qualified doctor and their informed consent should be sought for any procedure they undergo. Medical students abroad are representatives of their country and medical school and it is important that they should behave in a mature and responsible way. Professional values should be the same as those used at home. Students should be dressed respectably even in hot weather. They should be polite and courteous to patients, their relatives and everyone else working in the hospital.

Electives can be an amazing and memorable experience. Students should not let preventable bad experiences impact on the rest of their medical career.

 KEY POINTS

- Electives abroad are a useful learning experience and a fantastic opportunity to travel.
- Medical students should follow the same ethical principles that they do when working in the UK.
- Students should never perform procedures they are not able to do without appropriate supervision.

CASE 100: A MEDICAL STUDENT'S EXPERIENCE OF ILLNESS

'I was a final-year medical student when I was diagnosed with Hodgkin's lymphoma. In the space of 3 weeks I went from initial presentation at the general practitioner to disease diagnosis, including grading and staging. Pretty impressive, considering this involved going for two consultations (one with a hospital specialist), a blood test, chest X-ray, computed tomography (CT) scan, fine needle aspiration and biopsy under general anaesthetic. My world had been turned upside down.

'Looking back the majority of those 3 weeks are a hazy memory. However, my first consultation with the hospital specialist sticks in my head, but for all the wrong reasons. Initially there were no introductions, which meant I had no idea who anyone was. I remember there being another person in the room besides the doctor, my mother and myself. I assumed at the time that she was a student nurse, but this is pure supposition based on my own experiences as a student in outpatient clinics. I certainly was not asked whether I minded her being present and she did not say or do anything to indicate that her being there was necessary. The consultant appeared in a hurry and spent most of the consultation speaking to my mother about everything that had happened, despite the fact that at 23 I was not only the patient, but also a competent adult (and nearly qualified medical professional!). The worst thing about the consultation was the provisional diagnosis. It was not broken to me in the way I would have expected. The consultant asked me what I thought was wrong with me. By that point, most differentials had been ruled out; the only one left was Hodgkin's, yet still I thought I was just being a hypochondriac. I made my suggestion and the consultant responded, but not with the answer I'd been expecting: 'Yes, I think it's Hodgkin's too.' From that point on, the rest of that consultation is a blur. I can't remember any of the other information I was given; my mind had gone into overdrive and the only thing I could think was that I had cancer and might die.

'A week later, after the diagnosis had been confirmed histologically, I went for CT staging. Again, I found this a terrifying experience. I was scared it might show the cancer had already metastasized, but also of having the scan itself. Nobody had explained the procedure to me – that I needed to be cannulated and have intravenous contrast injected. By the time I got into the CT scanner, I was hysterically upset. A form was thrust at me, which I was asked to sign. To this day I have no idea what I signed for, whether it was to consent to the scan, confirm I didn't have any allergies to iodine/shellfish or to confirm I wasn't pregnant.

'Despite having spent 2 years on hospital ward as a student, being an inpatient while I received chemotherapy was a completely different experience. It made me really think about what my own patients must have been going through. There are things that you don't appreciate as a student (and perhaps even as a junior doctor). Privacy was a big problem. I was paranoid about sleeping since everyone would see me and possibly hear me snore. I was constantly tired as the nurses are always coming to do observations or give drugs. Machines bleeping constantly was also a huge annoyance! I was also always asked about how I was feeling and about my intimate bodily functions in front of an entire ward of patients and relatives. It was also very lonely being a patient; I would see doctors on their rounds for less than 10 minutes and then speak to no one till visiting hours in the afternoon.

'I spent 6 months as a patient, and thankfully now I'm a doctor. But my experience was more valuable than any lectures or clinics. It made me think a lot about the way we treat our patients, and if reading about it makes you do the same, then writing this will have been worthwhile.'

Questions

- Should I have been treated quicker just because I am a medical professional?
- Should the consultant have assumed I knew what all the investigations and treatments involved?
- Is informed consent ever possible when a patient is scared? Or in pain? Or in emergency situations?
- Can confidentiality ever be kept when information about patients is discussed in open wards?

ANSWER 100

Using your knowledge of medical ethics, write your answers to the questions regarding this scenario here.

ADDITIONAL RESOURCES

Websites

All websites were accessed in October 2007.

British Association for Sexual Health and HIV. 2006 United Kingdom National Guideline on the Sexual Health of People with HIV: Sexually Transmitted Infections.
www.bashh.org/guidelines/2006/sexual_health_hiv_0406.pdf

British HIV Association. HIV transmission, the law and work of the clinical team. March, 2006: www.bhiva.org/cms1191673.asp

British Medical Association:
www.bma.org.uk

British Medical Association, Medical ethics:
www.bma.org.uk/ethics/index.jsp/

Department of Health
www.dh.gov.uk/en/index.htm

Directgov, Living wills: Advance decision or directive:
www.direct.gov.uk/en/Governmentcitizensandrights/Death/Preparation/DG_10029683

General Medical Council:
www.gmc-uk.org

General Medical Council, A-Z of ethical guidance:
www.gmc-uk.org/guidance/a_z_guidance/index.asp

Human Genetics Commission. *Inside Information. Balancing Interests in The Use of Personal Genetic Data*, 2002:
www.hgc.gov.uk/UploadDocs/DocPub/Document/insideinformation_summary.pdf

National Institute for Health and Clinical Excellence:
www.nice.org.uk

NHS, Care and Evidence (advice for professionals who may come into contact with victims of sexual assault):
www.careandevidence.org/7.asp

Nuffield Council on Bioethics. *Critical Care Decisions in Fetal and Neonatal Medicine: Ethical Issues,* 2006:
www.nuffieldbioethics.org/go/ourwork/neonatal/introduction

Patient Advice and Liaison Service (PALS):
www.pals.nhs.uk

Royal College of General Practitioners, GP Guidance Database:
www.rcgp.org.uk/extras/guidance/query.asp

UK Clinical Ethics Network:
www.ethics-network/org.uk

Legislation and cases

UK Parliament – Bills and Legislation:
www.parliament.uk/business/bills_and_legislation.cfm

British and Irish Legal Information Institute (search engine for court cases):
www.bailii.org

Coroners and Justice Act 2009
www.justice.gov.uk/publications/coroners-justice-bill.htm

Human Fertilisation and Embryology Acts 1990 and 2008.

Human Tissue Act 2004:
www.opsi.gov.uk/acts/acts2004/20040030.htm

Mental Capacity Act 2005:
www.opsi.gov.uk/acts/acts2005/20050009.htm
Mental Capacity Act, Explanatory Notes:
www.opsi.gov.uk/acts/en2005/2005en09.htm
Mental Health Act 2007:
www.opsi.gov.uk/acts/acts2007/20070012.htm
Surrogacy Arrangements Act 1985

Professional Guidance and Information
General Medical Council

0-18 Years: Guidance for All Doctors. London: GMC, 2007.
Consent: Patients and Doctors Making Decisions Together. London: GMC, 2008.
Confidentiality. London: GMC, 2009.
Good Medical Practice. London: GMC, 2006.
Maintaining Boundaries. London: GMC, 2006.
Medical Students: Professional Behaviour and Fitness to Practice. London: GMC and MSC, 2007.
Tomorrow's Doctors. London: GMC, 2009.
Treatment and care towards the end of life: good practice in decision making. London: GMC, 2010.

British Medical Association

Incentives to GPs for Referral or Prescribing. London: BMA, 1995 (revised 1997).
Confidentiality and Disclosure of Health Information Toolkit. London: BMA, 2009.
BMA Consent Toolkit, 5th edn. London: BMA, 2009.
Doctors' Responsibilities in Child Protection Cases. London: BMA, 2004.
Female Genital Mutilation – Caring for Patients and Child Protection. London: BMA, 2006.
Referral to Complementary Therapists: Guidance for GPs. London: BMA, 2006.
The Law and Ethics of Male Circumcision – Guidance for Doctors. London: BMA, 2006.

Department of Health

Donaldson L, Chief Medical Officer. Making amends: a consultation paper setting out proposals for reforming the approach to clinical negligence in the NHS. A report by the Chief Medical Officer. London: Department of Health, 2003. Available at: www.dh.gov.uk/en/Publicationsandstatistics/Publications/PublicationsPolicyAndGuidance/DH_4010641.
Best practice guidance for doctors and other health professionals on the provision of advice and treatment to young people under 16 on contraception, sexual and reproductive health. London: DH, 2004.
Mental Capacity Act 2005, Core Training Set. London: DH, 2007.
Mental Capacity Act 2005, Acute Hospital Training Set. London: DH, 2007.
Policy consultation on confidentiality and disclosure of patient information: HIV and sexually transmitted infection. London: DH, 2006.

National Institute for Health and Clinical Excellence

NICE Guidance. *Fertility: assessment and treatment for people with fertility problems.* London: RCOG Press, 2004.

Ethical Principles

Beauchamp TL, Childress JF. *Principles of Biomedical Ethics*, 5th edn. Oxford: Oxford University Press, 2001.

BMA Ethics Department. *Medical Ethics Today: The BMA Handbook of Ethics and Law*, 2nd edn. London: BMJ Books, 2004.

Calman KC. Evolutionary ethics: can values change? *J Med Ethics* 2004;**30**:366–70.

Gardiner P. A virtue ethics approach to moral dilemmas in medicine. *J Med Ethics* 2003;**29**:297–302.

Gillon R. Medical ethics: four principles plus attention to scope. *BMJ* 1994;**309**:184.

Gillon R. Four scenarios. *J Med Ethics* 2003;**29**:267–8.

McCarthy J. Principlism or narrative ethics: must we choose between them? *Med Humanities* 2003;**29**:65–71.

Sommerville A. Juggling law, ethics, and intuition: practical answers to awkward questions. *J Med Ethics* 2003;**29**:281–6.

Ethics and Law in Clinical Medicine

British Medical Association, the Resuscitation Council (UK), Royal College of Nursing. *Decisions Relating to Cardiopulmonary Resuscitation.* A Joint Statement by the British Medical Association, the Resuscitation Council (UK), and the Royal College of Nursing. London: BMA, 2007.

Chalmers J. Criminalization of HIV transmission: can doctors be liable for the onward transmission of HIV? *Int J STD and AIDS* 2004;**15**:782–7.

Erin C, Harris J. An ethical market in human organs. *J Med Ethics* 2003;**29**:137–8.

Glover J. *Causing Death and Saving Lives.* Harmondsworth: Penguin, 1977.

Glover J. Should the child live? Doctors, families and conflict. *Clin Ethics* 2006;**1**:52–9.

Hallowell N, Foster C, Eeles R, *et al.* Balancing autonomy and responsibility: the ethics of generating and disclosing genetic information. *J Med Ethics* 2003;**29**:74–83.

Harris J. The Value of Life. London: Routledge, 1985.

Higgs R. On telling patients the truth. In: Lockwood M (ed.). *Moral Dilemmas in Modern Medicine.* Oxford: Oxford University Press, 1985.

Human Fertilisation and Embryology Authority. Sex selection: options for regulation. London: HFEA, 2003.

Human Fertilisation and Embryology Authority. *Tomorrow's Children, Review of the HFEA's guidance on Welfare of the Child.* London: HFEA, 2005.

Johnston C. The Mental Capacity Act 2005 and advance decisions. *Clin Ethics* 2007;**5**:80–4.

Kennedy R, Kingsland C, Rutherford A, *et al.* Implementation of the NICE guidelines – recommendations from the British Fertility Society for national criteria for NHS funding for assisted conception. *Human Fertility* 2006; 3:181–9.

Mental Health Foundation and Camelot Foundation. *Truth Hurts. Report of the National Inquiry into Self-harm among Young People.* London: Mental Health Foundation, 2004.

Peterson M. Assisted reproductive technologies and equity of access issues. *J Med Ethics* 2005;**31**:280–5.

Royal College of Obstetricians and Gynaecologists. *Law and Ethics in Relation to Court-authorised Obstetric Intervention.* Ethics Committee Guideline no. 1. London: RCOG, 2006.

Savulescu J. Procreative beneficence: why should we select the best children? *Bioethics* 2001;**15**:413–26.

Savulescu J. Is there a 'right not to be born'? Reproductive decision making, options and the right to information. *J Med Ethics* 2002;**28**:65–7.

Slowther AM. Medical futility and 'do not attempt resuscitation' orders. *Clin Ethics* 2006;**3**:18–20.

Spriggs M. Lesbian couple create a child who is deaf like them. *J Med Ethics* 2002; **28**:283.

Spriggs M. Is conceiving a child to benefit another against the interests of the new child? *J Med Ethics* 2005;**31**:341–2.

Sullivan R, Menapace L, White R. Truth-telling and patient diagnoses. *J Med Ethics* 2001;**27**:192–7.

Szmukler G, Dawson J. Commentary: toward resolving some dilemmas concerning psychiatric advance directives. *J Am Acad Psychiatry Law* 2006;**34**:398–401.

Wheeler R. Gillick or Fraser? A plea for consistency over competence in children. *BMJ* 2006;**332**:807.

Wong J, Poon Y, Hui E. 'I can put the medicine in his soup, Doctor!' *J Med Ethics* 2005;**31**:262–5.

Duties of a Doctor

Alberti K. Medical errors: a common problem. *BMJ* 2001;**322**:501–2.

Chalmers J. Criminalization of HIV transmission: can doctors be liable for the onward transmission of HIV? *Int J STD AIDS* 2004;**15**:782–7.

Cole P. Human rights and the national interest: migrants, healthcare and social justice. *J Med Ethics* 2007;**33**:269–72.

Furniss R, Ormond-Walshe S. An alternative to the clinical negligence system. *BMJ* 2007;**334**:400–2.

Hope T. Rationing and live-saving treatment: should identifiable patients have higher priority? *J Med Ethics* 2001;**27**:179–85.

Koschorke A, Tilzey A, Welch J. Should medical students be taught about rape? A survey of UK medical schools. BJOG 2007;**114**:224–5.

Maynard A. Ethics and healthcare 'underfunding'. *J Med Ethics* 2001;**27**:223–7.

Mills S. Regulation in complementary and alternative medicine. *BMJ* 2001;**322**:158–160.

Pollard J, Savulescu J. Eligibility of overseas visitors and people of uncertain residential status for NHS treatment. *BMJ* 2004;**329**:346–9.

Tallis R. *Hippocratic Oaths: Medicine and its Discontents*. London: Atlantic Books, 2004.

Faith, Values and Culture

Crawley L, Marshall P. Lo B *et al*. Strategies for culturally effective end-of-life care. *Ann Intern Med* 2002;**136**:673–9.

Qureshi B. Diabetes in Ramadan. *J R Soc Med* 2002;**95**:489–90.

Spiegel W, Colella T, Lupton P. Private or intimate relationships between patients: is zero tolerance warranted? *J Med Ethics* 2005;**31**:27–8.

Wade P. Treatment of patients who are Jehovah's Witnesses. *J Med Ethics* 2001;**27**:137–8.

INDEX

References are by case number with relevant page number(s) following in brackets. References with a page range e.g. 25(68–70) indicate that although the subject may be mentioned only on one page, it concerns the whole case. There are a few exceptions outside case numbers where page number alone appears and these are shown in italics. Glossary references are given in Roman numerals.